THE MAGIC AND MYSTERIES OF MEXICO

The Arcane Secrets and Occult Lore of the Ancient Mexicans and Maya

LEWIS SPENCE

With Special Introduction By Dragonstar

ALSO: Does The Mayan Calendar Predict The End of the World in 2012?

A Report By Commander X

THE MAGIC AND MYSTERIES OF MEXICO
Or
THE ARCANE SECRETS AND OCCULT LORE OF THE ANCIENT MEXICANS AND MAYA

By
LEWIS SPENCE

Author Of:

THE CIVILIZATION OF ANCIENT MEXICO

•

THE MYTHS OF MEXICO AND PERU

•

THE PROBLEM OF ATLANTIS

•

THE HISTORY OF ATLANTIS

•

THE MYSTERIES OF BRITAIN

•

THE MYSTERIES OF EGYPT
(Titles Currently Out-of-Print)

Global Communications

THE MAGIC AND MYSTERIES OF MEXICO
Or
THE ARCANE SECRETS AND OCCULT LORE OF THE ANCIENT MEXICANS AND MAYA

Lewis Spence

ISBN: 978-1-60611-006-5
ISBN: 1-60611-006-3

Second Expanded Edition Newly Revised
Originally Published by The Mayflower Press (UK), 1943

Nonfiction – Metaphysics/Anthropology

Timothy Green Beckley: Editorial Director
Carol Rodriguez: Publishers Assistant
Sean Casteel: Associate Editor
William Kern: Editorial Assistant
Cover Art: Tim Swartz

Printed in the United States of America

For free catalog write:
Global Communications
P.O. Box 753
New Brunswick, NJ 08903

Free Subscription to Conspiracy Journal E-Mail Newsletter
www.conspiracyjournal.com

THE MAGIC AND MYSTERIES OF MEXICO

<u>CONTENTS</u>

TEZCATLIPOCA AS A WER-JAGUAR

THE MAGIC AND MYSTERIES OF MEXICO

Introduction
By Dragonstar

In North America, mystical and occult beliefs can be chiefly traced back to Old World influences. South of the border, however, the occult traditions of Mexico are an interesting mix of Old World Catholicism and Pre-Columbian Indian beliefs.

When we look beyond the influence of recent invaders to Central America, the religious, magical and philosophical beliefs of the aboriginal Native American cultures that evolved in Meso-America are both unique and strangely similar to magical practices from Europe, Africa and Asia. Even though these Old World mystical traditions supposedly arose under isolation from the other side of the world, it is obvious that when it comes to human spirituality in any form, they all seem to radiate out from one universal source.

History says that the Mayan civilization arose in Central America around 250 CE, influenced by the culture and religion of the Olmecs. The Mayan urban culture especially flourished until about 900 CE, but continued to thrive in various places until the Spanish conquest.

During this first 650 years, which scholars call the Classic Period, the Mayan civilization consisted of more than 40 large cities spread across modern-day Mexico, Guatemala, and northern Belize.

At its peak, the total population may have reached two million people, the majority of whom lived in modern-day Guatemala. The cities seem to have been mainly ceremonial centers, with the majority of the Maya living a rural, agricultural life around the cities.

Sometime after 900 CE, the Mayan culture declined dramatically and most of the cities were abandoned. Historians offer several explanations on this decline, chief being the loss of trade routes due to war.

Residents fled the great southern cities, but the cities of the Yucatan peninsula in Mexico (such as Chichén Itzá, Uxmal, and Mayapán) continued to thrive in the early part of the "Post-Classic Period" (900–1519). By the arrival of the Spanish in the early 16th century, however, most of the Maya were village-dwelling farmers.

The Maya had a highly sophisticated culture, and this included a written hieroglyphic language that was carved into stone monuments or pieces of bone, painted on pottery, and written on books (codices) of bark paper. Mayan texts describe religious rituals, astronomy, and divination, and are the most valuable source of information on the ancient civilization. Most of the Maya religious texts were destroyed by the Spanish because of their pagan religious content, but three main codices have survived. Named for the cities in which they are now kept, these are the *Dresden*, *Madrid*, and *Paris* codices. The *Dresden Codex* contains very precise tables of Venus and the moon and describes a method of predicting solar eclipses.

Perhaps the most famous of these texts is the *Popol Vuh* (1554-1558), which was written in Quiché, a highland Maya language, and translated into Spanish by a priest. This tells of the mythology and cosmology of the Post classic Guatemalan Maya, and shows central Mexican influences. It chronicles the creation of man, the actions of the gods, the origin and history of the Quiché people, and the chronology of their kings down to 1550.

Mexico was a land filled with magic; the gods were magical figures, and their rites arose out of magical practice. Like the Old World, the ancient Mexicans' believed in divination, the influence of the planets and stars on human affairs, and a rich spiritual world filled with ghosts, fairies, witches, and other supernatural entities.

At the beginning of the 21st century, the world has become aware of the Maya due to their ancient "long-count" calendar. In the mythology of the Maya, the first age of mankind ended with the animals devouring humans. The second age was finished by wind, the third by fire, and the fourth by water. The present fifth epoch is called Nahui-Olin (Sun of Earthquake), which will end on December 21, 2012.

There are different opinions on what is suppose to happen on that date. Even though Maya myths told of death and destruction at the end of each cycle, in real life the Maya celebrated the end of a cycle much as we celebrate New Years today. Others say that on the winter solstice in 2012, the sun will be aligned with the center of the Milky Way for the first time in about 26,000 years. This means that whatever energy typically streams to Earth from the center of the Milky Way will be disrupted.

The truth is nobody really knows what will happen. However, from this book, we can get a better understanding on how the ancient peoples of Mexico viewed their world. We owe a debt of gratitude to Lewis Spence, the author of this book, for his meticulous research on Maya magic. Without it, we could not even attempt to understand the magic and mysteries of Mexico.

PREFACE

This, the first effort to include in one volume all that is known regarding the arcane knowledge and occult lore of the ancient Mexican peoples and their neighbors, the Maya of Central America and Yucatan, is the result of more than thirty-five years of research in a sphere which has richly repaid the writer by the companionship of its fascination, and which he hopes will prove equally absorbing to the reader who seeks passing amusement and to the serious student.

The book is so compiled as to be useful to both, popular in its general treatment, yet sufficiently authoritative in its sources and data to be of avail either to the practical anthropologist or the student of Mysticism. The historical passages essential to the introduction of the main subject are necessarily sketchy, but embody sufficient information to permit the reader ignorant of Central American chronicles to approach the consideration of the curious knowledge of the more enlightened peoples of Isthmian America in the fields of pure Magic, Astrology, Witchcraft, Demonology and Symbolism.

The chapters on the difficult question of Mexican and Maya Astrology have been reduced to a simplicity of presentation which, it is hoped, will render this vexed subject plain to everyone, and its basic importance to the whole survey of Mexican occult knowledge has been demonstrated with an equal desire for clarity. That this astrological lore was inevitably accompanied by a philosophy of dualism, recalling that of ancient Persia, is also shown, and that a system of initiation resembling that connected with Asiatic and European wisdom-religions was also in vogue in Central America is now for the first time suggested, and, it is hoped, adequately proved.

The mystical books of the Mexicans and Maya are described and the relationships between the religions of these people and their magical beliefs fully discussed. Nor have minor questions, such as popular superstitions, augury, and the use of charms and amulets been neglected. In fact, every effort has been put forth to render the volume as complete a treasury of the occult lore of Central America as our present acquaintance with the facts permits.

The writer has, above all, striven to preserve the romance inherent in the subject, and has tried to cast light on the darker places by an occasional appeal to fiction, but when such an aid is invoked its imaginative character is duly indicated. The Magic of old Mexico, although it closely resembles that of other lands, has distinct racial characteristics of its own, and is capable of illuminating other systems through its peculiar preservation of what many of them have lost or cast aside.

Its inherent unity of idea with the arcane systems of the Old World makes it a valuable mine of analogy and comparison, even if the differences brought about by environment seem to render it superficially distinctive. But, above all, its indwelling spirit of gloomy wonder and mystical exclusiveness perhaps reveal it as the most fascinating of the world's secret systems.

Lewis Spence

MEXICO AT THE TIME OF THE MONTEZUMAS

CHAPTER I
A GLANCE AT ANCIENT MEXICO

The magic of ancient Mexico and the mysteries which accompanied it have been somewhat neglected owing to the extraordinary difficulties attending the consideration of the Mexican past. Only within the last generation has it been made possible to comprehend even dimly the civilization of ancient Mexico as a whole and that has been accomplished merely in a provisional manner. It is therefore not surprising that the occult side of Mexican life has been dealt with only in a fragmentary way, and chiefly in connection with the religious beliefs of the Aztecs and Maya.

The writings of the Spanish missionary friars who labored in Mexico subsequent to the period of its conquest by Cortes frequently touch in the passing on the question of the arcane beliefs of the Indians to whom they ministered, but in no very illuminating manner. Indeed, their notices of occult beliefs are confused and exhibit a not incomprehensible terror of the dark knowledge which they conceived it their duty to extirpate. It is therefore not easy to arrive at the facts and discover the principles underlying Mexican arcane science.

In the following pages I shall essay the task, aided, I hope, by a long acquaintance with the writings of the Spanish conquistadores and the missionary friars, and with practically all that has been penned within our times on the subject of old Mexico. And it may be that a strong personal predilection towards the mysterious may further assist me to make the dark places plain to the wayfaring reader.

Mexico possessed a magic of her own as mystical in its essence and as grimly romantic as that of any land, European or Asiatic. Yet its secrets are to be gauged only by treading many obscure and difficult pathways.

If those who follow me in the quest find any of these corridors too dark or too difficult of access they must not blame me, but rather the tortuous nature of the study. I would advise them to "skip" the obscure passages and to turn to those pages which retain more of the atmosphere of that purely dramatic interest which must ever cleave to the occult lore of Mexico and Central America. But the magic and sorcery of ancient Mexico cannot well be understood unless the somewhat shadowy path which leads to them is rendered more clear by a brief account of the general circumstances of Mexican life and custom in the past.

When Hernan Cortes conquered Mexico in 1519 he found it occupied by several races of people of Indian stock, who possessed a common culture, although they differed in language and to some extent in religious outlook. In the eastern regions the Nahua race, to which the Aztecs belonged, was in the ascendant, but the coastline was occupied by immigrant tribes of Maya or southern stock from Central America.

In the south-west the Mixtecs and Zapotecs, races which had embraced civilization before the Nahua, formed the bulk of the population, though Nahua elements were also largely present in that region. In the centre of the country dwelt the Otomi, the Zacatecs, and other long-settled tribes, whilst the northern pampas were the possession of nomadic bands. To the south-east of Mexico lived the Maya of Guatemala, Yucatan, and Central America, whose civilization greatly pre-dated that of Mexico proper, as we shall see when we come to consider their special conditions.

The Nahua, or Aztecs, with whom we are principally concerned, were a people of much later establishment in the country than most of the other races. They occupied a sphere extending from the present site of Tlascala, no great distance from Mexico City, to the Isthmus of Tehuantepec on the south, and were divided into tribes, most of whom owed allegiance to the Emperor of Mexico, although they were governed by their own immediate kings or chiefs. Research has established the distant relationship of the Nahua tribes with the Indians of British Columbia, whose language, customs, religion and art bear a close resemblance to those of the Mexicans, who, in all likelihood, migrated at various periods to the region in which they are presently situated.

At the time of the Spanish Conquest we find several Nahua tribes grouped round the lakes in the Valley of Mexico, the most notable being those which occupied the borders of the Lake of Tezcuco. The tribes composing these groups had entered the plateau of Mexico about the tenth century A.D., but had been preceded there by a much older civilization, the Toltec. Legend said that the Toltecs had settled there in the year 7 Tecpatl, or A.D. 387, coming from the north by way of the coast and then striking inland, a journey which occupied one hundred and four years. But the myth which recounts this exodus is almost certainly of artificial origin.

The Toltecs were regarded by the older writers on Mexican affairs as the great initiators and conservators of the occult sciences, magic and astrology. Perhaps no argument in the once passionate forum of American Archeology was formerly debated with such splenetic vigor and breadth of invective as the obscure and intricate question of the origin and identity of that earliest and most mysterious among the civilized races of Mexico, the Toltecs.

In their simplicity the first Castilian chroniclers of the affairs of New Spain accepted without demur the native traditions which exalted the culture of this shadowy race to a pitch which, as Prescott puts it, "almost transcends the human." They write of the clever architects and potters of the city of Tollan, which lay about forty miles north of Mexico, as inspired sages from whom none of the secrets of ancient civilization and few of those of modernity were hidden, and vaunt in epical periods the astonishing excellence of the culture which they were believed to have spread broadcast over North America.

The ruler of this Mexican Corinth was that Quetzalcoatl who is so frequently mentioned in Indian tradition as the bringer of all culture and enlightenment to the American isthmian regions. His descendants, we are assured, ruled in Tollan for several centuries, but were at last finally defeated and dispersed by barbarous Nahua invaders from the north, who destroyed the brilliant metropolis of the Toltecs, and scattered its inhabitants, noblesse and plebeians alike, to the ends of the American continent.

These accounts were, for the most part, based on the histories of the half-blood chronicler Ixtlilxochitl, whose relationship with the ancient kings of Tezcuco, a famous town near Mexico City, manifestly biased his conclusions. Nevertheless, these were credited by Mexican and foreign antiquaries alike from the end of the sixteenth century almost to the middle of the nineteenth. The doubts hesitated by Prescott, however, were more vigorously expressed by Daniel Garrison Brinton, the foremost Americanist of his day, who in 1887 published an essay, "Were the Toltecs an Historic Nationality?" in which he settled the question to his own satisfaction by the dogmatic assertion that the Toltecs were a sect of the Nahua or Aztec race whose sun-myths had surrounded their fragmentary history with a legendary brilliance which had the effect of dazzling those who chronicled them with visions of a civilization which never existed.

"The mythical Tollan," he wrote," and all its rulers and inhabitants, are the baseless dreams of poetic fancy, which we principally owe to the Tezcucan poets. I have no hesitation in repeating the words which I printed some years ago: 'Is it not time that we dismiss once for all these American myths from the domain of historical traditions? Why should we make an enlightened ruler of Quetzalcoatl, a cultured nation of the Toltecs, when the proof is of the strongest that they are the fictions of mythology?'"

For a couple of decades Brinton's statement was accepted, in official quarters at least, as final. But reaction from statements so positive was bound to set in. From 1873 to 1887 Charnay, the French archaeologist, had been excavating at intervals on the site of Tollan, the Toltec city, and his researches there made it evident that the locality had at some distant period produced a culture in some ways markedly dissimilar from that of the later Aztecs on the one hand, and on the other from the civilization of the Maya of Central America.

It became increasingly clear that some definite name and description must be conferred upon a civilization possessing such well marked architectural and other attributes of its own, and, by degrees almost imperceptible, the old name of "Toltec" was once more employed by archaeologists to designate the peculiar type of art and the strange symbolism which flourished not only in Tollan, but whose rather isolated monuments are to be encountered at intervals almost over the entire length of the isthmian area of America.

It was, however, universally admitted that Toltec culture could scarcely have preceded that of the Maya of Central America. The antiquity of the Maya cities of Guatemala indisputably reaches back to at least the first century before the Christian era, whereas no origin more venerable could possibly be assigned to Toltec civilization than the seventh century A.D.

The contention, too, that the Toltecs were themselves Maya who imported Central American progress into the Mexican tableland was regarded as impossible of acceptance for the good reason that the ancient chroniclers were unanimous that the Toltecs were a people of Mexican or Nahua origin, speaking a Nahua tongue. But the comparative study of their architecture, symbolism and traditions with that of the Maya clearly demonstrated that at some stage of their development they must have been in close touch with Maya civilization.

To render the puzzle still more involved, there were not wanting monumental evidences of a Toltec cultural invasion of the Maya country of Yucatan, especially in the religious and other edifices of the cities of

Ake, Uxmal, and Chichen Itza, where the peculiar Toltec serpent-shaped columns and balustrades, open-work decoration on the tops of the temple walls and caryatid pillars, as well as hieroglyphs of Toltec design, are to be found. But these were obviously later in date than the corresponding remains in Mexico.

By a careful review of all the available data, Holmes, Seler, Haebler and Spinden have made it clear that in the first place Mexico must have been indebted for her earliest culture to Maya sources. It was already known that an early Maya people, the Huaxtecs, had in primitive times worked their way from Central America up the east coast of Mexico, where their remains still show obvious Maya associations. A border tribe migrating between the races, the Kuikatecs, are also more than suspect of culture-carrying from south to north. The Nahua people of Oaxaca, too, the Zapotecs, possessed a culture mid-way between the Nahua and Maya types. The traditions were also insistent that progress in both the Maya and Mexican spheres of civilization had been introduced by a culture-hero known as Quetzalcoatl, who in the more northern area was regarded as a deified king of the Toltecs, while in Central America he was worshiped as a god of wind and moisture.

The cult of this god was markedly alien to Mexican ideas of human sacrifice, with which his worship was not associated; therefore it was manifest that his ritual must be of foreign and intrusive origin. Moreover, he was credited with the introduction of the Tonalamatl, or Book of Fate, which was certainly Mayan in its beginnings. Still, the clearly non-Maya racial origin of the Toltecs continued to perplex Americanists, who maintained a non-committal and conservative attitude on the question of Toltec origins.

Indeed, though the monuments traditionally connected with the race are now definitely classed as "Toltec," official Americanist science has not yet committed itself to any clear expression of opinion regarding the racial affinities of this mysterious people. If a solution may be ventured by one who has followed the controversy with fascinated interest for nearly a generation, some such explanation as that which follows may serve as a working hypothesis.

We are aware that at some time in the sixth century of the Christian era the Maya settlements in Guatemala were more or less suddenly vacated by their inhabitants. We do not know what prompted this hasty and wholesale desertion of the splendid cities of Palenque, Copan, and the neighboring states. Perhaps pestilence or invasion dictated their evacuation, but, judging from the almost perfect state of repair in which their temples and palaces still remain, it seems probable that their inhabitants set out on their northern pilgrimage on one of those religious quests which frequently inspired the Maya race.

They entered the peninsula of Yucatan, and in that region continued, if they did not surpass, the architectural triumphs of the southern fatherland. But, in the opinion of the writer, not all of them took this route. Others probably pushed northward into Mexico and found their way, perhaps in bands of restricted numbers, to the neighborhood of Tollan and elsewhere in that region, where, following the example of their kindred in Yucatan, they established new settlements.

Not only does the founding of Tollan synchronize with the Maya exodus, but the name of the city was that of the mythical home and starting-place of the Maya tribes and it is obvious from their traditions that the Mexican Tollan took its name from an older and probably legendary Maya locality. Tollan was probably founded in the seventh century of our era. It probably existed for several centuries before the gradual entrance of the barbarous Nahua peoples, the Chichimecs, Aztecs, and other tribes, into the Valley of Mexico.

Tradition says that they overthrew the city, but good grounds appear for the assumption that it had been deserted for some considerable time prior to their arrival. I believe an interregnum of comparative unoccupation to have occurred between the invasions of two separate waves of Nahua or Mexican immigration. But it seems inevitable that many people of Maya stock would have remained in the neighborhood of Tollan after the first Nahua invasion, and that they would mingle with the invaders, to whom they would pass on the Maya culture.

This mixed race, Maya and Mexican, I believe to have been the Toltecs, who, in their turn, were overwhelmed by the second wave of Nahua immigrants into the Valley of Mexico. This would account for the circumstance that the Toltecs were said to have been Nahua, and that they spoke the Nahua language. As regards their later entrance into the Central American sphere, where their architectural remains are found, it is definitely stated in many authentic documents that mercenaries of the Nahua race served in the armies of the Northern Maya Confederation in Yucatan, where they acted as a species of Mamelukes or Janissaries, helping the Maya rulers to keep their people in the grip of one of the cruelest ecclesiastical tyrannies the world has ever seen.

These mercenaries made Chichen Itza in Yucatan their headquarters towards the end of the twelfth century. This antedates the foundation of Mexico City and at that epoch Toltec art had not yet become merged into the more modern Mexican or Aztec phase in which Cortes and his companions found it.

If these conclusions are found acceptable and they have the support of historical fact, as well as that of their own inherent probability they may, perhaps, serve as a temporary solution of the problem of Toltec origins until such time as further excavation and research cast fresh light in an enigma which has baffled inquirers into the past of America since the credulous century of Las Casas and Torquemada.

THE FALL OF TOLTEC POWER

In the following narrative of the fall of the Toltec power I have associated legend and probability with fiction in an effort to supply the reader with a general view of the wondrous culture of the people of Quetzalcoatl and the cause of their national and racial disappearance.

Near a thousand years have passed since Tollan fell; and this is the saga of its ruin. Now shall you hear how that sin-laden city of the dark-souled Toltecs crashed to dust and death beneath the spite of the offended gods. Hearken, then; but remember that there is that which is stronger than the gods, stronger than time for while the memory of Tollan, the city of hidden ecstasies and of men whose thoughts were beyond good and evil, lives in the dreams of but a few, if these few are as its sons, Tollan lives still.

Is the soul of Pompeii dead? Is the spirit of Babylon a withered thing? Tollan, city of the Toltecs, the race that preceded the Nahua Aztec of Mexico, ruled the valley and its subject races for wellnigh half a thousand years. Great were its men in artistry, so that with the folk of those days to say "Toltec" was as who should say "craftsman."

Happy the people the use of whose name is a constant praise on the lips of men. Where are the songs of Tollan? Under the hard soil of the sad mound of Tula we still find its carven capitals, its curious cups, its gems and gauds, the variegated fragments of its glowing and many colored life. Its foundations are laid bare to the sun, its vases, its peristyles and columns, its chiseled portals even in the riot of ruin, in the despond of mutilation, fill men's mouths with praise and their eyes with tears.

But where are its songs? Do they still live in Indian lays, are they still to be heard when the tortillas are being rolled and the maguey tapped of its wine? One of its songs I heard, the song of Huemac, the saga of the downfall of Tollan, the city of artists.

On a day when the chiseled walls resounded to the chorus of the Festival of Flowers, Huemac the King took his instruments of music and his painting tools and, casting his crown on the floor of mosaic, called to his son to pick it up and wear it in his stead if so he chose and having done so, he went forth to his villa outside the walls, followed by a great company of musicians and men who were cunning in the drawing of poems, poems in which the written words were no mere meaningless signs, but birds, beasts, trees, flowers and mountains. Now, as Huemac passed through the forest-ways alone for he had bade those who accompanied him leave him to his thoughts of song he was astonished by a brightness which fell athwart his path; and behold, before him there stood the god Tlaloc, in the awfulness of his majesty.

His face was terrible with the lines of tempest, and from his curved snout projected the gleaming serpent fangs. The blue stripe palpitated upon his cheekbone; his eye gleamed as a fire behind a thicket. His robe was spangled with silver, symbol of the element he ruled.

For a space the great god of the clouds gloomed upon the King; then he spake, and his voice was as the seed of thunder when it has birth behind the mountains and ere yet it has grown into the fuller oratory of tempest.

"Huemac," said the god, "wherefore hast thou done this thing wherefore given thy crown to a bastard?"

Huemac trembled, and his heart became as water within him. No word could he utter.

"Speak!" cried the god, with an awful gesture of command.

"Let thine evil lips defend thy wicked heart if so they may, O Huemac."

"Is he not mine own flesh and blood, O divine one? " faltered Huemac.

"Many sons have I, but is he not the fairest and the most fitted of all to wear the crown?"

"Huemac," thundered the god, "from the first has thy heart been dark and alien to my law. But thou art of the blood of the gods, therefore shalt thou be spared. But not so thy son, in whose veins the divine blood has become polluted. Long hath thy race offended heaven, and now shall it be destroyed utterly along with the accursed city it has raised."

"Mercy, O divine one," gasped Huemac, prostrating himself. "Mercy, O lord of many waters."

"The day for mercy is past," replied the god harshly, and wrapped himself in a black cloud from which darted the mordant lines of lightning.

Huemac gazed after it until it disappeared as one deprived of sense and motion, and then rising slowly and mightily a-tremble, returned to the city. He found his son with Urendequa, chief of the dancers. Now this woman was past her prime and ill-favored of face. But of all the women in Tollan, she was most desired.

The Prince, now King, lay with his crowned head in her lap in the chamber of shells, picked from sea-beaches far away and encrusted on bricks of silver. The pair paid little attention to Huemac's entrance, but when they marked his face they rose hastily.

"Acxitl," he cried, embracing his son, "Acxitl, the prophecy has come to pass. We are a race accursed of the gods. I have seen and spoken with Tlaloc. He hath cursed us and our city because I have bestowed my place upon you."

"Since when did the gods dictate their way to the sons of Hueymatzin?" sneered Acxitl, slim, sallow, and languorous, with a heavy mouth and woman's brows.

"Since when did Tollan cry mercy from the dotards of heaven?" Urendequa laughed deep down in her bosom, but Huemac paled and trembled.

"Peace!" he cried. "We are a race accursed. We must no more blaspheme but placate the gods. Let us hasten to the Quetzalcoatl Teohuatzin, the High Priest, and hearken to him how perchance we may avoid the ruin that is near us."

But the sneer was heavy upon the thick lips of Acxitl.

"Let us hasten to where the scented octli glitters in the cup, O my father," he said soothingly but mockingly. "Let us forget what the god-fool hath uttered. Come!"

But Huemac shrank back.

"It may not be, son," he muttered. "Go thou and feast if so it please thee, but as for me, I will betake me to the temple."

"Every man to where his soul leads him," replied Acxitl, lightly. "Come, Urendequa," and linking his arm in that of the dancer, he went forth.

Huemac followed them, and watched them trip lightly down the carven staircase to the banqueting hall. Then he crossed the courtyard and wended slowly up the hillside to where stood the temple of Quetzal.

As he reached its portals he turned and surveyed the city beneath him, lying under the red veils of the evening, smoldering and glittering in the immense last outpourings of the sun. The walls rich with mosaic and rare stones glistened in faint pearl and argentine. Vermilion, iris, and the shimmer of sea-stone rose from roof and capital, cornice, and pilaster.

The city, planned after no plan but as in a dream-night's rhapsody, hung between the mists of the plain and the golden peninsulas of the clouds as an island of fantasy a rare shell for the enclosing of some rich and melodious secret, the coffer holding a life's desire, the inaccessible home of a music which it was not man's to grasp, of a fire which only a demi-god might come at and filch for earth-use.

As Huemac gazed on in love and dismay the soft innocence of evening descended with dove's wings upon the roofs and quenched the fires of sun-blood. A pale and curving moon swam pearl-like in the unimpassioned sea of air, quivering at first like a butterfly which sought to reach the sun's candle and fall into its heart.

The satyr-shapes of night came down, and dancing, skirted the forest, flowers folded and the stars came forth. A great and vastly solemn calm fell on everything even the very stones seemed to have found a deeper quality of death. The sun went out, and Huemac climbed the temple stairs in the darkness to drink the hope of prayer.

Right rich was that feast-chamber where Acxitl sat with Urendequa, they two alone. For the others had gone to the house of Huemac outside the walls, thinking there to find music and songs, little wotting that Huemac was stretched on his face in the white temple of Quetzal high up on the hill.

The soft chime of golden cups and the tinkle of the silver bells fringing the painted curtains as the evening air stole in and out of the place were louder than the whispers of Acxitl and Urendequa the dancer. The high chamber, with its narrow walls stamped in frette and painted in somber reds with a frieze of feathered gods in panoply of war or worship, was met for whisperers.

Stark, clean, complete, decisive its plan, yet shadowed, the strong thing veiled, the sharp thing rounded by shade rather than by chisel the primal and gigantesque screened by the mysterious. Here had been carven a bas-relief of the loves of Tlazolteotl, lewd goddess of luxury, the work done by the light of torches so that it might only be revealed beneath the tints of the glow in which it had been chiseled.

Urendequa spoke.

"So you do not tremble?" she asked.

Acxitl smiled slowly.

"Tremble?" he said, "at what, I pray you, Urendequa, at the wrath of the gods."

"My friend," he said," you have lived forty years as a dancer do you find aught to tremble at in the thought of death?"

"Aye," she replied. "Aye, one thing makes me tremble."

"That you may not dance in Mictlan?"

"Aye so; death ends all art."

"But age; does not that end the dancer's art?"

"It is so, Prince. I am weary; I cannot foot it as when I first danced before your father. My body grows heavy. Five years ago I feared death as the extinguisher of art; since then I had not thought of it. Now this night I see death as a disrobing-room where there is rest for those who have danced out their dance. But you are young and your limbs are supple. You are young and wise. Why should you desire death?"

"O Urendequa," replied the Prince, "well has it been said that the wisdom of women aye, even of the wisest woman is tethered to the earth. I am wise therefore I see this love of life and art to be but a snare, a bait which the unskillful gods have laid to keep us here. Who lacking the instinct of life or the love of art would not willingly go down into the vapors of Mictlan? I tell you these gods they have miscarven this ugly world, but for the credit of their godhead they must pretend that it is good. Hence have they cursed us with a love of life so that we may not affront them by fleeing the prison to which they have doomed us.

"Tis well for them to measure out a way for us. Oh, how easy it is for a god to point the way to man, and how simple it were for a man to play the god. But this curse; no philosophy will. I do not seek to meet it with philosophy. I will play my manhood against their divinity. They curse me because I am a man and not of their blood. I do not seek life. But let the blame for my taking off rest upon them alone. So shall it be said, ' They slew him because he found them out."

A sound as of a great tempest rushed through the chamber and the torches flickered, waved, and went out. Urendequa screamed; Acxitl laughed.

"Fools," he snarled. "Strike if ye will, but spare me such buffoonery as this!" And he called for torches. The faces of those who brought them seemed pallid, and they trembled greatly.

"There is small need for torches, lord," faltered one.

"Behold!" and drawing aside the curtain from an open casement, he pointed to where two great volcanoes which overlooked Tollan belched black and red into the emerald night. Above them, shadowed on the sky, grisly apparitions reared their heads, threatening the city with terrible menace.

Urendequa clapped her hands over her eyes and sank into her seat, moaning softly. Acxitl gave a thin, sneering laugh and stood looking on as at a juggling entertainment, applauding now and again when a more than usually gorgeous effect of color emanated from one or other of the volcanoes, or when the gestures of the mighty shades above them waxed more vehement and threatening.

There was a hurrying of crowds through the streets as people sought the temple. Voices cried out in the extreme of woe and terror. Far away sounded the monotonous beating of a great drum. The sin of the Toltecs had found them out.

The air was thick with falling ashes and scoriae, and the vengeful mutterings coming from the volcanoes had now swelled into the most terrific reverberations, which shook the city from wall to wall, so that the gorgeous houses rocked and the place of banquet in which Acxitl and Urendequa still remained swayed like a ship in the hollows of the sea.

"Save thyself, Prince!" cried a voice in passing, the owner of which had evidently recognized Acxitl.

"Save thyself, for the anger of the gods has come upon us."

But Acxitl only smiled. A great stone from one of the volcanoes struck the casement above his head, but he moved not. Urendequa seized and dragged him from the window as Huemac dashed into the room.

In the awful half-light of the smoky conflagration they saw that the old King's face was white as parchment and his eyes a deeper red than fire.

"Fly," he cried.

"Waste not a moment, boy. The Chichimecs are at the gates!"

The Chichimecs, the Huns of the Mexican plateau, hung ever upon the Toltec borders, their wolfish bands patrolling it for the capture of merchant caravans or wealthy travellers. For generations they had menaced Tollan. Now they were at her gates clamoring for entrance so that they might spoil her and return to enrich their mound-temples with her golden cups and gauds of ritual.

Already the clash of weapons and the shouts of men in combat could be heard at the gate hard by the palace. But Acxitl stirred not.

"Up, Prince!" cried Urendequa, "will you not fight?"

"My quarrel is not with the Chichimecs," replied Acxitl, "but with the gods."

"Madman!" cried Huemac. "Quick, with me to the temple. Let us prostrate ourselves. Even yet there is time."

"Wherefore has this thing happened?" asked Acxitl dully. "Because, forsooth, our way has not pleased the gods. Must we walk according to their vanity? Shall we toil constantly so that they may have seed; shall we fight constantly so that they may have blood; shall we pray constantly so that their vanity may increase? Do thou those things if thou wilt; but as for me, I have surprised their secret, and I am no more their slave. The door of escape from their prison-house is death, and he who, knowing this will not pass its portals is a slave. This door I shall force them to open to me.

"Tollan has been a city of music, of love, of rare converse, of a secret spirit, of many rich pleasantries and richer tears. Here have dwelt men who reveled in the making of things. Of all this the dotards of heaven are a- weary. They pine for praise, which is their food as much as blood is."

A terrific shock caused the palace to rock to its foundations. A great pillar, heavy with symbols, swayed and crashed downwards, the sound of its fall lost in the tumult of subterranean thunder. A shaft of lightning clove the darkness and showed them the face of Urendequa lying crushed beneath the painted capital.

A dry sob sounded in Acxitl's throat, but with a maniac shriek Huemac fled from the banqueting hall into the street. Never again was the last King of Tollan beheld by mortal man, Toltec or Chichimec.

Another lightning flash and Acxitl groped his way to a trophy of arms hard by the painted altar. Seizing a maquahuitl, a club set with obsidian edges, he staggered through the gloom out into the causeway.

The streets were knee-deep with ashes, and great stones hurtling through the air rang on roof and wall, crushing the fine details of capital and portico, mutilating wondrous carving. Still he groped onwards, until he came to the place where stood the temple of Tlaloc.

Before the fane was a great statue of the god, recumbent on elbows and with huddled knees, typifying the hill-land whence came the rains. As Acxitl gazed upon the massive block of greenstone the tramp of armed men resounded on the cobbles and gave him pause. Through the gloom he could see a band of Chichimecs, a befeathered chief at their head.

"Stand, brothers," he cried, "and hearken to me. Today I was King in Tollan; we were too happy here, and the gods grew wroth against us because we neglected their worship. Happy, too, was I, until I found that man cannot live save on sufferance of the gods, and no snare of life or art shall now hold me in such servitude. Thus do I force the gods to open the door of death."

And raising high his maquahuitl, he smote the image of Tlaloc full on the bended neck. The weapon shattered, and its flinty blade tinkled in fragments to the ground; but the head, mayhap by reason of a flaw in the stone, nodded, fell, and rolled into the gutter. Acxitl laughed aloud. A jagged circle of flame burst from the heavens, and a great thunderbolt hurtled earthward. Acxitl was one with the ashes which littered the causeway.

"Great indeed are the gods!" whispered the Chichimec chief in profoundest awe.

"Great indeed are they of whom we are the unworthy instruments. This city was full of sin and its King was rnad. His fate be upon his head."

"Yet," said a shield-bearer beside him, "it is not every man who can force the gods to slay him, so that his blood may witness against them. Is not he who can coerce the gods almost as a god himself?"

THE RISE OF THE CRANE PEOPLE

After the "disappearance" of the Toltecs, one wave of Nahua after another descended upon the Valley of Mexico, until at last the Aztecs, or "Crane People" settled on the borders of Lake Tezcuco. They were a warlike and somewhat taciturn folk, with a deeply rooted love of the mysterious, fond of dancing and flowers, but dwelling under the shadow of one of the most gloomy religions ever established by mankind, a faith which chiefly manifested itself in human sacrifice and penitential exercises of a severe nature. Yet they were and are, whatever some Europeans and Americans may think, a people gifted with an ability to regard the subtle side of things with extraordinary nicety, as is shown by the rich and involved character of the mythology they developed.

They entered the Mexican Valley at the beginning of the fourteenth century, and in the course of the two centuries or so between their settlement there and the conquest of Cortes succeeded by warlike prowess in bringing under their dominion nearly all the tribes then dwelling in Mexico. At the period of the Conquest the lacustrine city of Mexico-Tenochtitlan contained 60,000 houses and about 300,000 inhabitants, and the Lake of Tezcuco, on which it was partly built, was ringed round with other large cities.

The site was intersected by four great road- ways or avenues built at right angles to one another, and laid four-square with the cardinal points. Situated as it was in the midst of a lake, it was traversed by numerous canals, which were used as thorough- fares for traffic.

The four principal ways described above were extended across the lake as dykes or viaducts until they met its shores. The dwellings of the poorer classes were chiefly composed of adobe, but those of the nobility were built of a red porous stone quarried close by. They were usually of one story only, but occupied a goodly area, and had flat roofs, many of which were covered with flowers.

They were usually coated with hard white cement, which gave them an added resemblance to the Oriental type of building. Towering high among these, and a little apart from the vast squares and market-places, were the teocallis, or temples. These were not covered-in buildings, but "high places," great pyramids of stone, built platform on platform, and a coiling staircase led to the summit, on which was usually erected a small shrine containing the tutelary deity to whom the teocalli had been raised.

The great temple of Uitzilopochtli, the war-god, built by King Ahuizotl, was, besides being typical of all, by far the greatest of these votive piles. The enclosing walls of the building were 4800 feet in circumference, and strikingly decorated by carvings representing festoons of intertwined reptiles, from which circumstance they were called coetpantli (walls of serpents). A kind of gatehouse on each side gave access to the enclosure.

The teocalli, or great temple, inside the court was in the shape of a parallelogram, measuring 375 feet by 300 feet, and was built in six platforms, growing smaller in area as they ascended. The mass of this structure was composed of a mixture of rubble, clay, and earth, covered with carefully worked stone slabs, cemented together with infinite care, and coated with hard gypsum.

A flight of 340 steps circled round the terraces and led to the upper platform, on which were raised two three- storied towers 56 feet in height, in which stood the great statues of the tutelary deities and the jasper stones of sacrifice. These sanctuaries, say the old Conquistadores who entered them, had the appearance and odor of shambles, and human blood was bespattered everywhere. In this weird chapel of horrors burned a fire, the extinction of which, it was supposed, would have precipitated the end of the Nahua power.

It was tended with a care as scrupulous as that with which the Roman Vestals guarded their sacred flame. No less than six hundred of these sacred braziers were kept alight in the city of Mexico alone. The civilization of the people who inhabited Mexico was of a much higher order than that of many communities which have enjoyed greater advantages.

Although its people were ignorant of the uses of iron and steel, for which they substituted the sharp sherds of the obsidian stone, they possessed many of the refinements of the most cultivated nations of Europe a noble if bizarre architecture, a high sense of the value of color, an art which owed little to imitation and much to nature and to their own imaginative capacity, a useful if primitive system of writing, a well-defined legal code and no mean skill in the military art.

If Aztec society was established on rather hard-and-fast lines, it was still so perfectly controlled that every individual had his niche, which was, indeed, marked out for him at birth. A caste system obtained in the case of craftsmen, but the position of women appears to have been much more free than in any other human society outside Europe.

The Aztecs, and indeed the entire Nahua race, employed a system of writing of the type scientifically described as "pictographic," in which events, persons, and ideas were recorded by means of drawings and colored sketches. These were executed on paper made from the agave plant, or were painted on the skins of animals.

By these means not only history and the principles of the Nahua mythology were communicated from generation to generation, but the transactions of daily life, the accountings of mer- chants, and the purchase and ownership of land were placed on record. That a phonetic system was rapidly being approached was manifest from the method by which the Nahua scribes depicted the names of individuals or cities.

These were represented by means of several objects, the names of which resembled that of the person for which they stood. The name of King Ixcoatl, for example, is represented by the drawing of a serpent (coatl) pierced by flint knives (Iztli), and that of Motequauhzoma (Montezuma) by a mouse-trap (montli), an eagle (quauhtli), a lancet (zo), and a hand (maitl).

The phonetic values employed by the scribes varied exceedingly, so that at times an entire syllable would be expressed by the painting of an object the name of which commenced with it, at other times only a letter would be represented by the same drawing. But the general intention of the scribes was undoubtedly more ideographic than phonetic; that is, they desired to convey their thoughts more by sketch than by sound.

These pinturas, as the Spanish conquerors called them, offer no very great difficulty in their elucidation to modern experts, at least so far as the general trend of their contents is concerned. In this they are unlike the manuscripts of the Maya of Central America, with which we shall make acquaintance farther on. Their interpretation was largely traditional, and was learned by rote, being passed on by one generation of amamatini (readers) to another, and they were by no means capable of being read by all and sundry.

The life of the people varied considerably with their caste and avocations. The lower classes in the country districts were almost wholly agricultural, and acted as laborers in the maize fields, or hunters, fowlers, and fishers, while the working folk in the towns wrought at such trades as building, the making of feather robes, jewelry, and so forth.

Vendors of flowers, fruit, vegetables, and fish crowded the large markets and public squares, and each of these trades and castes had its particular patron god. The upper class was aristocratic and exclusive. The monarch was regarded as a deity, and his office was an elective one, but he might be appointed from the royal family only, and at the instance of the great nobles alone.

The gulf betwixt the autocratic class and the people was a wide one, though prowess in war was capable of bridging it and a doughty soldier might well be advanced to the position of a knight. The architecture of ancient Mexico, if bizarre, was not undistinguished. In the cities the better houses were built of stone, four-square and stable, and ornamented with designs taken from Aztec symbolism.

They had flat roofs or azoteas, and heavily eaved doorways. The city of Mexico has already been described, but it behoves to pay some attention to the more celebrated architectural monuments in other parts of the country.

Although Mexico is not as rich in ruins of her great past as are Yucatan or Guatemala, where the growth of forests has protected the architectural antiquities of these countries, it is not without several striking examples of native building. In the northern part of the states of Vera Cruz are to be found the great pyramids of Teotihuacan and the beautiful teocalli of Xochicalco.

The former place was the Mecca of the Nahua races, and its pyramids of the Sun and Moon are surrounded by extensive cemeteries where the devout had been interred in the hope that their souls would thus find entrance to the paradise of the sun. The teocalli of the moon has a base covering 426 feet and a height of 137 feet. That of the sun is of greater dimensions, with a base of 735 feet and a height of 203 feet.

These pyramids were divided into four stories, three of which remain in each case. On the summit of that of the sun stood a temple containing a great image of that luminary carved from a rough block of stone. In the breast was inlaid a star of the purest gold, seized afterwards as loot by the insatiable followers of Cortes. From the teocalli of the moon a path runs to where a little rivulet flanks the "Citadel."

This path is known as "The Path of the Dead," it is surrounded by some nine square miles of tombs and tumuli, and, indeed, forms a road through the great cemetery. Xochicalco, "The Hill of Flowers," near Tezcuco, is a teocalli or pyramid of amazing beauty, built of richly sculptured blocks of porphyry 12 feet in length, depicting the god Quetzalcoatl as the great serpent-bird.

The site of Tollan, the Toltec city, is equally impressive as regards its remains discovered by excavation. Charnay unearthed there gigantic fragments of caryatids, each some seven feet high. He also found columns of two pieces, which were fitted together by means of mortise and tenon, bas-reliefs of archaic figures of undoubted Nahua type, and many fragments of great antiquity.

On the hill of Palpan, above Tollan, he found the ground-plans of several houses with numerous apartments, frescoed, columned, and having benches and cisterns recalling the impluvium of a Roman villa. Water-pipes were also actually unearthed, and a wealth of pottery, many pieces of which resembled old Japanese china.

The ground-plan or foundations of the houses uncovered at Palpan showed that they had been designed by practical architects, and had not been built in merely haphazard fashion. The cement which covered the walls and floors was of excellent quality, and recalled that found in ancient Italian excavations. The roofs had been of wood, supported by pillars. Only the briefest sketch of Aztec history can be offered here. At the period when the Nahua tribes proper first settled on the borders of Lake Tezcuco their communities grouped themselves around two of the larger sites, Azcapozalco and Tezcuco, which may be described as the Athens of Mexico, the literary and artistic capital. A fierce rivalry sprang up between these cities, and ended in the discomfiture of the former.

From this time Mexican history may be said to commence, the Tezcucan power over- running the entire area from the Mexican Gulf to the Pacific. On the rise of the Aztecs in the fourteenth century they allied themselves with the tribe of the Tecpanecs of Tlacopan, and little by little subdued most of the lacustrine communities, penetrating also into the Otomi country to the north. Finally, they subdued Tezcuco itself.

The Tezcucans had levied an embargo against their goods and refused them intercourse. War followed, probably about 1428, and the Aztecs defeated the Tezcucan confederacy with great slaughter. An alliance ensued between Aztec Mexico, Tezcuco and Tlacopan, the allies overran many states far beyond the confines of the Valley, and by the period of the Spanish Conquest had extended their boundaries almost to the limits of the present Mexican Republic. They levied a strictly collected tribute from their conquered subjects, manufacturing the raw material exacted from them, which they sold again in its finished state to the tribes under their sway, until at last Mexico became the chief market of the empire.

When Montezuma I. came to the throne in 1440 he almost at once began to extend the Aztec dominions. He had been both high priest of the kingdom and its commander-in-chief, but now he displayed ability as a town-planner, building beautiful palaces and temples and the dykes or passage-ways which connected the city with the mainland, and constructing canals. But horrible human sacrifices disfigured the civilization of this people, growing with the power of the Aztec state, regarded as they were as a sign of heavenly favor as manifested in conquest and prosperity.

The peoples surrounding the Aztecs came to loathe the hateful power which drew countless thousands of victims to the smoking altar of the war-god Uitzilopochtli, and when Axayacatl became king in 1468 several revolts broke out. But these were broken, and when Montezuma II. began to reign, Mexico and all its dependencies were ripe for rebellion once more. No need to repeat here the story of the Spanish Conquest. But that Castilian rule shattered a hegemony of monstrous evil, who can question?

The Aztec state seemed never to have even a doubt as to the inherent virtue resident in its sanguinary regime. But Beneficence, which will not permit evil to reign for ever, set over the Aztec people the rod of an iron tyranny which seems in some measure the just due of a race which had so wantonly flouted those common dictates of mercy and humanity which peoples far less cultured than the Aztec have displayed.

Whether the Mexican peoples are inherently cruel, or whether the awful devil-worship they once indulged in has rendered them so, who shall presume to say? But an examination of their subsequent history lends color to the assumption that if they are not natively the most barbarous among the world's nations they have in this respect, along with outstanding virtues, a "bad eminence" which even their well-wishers cannot but deplore.

CHAPTER II
THE MAGICAL ASSOCIATIONS OF MEXICAN RELIGION

To understand Mexican Magic and the attitude of the ancient Mexicans towards the supernatural, it is necessary to explain the fundamental tendencies of religion as understood on the plateau of Mexico. At first sight these appear as inextricable, but in reality they are capable of very simple treatment indeed.

The basis of Mexican religion, it will be found, is really a magical one, the gods are magical figures, and their rites arose out of magical practice. As observed at the period of the Spanish Conquest, Mexican religion appears complex enough, but research has succeeded in referring almost every one of its beliefs to very simple and even primitive ideas, however, which contain the root elements of magical knowledge and practice. The tales which give us the clue to early religious influences in Mexico are mostly associated with the pre-Aztec or Toltec civilization.

Many of them refer to a god or culture-hero called Quetzalcoatl, who is described as a magician and the inventor of the astrological tonalamatl, or *Book of Fate*. The faith he introduced differed greatly from that in vogue at the period of the Conquest. It inculcated purification and penance by the drawing of blood from the tongue and thighs, and was unfriendly to the cannibal rites later practiced. But this cult was to a great extent superseded by that of other and earlier deities.

Beneath the worship of these we can descry one out- standing purpose the desire to ensure such a supply of rain by magical means as would result in a crop of maize sufficient to keep the people in life. Out of this was developed a rain-cult of such elaborate character that a most complex theology, pantheon, and system of ethical conduct came in turn to be associated with it.

The original native deities of Mexico presided over vegetable and cereal growth, and those who came to be identified with the creative idea or with the heavenly bodies were either gods of growth to whom these attributes had become fortuitously attached, or were the products of later priestly speculation. In a land as arid as Mexico it is scarcely surprising that the magical production of rain should have become the chief religious endeavor of the people.

Famine and its accompanying evils followed upon a dry agricultural season and subjected the race to all the miseries of hunger and thirst. What wonder, then, that they deified the powers of rain, exalted them above all others, and by every supernatural means strove to avert the disaster of a dry season? The earth they regarded as the cipactli or dragon-beast which brought forth the grain and which might fail in its powers unless nurtured by draughts of human blood.

The more she was nourished by this dreadful wine the more she was capable of bringing forth. Blood, human or animal, was conceived of as rain in another form, of being capable of transformation into rain, the fructifying essence which descended from above. The earth became in the popular idea the goddess Coatlicue, to whom thousands of hearts must annually be offered up in the hope of a good harvest.

There were many other deities of growth, probably of foreign importation, that is originally belonging to other tribes than the Aztecs, but the dragon-statue of this goddess, still preserved in the National Museum at Mexico City, displays her as the Earth-Mother par excellence, clad in her serpent-robe and hung with the skin of a sacrificed woman, her merciless countenance covered by a serpent or dragon's mask, surmounting the grotesque riot of symbolic attributes by which she is covered.

GODS THAT THIRST FOR HUMAN BLOOD

Deeply rooted in the Mexican mind was the idea that unless the gods were abundantly refreshed with human blood they would perish of hunger and old age and would be unable to undertake their labors in connection with the growth of the crops. Whence came this idea?

Undoubtedly from that process of barbaric reasoning through which Mexican man had convinced himself that the amount of rainfall would be in ratio to the amount of blood shed sacrificially. Eduard Seler, the German savant, has indicated his belief in such a process of reasoning by stating that "the one was intended to draw down the other, the blood which was offered was intended to bring down the rain upon the fields."

This, then, is the precise nature of the compact between Mexican man and his gods: Do ut des, "Give us rain, and we shall give you blood." Once this is understood the basic nature of Mexican religion becomes clear, and all the later additions of theology and priestly invention can be viewed as mere excrescences and ornaments upon the simple architecture of the temple of the rain-cult.

Many were the methods by which blood and hearts were offered up to the gods, and the several festivals at which this rite was in vogue differed slightly from each other in ritual and procedure. But that which may be regarded as supplying perhaps the most general form of the horrid rite was that of the Xalaquia, a festival held at the season when the magic plant had attained its full growth.

The women of the city wore their hair unbound, and shook and tossed it so that by sympathetic magic the maize might grow correspondingly long. Hymns were sung to the earth- goddess Chicomecohuatl, a variant of Coatlicue, and hilarious dances were nightly performed in the teopan (temple), the central figure in which was the Xalaquia, a female captive or slave, with face painted red and yellow to represent the colors of the maize plant.

She had previously undergone a long course of training in the dancing-school, and now, all unaware of the horrible fate awaiting her, she danced and pirouetted gaily among the rest. Throughout the duration of the festival she danced, and on its expiring night she was accompanied in a kind of ballet by the women of the community, who circled round her, chanting the deeds of Chicomecohuatl.

When day- break appeared the company was joined by the chiefs and headmen, who, along with the exhausted and half-fainting victim, danced the solemn death-dance. The entire community then approached the teocalli (pyramid of sacrifice), and, its summit reached, the victim was stripped to a nude condition, the priest plunged a knife of flint into her bosom, and, tearing out the still palpitating heart, offered it up to Chicomecohuatl.

In this manner the venerable goddess, weary with the labors of inducing growth in the maize-plant, was supposed to be revivified and refreshed. Hence the victim's name Xalaquia, which signifies "She who is clothed with the Sand." Apart altogether from the more primitive deities of grain, were gods of somewhat higher status, several of whom were thought of as having introduced the practice of magic into Mexico.

The most remarkable of these was Quetzalcoatl, the grand enchanter. Regarding this Quetzalcoatl, we possess an extraordinary amount of material which alone makes it certain that he was a figure of primary importance. Indeed, some modern authorities have proved to their own satisfaction that he was a veritable human personage, and with this view I am in general agreement.

Perhaps the best account of his history is that of Sahagun, a Spanish friar of the sixteenth century, who had exceptional opportunities of collecting the traditions of the Aztecs. Quetzalcoatl, he tells us, was a great civilizing agent, who entered Mexico at the head of a band of strangers, the Toltecs. He imported the arts into the country and especially fostered agriculture.

In his time maize was so large in the head that a man might not carry more than one stalk at a time, and cotton grew in all colors without having to be dyed. He built spacious and elegant houses, and inculcated a type of religion which fostered peace, and the rites of which included the drawing of blood by way of penance. But sorcerers came against Quetzalcoatl and his people, the Toltecs, and these, we are told, were the gods Tezcatlipoca, Uitzilopochtli, and Tlacuepan. Tezcatlipoca visited the house of Quetzalcoatl in the guise of an old man, but was told that he was sick, and was at first refused entrance.

Later, however, he was admitted, Quetzalcoatl observing that he had waited for him for many days. Tezcatlipoca then produced a draught of medicine which, he assured the sick king, would intoxicate him, ease his heart, and carry his thoughts away from the trials and fatigues of death and departure. This latter statement inspired Quetzalcoatl to ask whence he must go, for that he had a premonition of departure seems clear.

"To Tollantlapallan," replied Tezcatlipoca, "where another old man awaits thee. He and you shall speak together, and on thy return thou shalt be as a youth, yea as a boy."

With little goodwill Quetzalcoatl quaffed the medicine, and having once tasted of it, he drank more deeply, so that at last he became intoxicated and maudlin. That which he had drunk was the wine made from the maguey-plant, called teoncetl ("drink of the gods"). And so great a longing to depart came upon him that at length he arose and went from Tollan. Ere departing, Quetzalcoatl burned his houses of shells and silver and buried many precious things in the mountains.

He reached the coast after many adventures, incidentally losing all his servants, who perished through cold whilst traversing the snowy sides of a volcano. At length he came to the sea, where he commanded that a raft of serpents should appear, and in this he seated himself as in a canoe, and set out for Tlapallan, the mysterious country whence he had come. Another Spanish friar, Torquemada, says of Quetzalcoatl and his comrades that they came from the north by way of Panuco, dressed in long robes of black linen, cut low at the neck, with short sleeves.

They came to Tollan, but finding the country there too thickly peopled, passed on to Cholula, where they were well received. Their chief was Quetzalcoatl, a man with ruddy complexion and long beard. These people multiplied and sent colonists to the Mixtec and Zapotec countries, raising the great buildings at Mitla.

They were cunning handicraftsmen, not so good at masonry as at jewelers' work, sculpture, and agriculture. Tezcatlipoca and Huemac conceived an enmity to Quetzalcoatl, and as he did not wish to go to war with them he and his folk removed to Onohualco (Yucatan, Tabasco, and Campeche). Mendieta, a Castilian author, alludes to the manner in which Quetzalcoatl originated the astrological calendar. He says that the gods thought it well that the people should have some means of writing by which they might direct themselves, and two of their number, Oxomoco and Cipactonal, who dwelt in a cave in Cuernavaca, especially considered the matter. Cipactonal thought that her descendant Quetzalcoatl should be consulted, and she called him into counsel. He, too, thought the idea of a calendar good, and the two addressed themselves to the task of making the tonalamatl, or Book of Fate.

To Cipactonal was given the privilege of choosing and writing the first sign or day-symbol of the calendar. She painted the cipactli or dragon animal, and called the sign ce cipactli ("one cipactli"). Oxomoco then wrote ome acatl ("two cane"), and Quetzalcoatl" three house," and so on, until the thirteen signs were completed.

We will also find Quetzalcoatl in Maya lore when we come to consider it, under the names of Kukulcan, Gucumatz, and Votan. Quetzalcoatl later became sanctified in godlike guise, and was worshiped as the god of the trade wind which brings the fructifying rains to Mexico. It was in this character that he was supposed to depart to the land of refreshment to seek the new rain. But that originally he was a real man we cannot doubt, as indeed Dr. H. J. Spinden has proved, and in my belief he was a primitive wizard or medicine-man who introduced the magical art and astrology into Mexico and Central America.

Regarded as the inventor of the tonalamatl, or *Book of Fate*, he gained a reputation as the possessor of profound wisdom, and came to be looked upon as the magician or sage par excellence. The name implies "feathered serpent," or, according to some other authorities, "Precious Twin."

It is chiefly in the myths of Central America rather than in those of Mexico that the magical character of Quetzalcoatl is to be remarked.

These speak of him most definitely as a magician, and the cult of the Nagualists, a magical society, regarded him as its peculiar patron. The next magician-god we encounter is Tezcatlipoca, or "Fiery Mirror," so-called because he took his name from the obsidian scrying-stone of the Mexican seers.

This stone had an especial sanctity for the Mexicans, as it provided the sacrificial knives employed by the priests, and we possess good evidence that obsidian in its fetish form was worshiped even so late as the eighteenth century by the Nahuatl-speaking Chotas, who comprised it in a trinity with the Dawn and the Serpent. But another important link connects Tezcatlipoca with obsidian. Bernal Diaz states that they called this stone or vitreous glass "Tezcat." From it mirrors were manufactured as divinatory media to be used by the wizards.

Sahagun says that it was known as aitztli (water obsidian), probably because of the high polish of which it was capable. Another such stone he mentions was called tepochtli, which I would translate "wizard stone," and from which I think, by a process of etymological confusion, Tezcatlipoca received one of his minor names, Telpochtli, "the youth." The name of the god means "Smoking Mirror," and Acosta says that the Mexicans called Tezcatlipoca's mirror irlacheaya (an obvious error for tlachialoni), "his glass to look in," otherwise the mirror or scrying-stone in which he was able to witness the doings of mankind.

It is possible that the "smoke" which was said to rise from this mirror symbolized the haziness which clouds the surface of a divinatory glass prior to the phenomenon of vision therein. Thus from the shape beheld in the seer's mirror Tezcatlipoca came to be regarded as the seer. That into which the wizard gazed became so closely identified with sorcery as to be thought of as wizard-like itself; for Tezcatlipoca is, of all Mexican deities, the one most nearly connected with the wizard's art, the art of Black Magic.

He is distinctively the nocturnal god who haunts the crossways and appears in a myriad phantom guises to the night-bound wayfarer. "These," says Sahagun, "were masks that Tezcatlipoca assumed to frighten the people."

He wears the symbol of night upon his forehead; he is the moon, ruler of the night, the wizard who veils himself behind the clouds; he bears as a magical instrument the severed arm of a woman who has died in childbed, as did the naualli or sorcerers of old Mexico. From him all ominous and uncanny sounds proceed: the howl of the jaguar (in which we perceive Tezcatlipoca as the wizard metamorphosed into the wer-animal), and the foreboding cry of the uactli bird, the voc, the prophesying bird of Hurakan in the "Popol Vuh," the magical book of Central America. Tezcatlipoca, at the period of the Conquest, had developed attributes of a more lofty kind than any of those deities already described.

Like Quetzalcoatl, and because he was a god of the wind or atmosphere, he came to be regarded as the personification of the breath of life. In the mind of savage man the wind is usually the giver of breath, the great storehouse of respiration, the source of immediate life. In many mythologies the name of the principal deity is synonymous with that for wind, and in many languages the words "soul" and "breath" have a common origin. But it is as a sorcerer that we must regard Tezcatlipoca in this place, and that side of his character is well depicted in the myths concerning the manner in which he plagued the Toltecs.

Sahagun recounts a myth which tells how, disguised as a peddler named Toveyo, he behaved much as did the Pied Piper. "This Toveyo adorned all his body with the rich feathers called tocivitl, and commanded the Toltecs to gather together for a festival, and sent a crier up to the top of the mountain Tzatzitepec, to call in the strangers and the people afar off to dance and to feast. A numberless multitude gathered to Tollan. When they were all gathered, Toveyo led them out, young men and girls, to a place called Texcalapa, where he himself began and led the dancing, playing on a drum. He sang, too, singing each verse to the dancers, who sang it after him, though they knew not the song beforehand. Then was to be seen a marvelous and terrible thing. A panic seized the Toltecs. There was a gorge or ravine there, with a river rushing through it called the Texcaltlauhco. A stone bridge led over the river. Toveyo broke down this bridge as the people fled. He saw them tread and crush each other down, under-foot and over into the abyss. They that fell were turned into rocks and stones; as for those that escaped, they did not see nor think that it was Toveyo and his sorceries that had wrought this great destruction; they were blinded by the witchcraft of the god, and out of their senses, like drunken men."

Another of his sorceries is described as follows: "And after this Tezcatlipoca wrought another witchcraft against the Toltecs. He called himself Tlacavepan, or Acexcoch, and came and sat down in the midst of the market-place of Tulla, having a little manikin (said to have been the god Uitzilopochtli) dancing upon his hand. There was an instant uproar of all the buyers and sellers and a rush to see the miracle. The people crushed and trod each other down, so that many were killed there; and all this happened many times. At last the god-sorcerer cried out on one such occasion: 'What is this? Do you not see that you are befooled by us? Stone and kill us.' So the people took up stones and killed the said sorcerer and his little dancing manikin. But when the body of the sorcerer had lain in the market-place for some time it began to stink and to taint the air, and the wind of it poisoned many. Then the dead sorcerer spoke again, saying: 'Cast this body outside the town, for many Toltecs die because of it.' So they prepared to cast out the body, and fastened ropes thereto and pulled. But the ill-smelling corpse was so heavy that they could not move it. Then a crier made a proclamation, saying: 'Come, all ye Toltecs, and bring ropes with you, that we may drag out and get rid of this pestilential carcass.' All came accordingly, bringing ropes, and the ropes were fastened to the body and all pulled. It was utterly in vain. Rope after rope broke with a sudden snap, and those that dragged on a rope fell and were killed when it broke. Then the dead wizard looked up and said: 'O Toltecs, a verse of song is needed.' And he himself gave them a verse. They repeated the verse after him, and, singing it, pulled all together, so that with shouts they hauled the body out of the city, though still not without many ropes breaking and many persons being killed as before. All this being over, those Toltecs that remained unhurt returned every man to his place, not remembering anything of what had happened, for they were all as drunken."

Other signs and wonders were wrought by Tezcatlipoca in his role of sorcerer. A white bird called Iztac cuixtli was clearly seen flying over Tollan, transfixed with a dart. At night also the sierra called Zapatec burned, and the flames were seen from afar. All the people were stirred up and affrighted, saying one to another, "O Toltecs, it is all over with us now; the time of the end of Tollan is come; alas for us, whither shall we go?"

Wizard-like also was the god Uitzilopochtli. Indeed the derivation of his name, "Humming-bird wizard," makes this plain enough. "He was," says Sahagun, "a necromancer and friend of disguises."

The older derivation of his name, "Humming-bird to the left," seems to me fantastic. "Left" in Mexican, as in some other tongues, has the significance of wizardry, of the "sinister." His other name, Uitznauitl, shows that he was associated also with prophecy and oracular speech, to deliver which he sometimes took the shape of a bird. He was, too, the brother of the "Four Hundred Southerners," the stars of the Southern Hemisphere, who were regarded as demons, and seem to have been the same as the Tzitzimime demons, to be alluded to later.

Clavigero, relating this myth, says: "Huitzilopochtli, or Mexitli, was the god of war; the deity the most honored by the Mexicans, and their chief protector. Of this god some said he was a pure spirit, others that he was born of a woman, but without the assistance of a man, and described his birth in the following manner: There lived, said they, in Coatepec, a place near to the ancient city of Tula (Tollan), a woman called Coatlicue, mother of the Centzonhuiznahuas (or Four Hundred Southerners), who was extremely devoted to the worship of the gods. One day, as she was employed, according to her usual custom, in walking in the temple, she beheld descending in the air a ball made of various feathers. She seized it and kept it in her bosom, intending afterwards to employ the feathers in the decoration of the altar; but when she sought it after her walk was at an end she could not find it, at which she was extremely surprised, and her wonder was very greatly increased when she began to perceive from that moment that she was pregnant. Her pregnancy advanced till it was discovered by her children, who, although they could not themselves suspect their mother's virtue, yet fearing the disgrace she would suffer upon her delivery, determined to prevent it by putting her to death. They could not take their resolution so secretly as to conceal it from their mother, who, while she was in deep affliction at the thought of dying by the hands of her own children, heard an unexpected voice issue from her womb, saying, 'Be not afraid, mother, I shall save you with the greatest honor to yourself and glory to me.'

"Her hard-hearted sons, guided and encouraged by their sister Cojolxauhqui, who had been the most keenly bent upon the deed, were now just upon the point of executing their purpose, when Huitzilopochtli was born, with a shield in his left hand, a spear in his right, and a crest of green feathers on his head; his left leg adorned with feathers, and his face, arms, and thighs streaked with blue lines. As soon as he came into the world he displayed a twisted pine, and commanded one of his soldiers, called Tochchancalqui, to fell with it Cojolxauhqui, as the one who had been the most guilty; and he himself attacked the rest with so much fury that, in spite of their efforts, their arms, or their entreaties, he killed them all, plundered their houses, and presented the spoils to his mother. Mankind was so terrified by this event that from that time they called him Tetzahuitl (terror) and Tetzauhteotl (terrible god)."

This was the god who, as they said, becoming the protector of the Mexicans, conducted them for so many years in their pilgrimage, and at length settled them where they afterwards founded the great city of Mexico. They raised to him that superb temple, so much celebrated, even by the Spaniards, in which were annually holden three solemn festivals in the fifth, ninth, and fifteenth months; besides those kept every four years, every thirteen years, and at the beginning of every century.

His statue was of gigantic size, in the posture of a man seated on a blue-colored bench, from the four corners of which issued four huge snakes. His forehead was blue, but his face was covered with a golden mask, while another of the same kind covered the back of his head. Upon his head he carried a beautiful crest, shaped like the beak of a bird; upon his neck a collar consisting of ten figures of the human heart; in his right hand a large blue twisted club; in his left a shield, or quincuncc, on which appeared five balls of feathers disposed in the form of a cross, and from the upper part of the shield rose a golden flag with four arrows, which the Mexicans pretended to have been sent to them from heaven to perform those glorious actions which we have seen in their history.

His body was girt with a large golden snake and adorned with lesser figures of animals made of gold and precious stones, which ornaments and insignia had each their peculiar meaning. They never deliberated upon making war without imploring the protection of this god with prayers and sacrifices; and offered up a greater number of human victims to him than to any other of the gods.

Acosta says of his appearance: "The chief idol of Mexico was, as I have said, Vitziliputzli. It was an image of wood like to a man, set upon a stool of the color of azure, in a brankard or litter, in every corner was a piece of wood in form of a serpent's head. The stool signified that he was set in heaven. This idol had all the forehead azure, and had a band of azure under the nose from one ear to another. Upon his head he had a rich plume of feathers like to the beak of a small bird, the idol was covered on the top with gold burnished very brown. He had in his left hand a small target, with the figures of five pineapples made in white feathers set in a cross. And from above issued forth a crest in gold, and at his sides he had four darts, which (the Mexicans say) had been sent from heaven, which shall be spoken of. In his right hand he had an azured staff cut in the fashion of a waving snake. All those ornaments with the rest he had, carried his sense as the Mexicans doe shew."

Horrible human sacrifices took place in honor of this god, but with this side of his worship we have no concern here. Cinteotl, the young god of the maize-plant, has certain affinities with witchcraft. A song in his honor says: "I came to the place where the roads meet, I, the Maize-god. Where shall I now go? Which way shall I take? "

GHOSTS AND WITCHES

The place where the roads meet is of course the haunting-place of the Ciuateteo, or witches, later to be described. The god complains that he has a difficulty in finding his way at the cross-roads. This was the precise reason for which they were made, so that the witches should be puzzled by them and know not which route to take to approach their victims.

Witches all the world over are baffled by cross-roads, and formerly the bodies of suicides and vampires were buried beneath them, so that, did their evil ghosts arise, they would be puzzled by the multiplicity of directions, "wandered," as the Scottish country folk say, and baffled in their intent to haunt the living.

Cinteotl's mother, Tlazolteotl, as we shall see later, fulfilled the Mexican idea of the Queen of the witches, and he was the husband of Xochiquetzal, who may be described as the ruler of the Mexican Fairyland. Cinteotl must also be regarded as one of the plutonic deities, as, indeed, most grain-gods are, a figure associated with the Underworld, the place of the dead, the realm in which the seed germinates ere it sprouts above ground.

A terrible and phantom-like goddess was Ciuacoatl, or "Serpent Woman," another of the deities of grain. She is depicted as dressed in gorgeous robes, but with the face of a skull, her headdress ornamented with sacrificial flint knives. She dispensed bad fortune, abjectness and misery. She was wont to appear to men in the guise of a richly dressed lady, such as frequented the court. Through the night she wandered, howling and bellowing.

Occasionally this ghost-like divinity was seen carrying a cradle, and when she vanished, examination showed that the resting-place of what was believed to be an infant contained nothing but an obsidian knife, such as was used in human sacrifice. Xipe Totec was a dismal god of human sacrifice, who had likewise fiendish or ghostly characteristics. He was the god of penance, once a man, who betook himself to the mountain Catcitepulz, a height covered with thorns, to lead a life of seclusion.

The interpreter of the "Codex Vaticanus" says of him: "They hold him in the utmost veneration, for they say that he was the first who opened to them the way to heaven; for they were under this error amongst others: they supposed that only those who died in war went to heaven, as we have already said. Whilst Totec still continued doing penance, preaching and crying from the top of the mountain which has been named, they pretend that he dreamed this night that he beheld a horrible figure with its bowels protruding, which was the cause of the great abomination of his people. On this, praying to his god to reveal to him what the figure signified, he answered that it was the sin of his people, and that he should issue an order to the people, and cause them all to be assembled, charging them to bring thick ropes and to bind that miserable spectre, as it was the cause of all their sins, and that, dragging it away, they should remove it from the people, who, giving faith to the words of Totec, were by him conducted to a certain wild place, where they found the figure of death, which, having bound, they dragged it to a distance, and drawing it backwards, they fell all into a cavity between the two mountains, which closed together, and there they have remained buried ever since; none of them having effected their escape, with the exception of the innocent children, who remained in Tulan."

That portion of the story which details the mass burial of the Toltecs is, of course, the widespread tale of the disappearance of the old hero-race under- ground the fate which overtook Charlemagne and his peers, King Arthur and "the auld Picts" at Arthur's Seat, near Edinburgh, Barbarossa and his men, and many another group of paladins. The whole may allude, in the ultimate, to mound-burial.

It is strange too or quite natural, as we believe in, or doubt, the penetration of America by alien influences to find in Mexico an incomplete variant of the legend of the Pied Piper of Hamelin. I should not be surprised to find that Xipe piped the Toltec people into the Underworld, for Tezcatlipoca, with whom he was identified, or at least the captive who represented that god at the Toxcatl festival, and who had a year of merriment in which to prepare himself for his fate, went through the city at intervals, playing upon a flute.

This almost universal myth may allude to the ancient belief that the souls of the dead traveled with the wind, and were the cause of its sighing and whistling. We know, too, that the whistling of the night wind through the mountains was regarded by the Mexicans as of evil omen, and that Yoalli Eecatl (The Wind of Night) was one of the names of Tezcatlipoca. Xipe was also the "night drinker," the vampire- being who sucked the blood of penitents during the hours of slumber.

Few deities were more dreaded by the wretched Mexican peasants, by malefactors, and by the tribal enemies of the Aztecs, who were usually sacrificed to him after a mock combat. That this bloodthirsty being was regarded as the god of penitence arose, of course, out of the extraordinary importance of blood in the Mexican religion, the vehicle which sustained the gods in life and which the Aztec penitents shed on the altars by pricking their tongues and thighs with thorns.

Itzpapalotl, the horrible "obsidian-knife butterfly," was a supernatural being who combined attributes of the butterfly, or soul, with the knife of sacrifice. The butterfly in many mythologies is the ghost of the dead, and in this ghastly creature we find it associated with the horror of the altars of blood. Indeed the very name appears as of deathly and hideous omen.

This goddess of weird propensity has butterfly wings edged round with stone knives. Her dreadful face is tricked out with the cosmetics of the Mexican court ladies, rubber patches and white chalk. Her claws are borrowed from the jaguar, and sometimes she is represented as having a skull instead of a face, in the nasal orifice of which is set a sacrificial knife. In other pictures she is painted as wearing a naualli, or disguise of butterfly form, a magical cloak worn by all necromancers to change their appearance.

She also wears the witches' loin-cloth trimmed with a hem of human teeth, probably taken from a graveyard. When she "appeared" to men they could see only her claw-edged feet. That she was a demon is plain not only from her general appearance, but from the fact that she is enumerated along with those who fell from heaven, Uitzilopochtli and Tezcatlipoca among the rest.

That Itzpapalotl was associated with the story of the fall from heaven or paradise is plain from the account of her furnished by the interpreter of the "Codex Vaticanus A," who, however, errs in regarding her as a male deity. He says: "Yxpapalotl signifies a knife of butterflies. He was one of those gods who, as they affirm, were expelled from heaven; and on this account they paint him surrounded with knives and wings of butterflies. They represent him with the feet of an eagle, because they say that he occasionally appears to them, and they only see the feet of an eagle. They further add that, being in a garden of great delight, he pulled some roses, but that suddenly the tree broke and blood streamed from it; and that in consequence of this they were deprived of that place of enjoyment and were cast into this world because Tonacatecutli and his wife became incensed, and accordingly they came some of them to the earth, and others went to hell. He presided over these thirteen signs (certain symbols of the calendar), the first of which the house (calli) they considered unfortunate, because they said that demons came through the air on that sign in the figures of women such as we call witches, who usually went to the highways, where they met in the form of a cross."

Itzpapalotl was one of the Tzitzimime, or demons of darkness, and as such symbolically took insect shape. I believe her to have been developed from the idea of the deer, which is, after all, a surrogate of the dragon, and indeed she is identified in one tale with the mythical deer Itzcueye. We know, too, that the butterfly, or ghost-symbol, was associated with the Ciuateted or dead witches, to whose spirits the people offered cakes stamped with a butterfly symbol.

The gods of death and the Underworld naturally had a plutonic and magical significance. At the head of these was Mictlantecutli, or "Lord of Mictlampa," the region of death, or Hades. He was depicted as a skeleton, the arms and legs of which were painted white with yellow spots pricked in red to symbolize the bones of a newly flayed person. Beside him are depicted the ominous symbols of the witches' crossroads and the owl, the mummy-bundle and the grass of the desert, along with a smoking dish of human hearts.

The interpreter of "Codex Vaticanus A" says of Mict-lantecutli: "He descends for souls as a spider lowers itself with its head downwards from the web." Later on he states that "he is the great lord of the dead below in hell, who alone after Tonacatecutli (Lord of the Sun) was painted with a crown. . . . They painted this demon near the sun, for in the same way as they believed that the one conducted souls to heaven, so they supposed that the other carried them to hell. He is here represented (that is in the codex) with his hands open and stretched towards the sun to seize on any soul that might escape from him."

Mictlantecutli, it would seem, is neither more nor less than a god of the dead, that is, his original conception was probably that of a prince of Hades, a ruler of the realm of the departed, who in time came to possess the terrific aspect and the punitive attributes of a deity whose office it was to torment the souls of the erring. The fact that he presides over the eleventh hour the hour of sunset indicates that he was in a measure identified with the night, as indeed certain aspects of his insignia would appear to show. In a manner he must be regarded as the earth which, in its form of the grave, yawns or gapes insatiably for the bodies of the dead.

His terrible wife, Mictecaciuatl, strongly resembles him. Tepeyollotl, another of the Tzitzimimes, seems to have represented both ghost and grave, earthquake and cave, a horrid blending of the attributes of mortality. But he seems also to have been the jaguar in his form of wer-beast, something devouring, annihilating. From all this we clearly discern the true tendency of Mexican magic. The gods were not so much gods in the usual acceptance of the term as magical forces personalized, divine figures, who, in some cases, had once been sorcerers or medicine-men.

We have a similar example in ancient Britain, where Merlin, the supreme wizard, came in time to be regarded as a deity, and the whole island as his "place" or "enclosure," the area of his magical scope. Small wonder, then, that the ignorant among the Mexicans, the people at large, feared and dreaded the gods. But the instructed classes and the priest-hood regarded them very differently. They strove to understand the magical system which these beings were thought to have initiated, and to wield it for the general behoof according to their lights. They were men engaged in the effort of comprehending and elucidating a vast system of philosophical magic, contained in myth, symbolism, and astrology, just as the European magicians, astrologers, and alchemists of the Middle Ages were in a similar manner devoted to the study of a magical system of more various origin bequeathed to them from the past in East and West, which they attempted to standardize and use.

In the Mexican occult system, which was also the Mexican religion, we behold a stage of the development of magical science not at its most delectable, perhaps, but rather at such an evolutionary phase as all such wisdom-religions or occult philosophies must pass through on the road to perfection, and there is every indication that, had it not been cut short by the Spanish invasion, it would have in time developed into a system of magico-religious thought such as is to be observed in earlier Brahmanism or in the philosophy of ancient Egypt.

At the period when Cortes dealt it its first reverse, this system was slowly emerging from a phase in which the minds of its ministers were engaged in grappling with the problem of demonism. They were in the process of discovering how, precisely, those dark powers to whom they attributed the rule and hegemony of this world and human society might be persuaded to employ their might for the good of man.

The one means by which they considered it possible to enlist the sympathies of the agencies in which they believed was by regaling them with human sacrifices. We see in the earlier form of British Druidism a similar condition and belief.

We know that the ancient system of worship once in vogue in our islands inculcated the need for human sacrifice, but that it also contained the germs of much loftier ideas, that, in the course of centuries, it excogitated a large philosophy of occult lore of a most sublime character. Similarly, then, the Mexican dispensation in vogue at the time of the coming of the Spaniards contained within itself the seeds and promise of greatly higher development.

In the exalted prayers to the gods, in the explanations of the priesthood, in the extraordinary mythology of the Aztecs, we can trace the underlying conditions and psychology of a great magical lore slowly coming to fruition. Twisted and distorted out of all semblance to its original form as it has been by the worthy friars who have bequeathed to us its broken fragments, is it remarkable that we have not so far estimated it at its true worth, but have regarded it as the mere devil-worship of degenerate barbarism?

Let us probe beneath the surface and try to discern the inner significance of what was actually a well-considered body of occult learning. In the first place we find an ancient and well-founded belief in a supreme being, an all-father, a god behind the gods, who, however, appears to have adopted a somewhat remote attitude towards human affairs. This First Cause the Aztecs called Teotl, or "the god," and that he was eternal and unfathomable in his nature all authorities are agreed.

The myths regarding the creator of the universe are somewhat conflicting, but display a belief in the various demiurgic processes familiar to most mythologies, and scarcely concern us in this place. A myth of wide acceptance was that which told of the periodic or epochal destruction of the world and of man by the agencies of fire, air, earthquake, and flood at dates the most distant and remote.

At the time of the Spanish invasion the Mexicans were awaiting with considerable dread the advent of a fifth cataclysm of the kind, and every fifty-two years the possibility of such a catastrophe came round and might only be avoided by sacrifice on a grand scale. But the grand arcanum or secret of the Mexican priests seems to have resided in the belief that the balance of the universe in which they lived could be held only by the observance of penitential proprieties which included not sacrifice alone, but the study of omens and portents. Augury and astrology were, indeed, the chief means by which humanity might be safeguarded from destruction or sorrow.

Nevertheless, the entire wisdom of the priesthood by no means resided in the proper use of the tonalamatl, or Book of Fate, or in the observance of auspices, as has too hastily been concluded. Side by side with them the hierophant cultivated mysteries which concealed and enshrined a system of thought of which the astrological and divinatory systems were merely the outward symbols, as will be shown later on.

THE MAGIC AND MYSTERIES OF MEXICO

CHAPTER III
MEXICAN MAGIC

The "official" magic of Mexico was almost entirely the preserve of a class of sorcerers known as naualli, who may have been a section of the priesthood especially deputed for this service, although many of them practiced their art separately. Regarding the powers of this caste, we possess sufficient information to give us a good general indication of their beliefs and practices.

The Spanish priesthood has bequeathed to us certain notices regarding the naualli which, however, give us a somewhat confused notion of their attributes. "The naualli" says the writer who first mentions them "is he who terrifies people and sucks the blood of children during the night."

"These are magicians," says Father Juan Bautista in his instructions to confessors, printed at Mexico in the year 1600," who conjure the clouds when there is danger of hail so that the crops may not be injured. They can also make a stick look like a serpent, a mat like a centipede, a piece of stone like a scorpion, and engage in similar deceptions. Others of them will transform themselves to all appearance into a tiger, a dog, or a weasel. Others, again, will take the form of an owl or a cock."

Nicolas de Leon, in a similar work, instructs the priest to ask the natives such questions as: "Art thou a soothsayer? Dost thou foretell events by reading signs, or by interpreting dreams, or by water, making circles or figures on its surface? Dost thou suck the blood of others, or dost thou wander about at night, calling upon the Demon to help thee? Hast thou drunk peyoil, or given it to others to drink, in order to find out secrets? Dost thou know how to speak to serpents in such words that they obey thee? "

The intoxicant peyotl, which the natives used to induce trance, is a species of vinagrilla having a white tuberous root, which was the part made use of. The Aztecs were said to have derived their knowledge of it from an older race that preceded them in the land.

The intoxication it caused lasted several days. The natives masticated it and then placed it in a wooden mortar, where it was left to ferment. Another medicine employed by the naualli for the purpose of inducing ecstatic visions was an unguent known as teopatli, or "the divine remedy," a compound of the seeds of certain plants, the ashes of spiders, scorpions, and other noxious insects. Magical enterprises and experiments were usually timed by sorcerers to take place during the second, fifth or seventh hours of the night, which were naturally the most dreaded by the common people because they were presided over by gods of evil repute, and thus were considered favorable to the appearance of demons or phantoms and the assemblies of witches.

CREATURES OF THE NIGHT

Night, too, was naturally the heyday of the sorcerer or naualli, and certain members of this caste seem to have practiced vampirism and to have taken the shape of werewolves, or rather wer-coyotes. Those who desired to injure an enemy by spells and other enchantments would go by night to the dwelling of the naualli and bargain for the drug or potion by means of which they hoped to be revenged. From certain passages in the old authorities it would seem that these sorcerers lived in huts built of wooden planks gaily painted perhaps a development of the lodge of the medicine-man with its brightly colored symbolism.

During the hours of darkness the priestly occupants of the teocallis or temples carefully replenished the braziers, whose fires were supposed to exercise a deterrent influence upon all evil visitants to the earth-sphere. At stated intervals, too, they beat drums and sounded conch-shells to drive off the demons of gloom, and the trembling peasant as he lay in his reed shack and listened to the reverberation of the tympani of serpent skins, the gongs, and the rude horns of the sacred guardians of his peace, must have been heartened by the distant and reassuring clamor.

All the terrors of Spanish ecclesiasticism could not put an end to the practice of magic among the Mexicans. The minor feats of sorcery flourished in every Mexican town and village. Sahagun tells us how a class of professional conjurers existed who could roast maize on a cloth without fire, produce as from nowhere a spring or well filled with fishes, and after setting fire to and burning huts, restore them to their original condition. The conjurer, asserts the chronicler, might on occasion even dismember himself and then achieve the miracle of self-resurrection. Perhaps higher castes of the naualli were the "master magicians," who were also known as teopixqui and teotecuhtli or "sacred companions-in-arms," and the nanahualtin, "those who know."

Entrance to these very select orders might be attained only after severe and prolonged tests of initiation. The chief naualli or magician of Mexico was a priest of high rank, an astrological adept, who was credited with the assumption of animal form at will and the power of levitation. He acted as the guardian of the city against sorcerers, and gave warning of famine or pestilence.

The naualli caste were therefore not only suspect of vampirism but had associations with witchcraft, as we shall see. They also practiced divination and astrology, as indeed did the Mexican priesthood as a whole. The Spanish priesthood quickly discovered that it was not so much a religion from which they had to wean the native mind as an elaborate ritual mingled with magical practice.

The dusk of magic which shadowed the bizarre, crowded cities could almost be felt by those courageous priests. It was easy enough to combat an idolatry regarding the higher conception of which the people had only loose ideas and legendary glimmerings. But the more popular devil-worship which accompanied it had a far stronger hold on the native affections. The Aztec was enthralled by it. His whole life from the cradle to the grave was ordered by its inevitable and ghastly provisions. No sooner had the Mexican aristocracy been accounted for by slaughter or conversion than a significant change took place in the tendency and character of the native faith.

The Aztec priesthood, realizing that if its doctrines were to survive at all it must make a powerful appeal to the mass mind of the nation, threw every ounce of energy into the task of shaping the superstitions of the lower orders into a deadly instrument of vengeance against the whites. In this new movement magic of a repellent kind was joined with political conspiracy against Spanish supremacy, and the extraordinary cult thus developed had for its chief deity Satan himself, if we are to credit the writings of those who opposed it and labored untiringly for its destruction.

This mysterious secret society had branches in all parts of the country, and its members were classed in varying degrees, initiation into which was granted only after prolonged and rigorous experience. Local brotherhoods or lodges were organized, and there were certain recognized centers of the cult. At each of these places was stationed a high priest or master magician, who had beneath his authority often as many as a thousand lesser priests, and who exercised control over a large district. The priesthood of this guild was handed down from father to son. The highest grade appears to have been that of Xochimalca, or "flower-weaver," probably because its members possessed the faculty of deceiving the senses of votaries by strange and pleasant visions.

Indeed, the Spanish clergy never were quite positive whether a native Mexican was a Christian or a pagan, and in many cases where it seemed the Indians were of the most devout character, subsequent investigation proved them to be unrepentant demon-worshippers. Father Burgoa describes very fully a case of this kind which came under his notice in 1652 in the Zapotec village of San Francisco de Cajonos.

He encountered on a tour of inspection an old native cacique, or chief, of great refinement of manners and of a stately presence, who dressed in costly garments after the Spanish fashion, and who was regarded by the Indians with much veneration. This man came to the priest for the purpose of reporting upon the progress in things spiritual and temporal in his village. Burgoa recognized his urbanity and wonderful command of the Spanish language, but perceived by certain signs which he had been taught to look for by long experience that the man was a pagan.

He communicated his suspicions to the vicar of the village, but met with such assurances of the cacique's soundness of faith that he believed himself to be in error for once. Shortly afterwards, however, a wandering Spaniard perceived the chief in a retired place in the mountains performing idolatrous ceremonies, and aroused the monks, two of whom accompanied him to the spot where the cacique had been seen indulging in his heathenish practices.

They found on the altar "feathers of many colors, sprinkled with blood which the Indians had drawn from the veins under their tongues and behind their ears, incense spoons and remains of copal, and in the middle a horrible stone figure, which was the god to whom they had offered this sacrifice in expiation of their sins, while they made their confessions to the blasphemous priests, and cast off their sins in the following manner: they had woven a kind of dish out of a strong herb, specially gathered for this purpose, and casting this before the priest, said to him that they came to beg mercy of their god, and pardon for their sins they had committed during that year, and that they brought them all carefully enumerated.

They then drew out of a cloth pairs of thin threads made of dry maize husks that they had tied two by two in the middle with a knot, by which they represented their sins. They laid these threads on the dishes of grass, and over them pierced their veins, and let the blood trickle upon them, and the priest took these offerings to the idol, and in a long speech he begged the god to forgive these, his sons, their sins which were brought to him, and to permit them to be joyful and hold feasts to him as their god and lord. Then the priest came back to those who had confessed, delivered a long discourse on the ceremonies they had still to perform, and told them that the god had pardoned them and that they might be glad again and sin.

Acosta, the Spanish chronicler, writing of the Mexican priests and their magical customs, says: "The priests of the idols in Mexico were anointed in this sort; they anointed the body from the foot to the head, and all the hair likewise, which hung like tresses or a horse's mane, for that they applied this unction wet and moist.

"Their hair grew so, as in time it hung down to their hams, so heavily that it was troublesome for them to bear it, for they did never cut it until they died, or that they were dispensed with for their great age, or being employed in governments, or some honorable charge in the commonwealth. They carried their hair in tresses of six fingers breadth, which they dyed black with the fume of sapine, of fir trees, or rosin; for in all antiquity it hath been an offering they made unto their idols and for this cause it was much esteemed and reverenced.

"They were always dyed with this tincture from the foot to the head, so as they were like unto shining negroes, and that was their ordinary unction: yet when as they went to sacrifice and give incense in the mountains, or on the tops thereof, or in any dark and obscure caves, where their idols were, they used another kind of unction very different, doing certain ceremonies to take away fear and to give them courage.

"This unction was made with divers little venomous beasts, as spiders, scorpions, palmers, salamanders, and vipers, the which the boys in the colleges took and gathered together, wherein they were so expert as they were always furnished when the priests called for them. The chief care of these boys was to hunt after these beasts; if they went any other way, and by chance met with any of these beasts, they stayed to take them with as great pain, as if their lives depended thereon.

"By the reason whereof the Indians commonly feared not these venomous beasts, making no more account than if they were not so, having been all bred in this exercise. To make an ointment of these beasts they took them all together and burnt them upon the hearth of the temple which was before the altar, until they were consumed to ashes: then did they put them in mortars with much tobacco or petum (being an herb that nation useth much to benumb the flesh that they may not feel their travail), with the which they mingle the ashes making them lose their force; they did likewise mingle with these ashes scorpions, spiders, and palmers alive, mingling all together, then they did put to it a certain seed being ground which they call ololuchqui, whereof the Indians make a drink to see visions, for that the virtue of this herb is to deprive man of sense.

"They did likewise grind with these ashes black and hairy worms, whose hair only are venomous, all which they mingled together with black or the fume of rosin, putting it in small pots which they set before their god, saying it was his meat. And therefore they called it a divine meat. By means of this ointment they became witches, and did see and speak with the devil. The priests being slobbered with this ointment lost all fear, putting on a spirit of cruelty.

"By reason whereof they did very boldly kill men in their sacrifices, going all alone in the night to the mountains, and into obscure caves, contemning all wild beasts, and holding it for certain and approved that both lions, tigers, serpents, and other furious beasts which breed in the mountains and forests fled from them, by virtue of this petum of their god.

"And in truth, though this petum had no power to make them fly, yet was the devil's picture sufficient whereinto they were transformed. This petum did also serve to cure the sick, and for children: and therefore all called it the divine physic: and so they came from all parts to the superiors and priests, as to their saviors, that they might apply this divine physic, wherewith they anointed those parts that were grieved.

"They said that they felt hereby a notable ease, which might be, for that tobacco and ololuchqui have this property of themselves, to benumb the flesh, being applied in manner of an emplaster, which must be by a stronger reason being mingled with poisons, and for that it did appease and benumb the pain, they held it for an effect of health and a divine virtue. And therefore ran they to these priests as to holy men, who kept the blind and ignorant in this error, persuading them what they pleased, and making them run after their inventions and devilish ceremonies, their authority being such, as their words were sufficient to induce belief as an article of their faith.

"And thus made they a thousand superstitions among the vulgar people in their manner of offering incense, in cutting their hair, tying small flowers about their necks, and strings with small bones of snakes, commanding them to bathe at a certain time; and that they should watch all night at the hearth lest the fire should die, that they should eat no other bread but that which had been offered to their gods, that they should upon any occasion repair unto their witches, who with certain grains told fortunes, and divines, looking into keelers and pails full of water.

"The sorcerers and ministers of the Devil used much to besmear themselves. There were an infinite number of these witches, diviners, enchanters, and other false prophets. There remains yet at this day of this infection, although they be secret, not daring publicly to exercise their sacrilegious devilish ceremonies and superstitions."

The statement that fortunes were told with grain is worthy of passing notice. Grains of maize or beans were used to discover whether a patient would get well, and the patroness of those diviners who used this medium was the golden Tozi, though the casting of grains was usually performed before an image of Quetzalcoatl, the patron of magic. Some twenty grains were cast upon a cloth.

If they fell in circular shape it was held to typify a grave, and therefore death, but if in a straight line, leaving two on each side, the illness would have a happy issue. If a knot tied in a string could be loosed by pulling it, recovery would ensue. A sick child would be held over a vessel of water. If his reflection was dim he might not recover, that is his "soul" or shadow was unhealthy.

Regarding these practices Father Clavigero says: "Besides the usual unction with ink, another extraordinary and more abominable one was practiced every time they went to make sacrifices on the tops of mountains, or in the dark caverns of the earth. They took a large quantity of poisonous insects, such as scorpions, spiders, and worms, and sometimes even small serpents, burned them over some stove of the temple, and beat their ashes in a mortar together with the foot of the ocotl, tobacco, the ololuchqui, and some live insects. They presented this diabolical mixture in small vessels to their gods, and afterwards rubbed their bodies with it. When thus anointed they became fearless to every danger, being persuaded they were rendered incapable of receiving any hurt from the most noxious reptiles of the earth or the wildest beast of the woods. They called it teopatli, or divine medicament, and imagined it to be a powerful remedy for several disorders; on which account those who were sick, and the young children, went frequently to the priests to be anointed with it. The young lads who were trained up in the seminaries were charged with the collecting of such kind of little animals; and by being accustomed at an early age to that kind of employment they soon lost the horror which attends the first familiarity with such reptiles. The priests not only made use of this unction but had likewise a ridiculous superstitious practice of blowing with their breath over the sick, and made them drink water which they had blessed after their manner. The priests of the god Ixtlilton were remarkable for this custom."

It is somewhat difficult to separate from religion proper those rite inteotl, stood by, and was regarded as the son conceived from this intercourse. Thus, by the aid of sympathetic magic, the new maize-spirit was born. The power of sympathetic magic was also invoked in the horrible human sacrifices to Tlaloc, the god of water, when the infants whose hair seemed to the priests to resemble eddies in the lake were ceremonially drowned so as to ensure "life" to the waves and whirlpools.

Magical, too, was the sham fight indulged in at the festival of Tlacaxipeualitzli, when young men, clad in the skins of the wretched sacrificed victims with others, typified, perhaps, the struggle of the renewed earth with the forces of dearth and drought, a drama similar to that of Osiris in Egypt. In fact, if we carefully examine the circumstances of the several Mexican religious festivals we find that they practically all had a magico-dramatic character, in which some particular mythical tale, the story of a god or fetish, was enacted, and that the rite so enacted was supposed by the power of sympathetic magic to be efficacious in producing the effects alluded to in the myth itself.

Thus at the festival of Tepeilhuitl, sacred to the gods of rain and moisture, little serpents and mountains were made of maize paste which were symbolical of the legend that the rain-gods dwelt in the hills and that they took the shapes of serpents, which typified water. Several women, called after the goddesses of fruitfulness, were sacrificed to give their representatives new life along with one man who typified water.

The paste images were afterwards broken up and eaten so that the people might partake of their qualities. But the very apogee of sympathetic magic is reached in what I will call the Obsidian Religion of Mexico, for in this strange cult, which I personally discovered, the obsidian stone was regarded as a magical substance which came to wield an extra-ordinary power over every department of Mexican life.

As everyone engaged in research is aware, there comes a time when the subject of study assumes an aspect so thoroughly at variance with one's original conception of it that the student is aghast at the extraordinary change presented. Generally, such an experience is the fruit of prolonged application and contemplation. In my own case it required more than twenty years of research and groping in the difficult field of Mexican religion to realize that underlying what I had always believed to be the official faith of the Aztecs was a still earlier cult connected with the obsidian stone.

I was, of course, well aware that obsidian played a certain part in Aztec religion as a ceremonial object in use on sacrificial and other occasions, but the full measure of its importance did not dawn on me until I began to arrange the gods of the Mexican pantheon into groups. During this process I observed that the names of at least three of these included the Mexican word for obsidian, itztli.

One of these gods, indeed, was known as Itztli, the other two being Itzpapalotl ("obsidian butterfly") and Itzlacoliuhqui ("curved obsidian knife"). I knew that Tezcatlipoca, one of the principal Mexican deities, was frequently represented as an obsidian knife, and that the native Aztec paintings were crowded with pictures of this symbol, which occurred so frequently that I could scarcely be mistaken in placing a high value on its religious significance. I had before me at least one other analogy.

The importance of jade in Chinese Religion and Folklore afforded me much food for thought. I knew that the implications of the beautiful jade stone permeated the whole of Chinese legend, folk-belief, and theology. Then I observed that several of the Mexican gods were represented as wearing sandals made of obsidian, and the sandal, I had formerly discovered, must often be taken as an indication of the significance of a Mexican god. In fact, the longer I searched the more traces of obsidian did I find in Mexican lore.

The image of the god Tezcatlipoca, the mirror in which he beheld the doings of humanity, his death-dealing arrows, was all of obsidian. The very cloak he wore was, I found, merely an adaptation of the net bag in which the Aztec hunter carried his obsidian arrow- heads. I found, too, that such deities as were connected with obsidian were exclusively those worshipped by the Aztec or Nahua tribes of Mexico, and that the cults of Quetzalcoatl and Tlaloc, the deities of older precedence in the land, were associated with it in a secondary manner only, and very slightly at that that, indeed, their associations were with the chalchihuitl stone, or native jadeite.

I resolved to follow up these clues, and did so with the following results: Obsidian is a vitreous natural glass, found in the upper volcanic strata of Mexico and California, which flakes readily from the core by pressure and gains by mere fracture a razor-like edge of considerable penetrative power. The principal quarry of this volcanic glass was the mountain known as the Cerro de las Navajas, or "Hill of the Knives," near Timapan, and from this centre obsidian was widely distributed by barter over a very considerable area. There would seem to be proof that this mineral, so suitable for the purposes of the nomadic hunter, was anciently known far to the north of Mexico. The observations of Dr. G. M. Dawson in British Columbia about 1890 satisfied him that trading intercourse was engaged in by the coast tribes with those of the interior along the Frazer River Valley and far to the south.

From the remotest times embraced in their native traditions, the Bilquila of Dean Inlet have possessed a trade route by way of the Bella Coola River to the Tinne Country, along which trail broken implements and chips of obsidian have been found. Many of the routes in British Columbia have also yielded chips and flakes of obsidian. The coast tribes of British Columbia have been traders for untold generations, exchanging oolactin oil for such materials as they could make implements from, and there seems to be no doubt that the Mound-builders of Ohio, Wisconsin, and Kentucky were also acquainted with obsidian, which they could only have obtained through the process of barter.

It was thus either to be found in the regions from which the Nahua of Mexico are thought to have come, or else obtainable through the channels of trade. The Nahua were thus probably acquainted with obsidian and its properties before their entrance into Mexico. This theory is strengthened by the material difference in workmanship between their tools and weapons made of this mineral and the stone and copper implements of the aboriginal peoples of Mexico.

It was naturally as a hunting people that they employed weapons of obsidian. The herds of deer, on the flesh of which they chiefly lived, roamed the steppes, and proof abounds that the customs of the chase strongly influenced the religious ideas of the early Nahua. Certain of their gods, indeed, seem to have been developed from deer forms, for among barbarous races the animal worshipped is frequently that which provides the tribe with its staple food, or, more correctly, a great eponymous figure of that animal is adored for example, the Great Deer who sends the smaller deer to keep the savage in life.

These deer-gods, or hunting-gods in some way connected with the deer Itzpapalotl, Itzcueye, Mixcoatl, Camaxtli had also stellar attributes. The deer was slain by the obsidian weapon, which, therefore, came to be regarded as the magical weapon, that by which food was procured. In the course of time it assumed a sacred significance, the hunting-gods themselves came to wield it, and it was thought of as coming from the stars or the heavens where the gods dwelt, in precisely the same manner as flint arrow-heads were regarded by the peasantry of Europe as "elf-arrows" or "thunder-stones" that is, as something supernatural, falling from above.

When the nomadic tribes, of which the Aztecs were one, adopted an agricultural existence, obsidian had doubtless been regarded as sacred for generations. It was by virtue of this supernatural stone that the nourishment of the gods was maintained by the sacrifice of deer. By the aid of lances and arrows fashioned from its flakes, deer were more easily slaughtered than with clumsier stone weapons.

With these primitive hunters obsidian took much the same place as bronze did with the Neolithic peoples, and came to be regarded as the chief agency through which the necessities of life were acquired. But when the Nahua embraced a more settled existence the nourishment of the gods had necessarily to be maintained by other means than the sacrifice of deer, which were gradually disappearing.

Slaves and war-captives were sacrificed in the place of deer, their wrists and ankles being tied together precisely in the manner in which a deer is trussed by the hunter. The transition of deer-sacrifice by obsidian to a human holocaust and from the hunting to the agricultural condition of life is well illustrated by an ancient hymn in praise of the goddess Itzpapalotl: "O, she has become a goddess of the melon-cactus, Our mother Itzpapalotl, the Obsidian Butterfly, Her food is on the Nine Plains, She was nurtured on the hearts of deer, Our mother the earth-goddess."

The inference in these lines seems to be that whereas Itzpapalotl was formerly a goddess of the Nahua nomads of the steppes in the north of Mexico, who sacrificed deer to her, she has now become the deity of the melon-cactus patch and an agricultural community. Mexican traditions make it very clear that obsidian, because of its blood and life-procuring properties, came to be regarded as the source of all life, as the very principle of existence.

Tonacaciuatl, the creative goddess, gave birth to an obsidian knife from which sprang sixteen hundred demi-gods who peopled the earth. In the native paintings, maize, the chief food of the people, is often pictured in the form of an obsidian knife-blade. Just as in many myths, both in the Old World and the New, flint was regarded as the great fertilizer because of its supposed connection with the lightning, so was obsidian.

Thus, all the elements which go to make for growth and life came to be regarded as having a connection with this mineral, even the sun itself being identified with the mirror of Tezcatlipoca. The hunter's obsidian weapon which supplied the necessary pabulum became in turn the weapon of the warrior who procured victims for the holocaust, and the sacred knife of the priest who sacrificed them to the deity. Obsidian was thus chiefly the war weapon and the sacrificial weapon, but the traditions relating to it are associated with all the offices of human art, industry, and activity, and well illustrate the inter-relations of early religion and magic with war, labor, art, and law.

Probably after a long career as a fetish, obsidian at last became personalized or deified, just as grain achieved a personality as Osiris or "John Barley-corn." The process of development from fetish to god is a fairly clear one. From obsidian were manufactured the mirrors or scrying-stones, in which wizards or necromancers pretended to see visions of the past or the future. These were known as aitzili, or "water obsidian," probably because of the high polish they were capable of.

One of these is carried by Tezcatlipoca. Many deities when they arrive at that stage of development when they take human shape continue to be represented along with their fetish or totem shape, and that this was so in the case of Tezcatlipoca admits of no doubt, as one of his minor names is Itztli, or "obsidian," and his principal title itself means merely " Smoking Mirror," and, as we have seen, his idol was carved from obsidian.

Obsidian, the great life-preserver and food-getter, became identified in the form of this god as one of those magical stones which are considered capable of raising a storm, and therefore with the wind, the cause or breath of life. Obsidian thus came to be looked upon as the symbol of life, with every manifestation of which it had inter- relations.

Just as the oak-cult of the Druids seems to have given an oak-like virtue to the oracular birds which dwelt within its branches, to the soil from which it grew, to the sky above it, to the priests who ministered to it, and to the sacred implements they employed, just as the idea of jade permeated all Chinese life and thought in early times, so the obsidian idea came to have ramifications in every department of Aztec life.

In course of time this magical idea gradually became amalgamated with the rather more "civilized" cults of Quetzalcoatl and Tlaloc. But it left its mark upon Mexican religion to the last, its symbolism persisted, and no view of Aztec life is complete which does not take it into consideration and regard it as a fundamental in the upbuilding of one of the world's most interesting magico-religious systems.

Thus the magic of obsidian assumed a religious phase, and became one of the chief considerations in Mexican life. It entered both into practical occultism as the medium for divination, and into thought as the supplier of blood. It had therefore a twofold effect on the general arcane outlook of Mexican man.

MAGICAL FOLK BELIEFS OF THE MEXICANS

Numerous superstitions came to be associated with the central occult ideas in Mexican life. If hair could be snatched from a sorcerer's head it was believed that he would die the same night unless he could steal or borrow something from the house of the person who had taken it. The animal world held many portents for man besides the ominous call of the owl, the bird of Mictlantecutli, the god of death, and it was considered unlucky to encounter a skunk or a weasel.

If rabbits or ants entered a house they were certain to bring bad luck, and if a certain kind of spider was found on the walls of a dwelling the inhabitant traced a cross upon the ground, in the centre of which he placed the insect. If it should crawl northwards it was regarded as a sign of death for him who caught it, as the north was the compass direction of the Underworld.

Scores of popular beliefs were current. Before maize was cooked it was blown upon "to give it courage" or life, and to neglect to pick up maize-grains lying on the ground was to court future want. To step over a child was to arrest its growth, although a backward step could avert the damage done. For a girl to eat standing was to risk the loss of a husband. Children's first teeth were placed in mouse-holes so that their subsequent teeth might grow strong, the idea being that the proximity of rodents to the first teeth would by sympathetic magic cause the next to have good growing power. Sneezing was an evil omen, and it was thought that ill was being spoken of the sneezer. The scent of flowers might be inhaled from the edge of a bouquet only, as the centre belonged to the god Tezcatlipoca.

In short, most of the superstitions which we ourselves still indulge in were to be encountered among the ancient Mexicans. I shall try through the medium of fiction to afford the reader a picture more or less complete of magic in Old Mexico, for to my way of thinking one of the most legitimate uses to which fiction can be put is the illumination of the past by its imaginary gleam.

From among the blue shadows of a night in Old Mexico arose the great pyramid temple of Uitzil, god of war, the braziers on its summit glowing sullenly in despite of a moon of full sovereignty. Half-way up the staircase which writhed around the white pile sat a little old man, bald and ragged, with a curious, carven face and wicked half-blind eyes. This was Total, the rag-picker. Raking among the gutters of the House of Archives, he had come upon a painted manuscript, and thinking it a contract or such-like, had pushed it into his sack with other street flotsam. But appraising his discovery at night in his waterside shack, he had spelled through its symbols, and as he was a rag-picker rather through idleness than insufficiency he did not fail to comprehend that it enshrined a mystery.

It read as follows, according to his interpretation, for writing by pictures lacks the exactitude of writing by letters, and a pictorial manuscript may find as many interpretations as it does readers: "Beneath the ninety-third step of the teocalli of Uitzil, the war-god, lies the casket of Huemac of the Strong Hand, the great and powerful magician. If anyone remove the stone and obtain possession of the casket and its contents he shall be as great as was Huemac."

That is why Total sat on the ninety-second step of the teocalli of the war-god and gazed sadly upon the ninety -third step. It was nearly four yards long, and weighed, perhaps, a ton. His imagination refused to soar with the shadow of such a weight upon it. The great block became his symbol for the impossible.

Wedged between its upper and under fellows in the flight of steps it seemed steadfast as the teocalli itself. Moreover, there was a never-ceasing traffic of priests and penitents from dawn till dusk and from sunset to sunrise. He peered over the sides of the pyramid. The stones of the retaining wall were even more massive than those of the stairway. Surely a devil had painted this script for his undoing, some evil fiend of Mictlan, the underworld of death and desolation.

Advice? He, a pariah, dare turn for that solace to none, much less to the priests or the mighty, who would at once award him doom on the count of premeditated profanation. No, he would seek out an adviser from among the outcast like himself. But that counselor would be no less learned or acute than priest or judge, even if he were reprobate, for he would go to a naualli a practitioner of black magic.

Making his way to the huddle of huts on the waterfront where he knew such an one dwelt, he debated with himself as to how much he would tell the naualli. If he told him all, would not the sorcerer desire for himself so great a treasure as the box of the mightiest of magicians?

Again, if he only told him so much would the naualli be able to help him at all? That was his dilemma.

Coming to the water-front, he sat down upon a little jetty which the waves licked dismally and tried to think. But he soon discovered that he had arrived at an impasse. Should he tell the magician his entire story the confidence might cost him his life; if he refrained from doing so he must for ever renounce all hope of possessing the casket of Huemac. Total was not a coward, but the thought of death by magic made him feel already half-way on the road to Mictlan.

When he had fortified himself at a drinking booth with a draught of octli, however, he took heart once more and quickened his steps to the hut of the naualli. Situated almost on the water's verge, it was built of rough boards covered with crudely painted protective symbols. Not a sound escaped from the hut, and Total, peering through the chinks in the boards, could discern nothing that was happening inside for black darkness. At last, frantically courageous, he pulled the skin curtain ever so little to one side and begged permission to enter. All he could see was a circle of glowing embers over which the shadow of a hand hovered for a moment. It thrust a half-burnt torch into the red ashes and in a halo of yellow light, mingled with moonshine, Total could see the naualli sitting, painted and fateful, with sullen unseeing eyes staring deadly through a thick fell of hair.

He invited Total to enter by a grunt, and the rag-picker drew near. Spite of his terror the rag-picker succeeded in making plain his errand. The naualli heard him in silence, then asked for the manuscript. Having perused it, he drew a small scrying-stone from among his rags and gazed long into its polished surface.

At length he spoke: "The casket is indeed underneath the ninety-third step," he said. "It rests immediately below it. A hollow has been made in the earth there to receive it. It contains the magical implements of the mighty Huemac of the Strong Hand."

"But how may it be recovered?" asked Total, unconvinced.

"That is a simple enough matter to one who has the sight," replied the naualli. "But what do you intend to pay me if I recover it for you?"

"I have thought of that," said Total, "and I do not know how I can pay you unless by sharing the contents of the box with you."

The naualli bowed. "The casket of Huemac of the Strong Hand should contain enough for two, even when one of them is a magician," he said. "Let us go to the pyramid of Huitzil."

He whistled sharply on his fingers and two young men not quite so disheveled as himself insinuated themselves into the hut. They were his pupils, and less distinguished in the art of appearing great though filthy.

The naualli addressed them peremptorily in what was evidently a caste dialect, and they quitted the hut as unobtrusively as they had entered it. The magician then rose and followed them, accompanied by Total. By this hour the streets were deserted, and when they reached the great pyramid all seemed lifeless below and above it save for the deep red glow of the braziers on its summit, the flames of which waved like bannerets in the thin night zephyrs.

At the foot of the teocalli they encountered one of the magician's pupils and he pointed upwards to signify that his companion had climbed to the summit in order to give notice to his master should anyone descend whilst the naualli was carrying out his operations. The sorcerer and the rag-picker mounted the teocalli side by side, eyeing each other aslant, and counting the steps as they went.

Arrived at the ninety-third step, they halted, and the naualli fumbled in the darkness at the side of the staircase. He must have touched a concealed spring, for the step swung outwards from the inner side of the staircase as if on hinges. He groped in the space where it had been and drew forth a curiously wrought box of some satin- like wood inlaid with silver symbols. Then he swung the step back into its original position.

Total and the naualli descended the steps, the rag- picker more or less dazed after what he had seen, and the magician thinking upon what he had achieved. So far he was too elated to have yet given any consideration as to whether he should strive to keep the casket and its contents for himself, and too interested in the possibility of what it might hold to actively covet it. They hurried back to the hut by the water's edge.

The naualli stirred up the dying embers with a new torch which, once alight, he placed in a socket in the wall. The casket was bound up by a silver chain, and, this burst in twain, a curious medley of objects lay before them. Here was a magic rattle which, if shaken in one way summoned spiritual assistance, if agitated in another, banned all demoniac forces. There was a mirror in whose surface might be espied fatal visions of days yet uncalendered.

On this side lay a heavy wand of power, cunningly inlaid; on that a drumstick with which to beat a magical tattoo such as would force multitudes to follow the drummer. Fetish necklaces of human fingers, an almanac in symbols more ancient than were known to either the naualli or Total, a cap of invisibility, phials of sleepful and potent draughts, and lastly, a book of spells such were the contents of the casket of Huemac of the Strong Hand.

By degrees the naualli's first rapture of interest wore off and the side glances which he directed at Total became more and more frequent. Then covetousness quickened speech.

"These things, O rag-picker, constitute the most marvelous collection of magical objects it has been my lot ever to behold," he said ungrudgingly and even enthusiastically. "They can be of small advantage to such a person as yourself, who cannot appreciate or make proper use of them. For what sum will you sell them? I will gladly pay you a goodly price for those treasures. You see, I do not attempt to belittle their value."

Total stood stock-still, only his eyes moving and shifting rapidly from side to side. He was thinking swiftly and evilly.

"I will sell the box and all it contains for three hundred quills of gold," he said, naming what seemed to him far more than the naualli was likely to possess.

The naualli turned, and groping in a recess of the hut, drew forth a stained and aged leather bag, from which he poured a bewildering heap of quills filled with gold-dust the higher currency of commerce in Old Mexico and began to count out the number Total had asked.

As he bent to his task, engrossed in the counting, he did not see the rag-picker lift the heavy wand out of the casket of Huemac. With a dexterous turn of the arm Total brought down the thick heavily mounted baton with all his force upon the nape of the naualli's bent neck, and the magician, without even a sigh, fell face forward into the circle of pink and grey ashes.

Total raised him and examined him carefully. But the fish-like eyes were fixed and the lines of the face were hard and grey as carven stone. Picking up the body as he might a sack of refuse, Total carried it to the water's edge.

Espying a canoe on the beach, he launched it, and tying a great stone to the naualli's neck with his sash, he threw the body aboard the tiny craft. Paddling out for some distance, he backed water and dropped the magician's body over the side. Then he returned to the shore and entered the hut.

He would be a magician. The naualli was dead; he, Total, would take his place. With the assistance of the casket of Huemac he would be the greatest worker of magic in Mexico.

First he gloated over the heap of gold quills; then he turned to the box and handled the implements it contained one by one. But the age-old symbols in the book of spells revealed no secret to him, the calendar was beyond him, the rattle he might shake continuously without succeeding in summoning a single spirit, and the mirror displayed no prophetic visions to his eyes.

Slowly it came to him that to be able to use these things successfully one must be a master in magic. But he would learn.

By the light of the still flickering torch he addressed himself fiercely to the task. All night he pondered upon the book of spells, but without unriddling a single symbol, and the dawn, peeping through the chinks of the windowless hut, found him still poring over the painted agave leaves in the patient determination of ignorance. And so sleep came to him. He did not know that magical secrets yield not themselves to the self-instructed, but must be taught. He slept long, and when he awoke it was late afternoon. With the dogged persistence of superstition he took up the task once more. Night fell. No one disturbed him. The naualli's pupils evidently had orders not to approach the hut unless expressly summoned. But he was not alone after the torch had flickered out.

At first Total only heard the faintest whisperings and rustlings. It was as if a number of very quiet children were in the hut playing in whispers. Then a voice named someone more loudly. It might be one of his pupils outside whispering to the magician through the chinks of the boards.

Then the name was spoken loudly, passionately, into Total's very ear. He leapt from where he sat with a cry, and stood trembling and quivering in horrible, irrational fear. Now he realized that the familiars of the naualli were with him, and that if he was to master the great art he must accustom himself to their visits.

Still trembling, he resumed his squatting attitude and his unavailing study of the book of spells. The disappearance of the lines of light from the chinks in the wall of the hut showed that night had fallen again. The horrid sounds around him multiplied. The flap and flitter of bats' wings sounded above his head or was it the sound of bats' wings?

Something alit and crouched for an instant upon his head. The black air felt as if it swarmed. Abominations shoaled about him. Once the leathern curtain before the door was agitated and a huge body bounded aimlessly round the hut and brushed behind him. Later the curtain sagged and was partly withdrawn and two eyes looked in upon him for a moment with glowing menace.

At last a hand stroked his face, and a cheek, hard and cold as stone was laid lovingly against his. With a sob of terror he stumbled into the night, never halting until he reached a little shrine of the Emerald Lady, spouse of the Water-god, the goddess of the fishers and fowlers of the waterside. Close to this he crouched, nor did he quit its vicinity till daylight. But with the first glimmer of day his ambitions returned to him. Such must be the experience of all magicians, he told himself, and he retraced his steps to the hut. Entering, he found all as before. The box of Huemac still lay where he had left it, half covered by the brilliant panoramic pages of the book of spells, and once more he set himself to its elucidation.

All day he labored over the inexorable symbols with no more success than before. The light waned and evening approached. When night fell he remembered that he had no fire. But he felt bolder. He was in process of becoming a naualli and the things of darkness must not prevail against him.

A soft yet ponderous body leapt upon his back. Something seized one of his hands. A smooth warm tongue brushed across his face. He could stand the sheer abomination of his environment no longer, and utterly broken down, he rushed from the hut into the moonlight, the casket of Huemac under his arm. In a frenzy of hate against the agency which had caused his suffering, he jumped into a canoe and paddled swiftly out into the lake.

In what direction he was going he knew not. But at a certain spot he stopped, and with a malediction hurled the casket of Huemac into the water. It floated lightly upon the surface. Apparently the silver which bound it was not sufficiently weighty to sink it. As it swam wickedly on the moonlit surface of the lake the water was suddenly agitated from below and a black hand with shriveled, tenuous fingers grasped avidly at the casket and seized it.

Too paralyzed at first to lift the paddles, Total watched the seizing hand in a transport of horror. As if pulling itself up by purchase upon the box, the body of the naualli slowly arose from the depths; first appeared the disheveled hair, then the dead fish-like eyes, fixed and unseeing, then the mouth, hard and grim.

With a shriek of anguish which rang far across the water Total seized the paddles and headed for the shore with a haste that made for little speed. He glanced over his shoulder. The naualli was swimming after him.

For five tense minutes he paddled, glancing ever behind as he did so. But the sorcerer followed in his very wake, the dark features showing against the line of foam with fearful and threatening distinctness. Ere he gained the beach Total leaped out into the shallows and floundered ashore. The naualli was not far behind him. Total's one hope was protection from his patron god, Uitzil. If magic had failed him, the strength of the war-god might still succor him.

Through the quiet streets and alleys he sped at the breakneck pace of a fear that was now delirious. And ever he heard the patter of speedful feet in his rear. It was dark in the lanes among the huddle of huts and houses and he could not now glimpse his pursuer.

At length he came to the foot of the great teocalli of Uitzil. He sprang upon its stairway with limbs which gave beneath him and a bursting heart. He had gained the twentieth step when, looking backwards and downwards, he saw the naualli leaping towards him. With a gasp he spurred his jaded body to the ascent. On, on he struggled and scrambled, but the naualli pressed him hard.

At last, just as he reached the ninety-third step, he felt hateful fingers grasp at his shoulders and seize his throat. Then with fiendish might he was lifted off his feet and hurled down the abyss-like slope of the teocalli.

The naualli descended and walked over the dead body of Total the rag-picker which lay at the base of the pyramid. He sneered down upon the white wicked features. Then he took his way to the waterside, and reentering his hut, squatted in front of the grey ashes, the casket of Huemac in his hands.

MEXICAN MAGICIANS CASTING LOTS

CHAPTER IV
MEXICAN MAGIC (continued)

The art of divination was widely practiced by the Mexican priesthood. In ancient or pre-Columbian Mexico there was a college of augurs, corresponding in purpose to the Auspices of ancient Rome, the alumni of which occupied themselves with observing the flight and listening to the songs of birds, from which they drew their conclusions and interpreted the speech of all winged creatures.

In Mexico the calmecac, or training college of the priests, had a department where divination was taught in all its phases, and that the occupation was no mere sinecure will appear later. Among the less advanced communities the services of the diviner or seer were much in request, and the forecasting of the future became, sooner or later, the chief concern of the higher classes of priests.

The methods adopted by the priests in the practice of divination scarcely differed with locality, but many various expedients were made use of to attain the same end. Thus, some practiced oracular methods in much the same way as did the priesthood in ancient Egypt and Greece. The idols became the direct medium by which Divine wishes were disclosed or the future made clear.

Necromancy was also extensively practiced, the priests pretending to raise the dead, whose instructions they communicated to those who had consulted them. Still other classes predicted by means of leaves of tobacco, or the grains or juice of coca, the shapes of grains of maize, taken at random, the casting of beans, the appearance of animal excrement, the forms assumed by the smoke rising from burning victims, the entrails and viscera of animals, the course taken by spiders, visions seen in dreams, the flight of birds, and the direction in which fruits might fall.

The professors of these several methods were distinguished by different ranks and titles, and their training was a long and arduous one, and undertaken in no mere spirit of flippancy. It has been already mentioned that the Mexican priesthood, or that class of it devoted to augury, made a practice of observing the flight of various birds and of listening to their songs. This observation of birds for the purpose of augury was common to other American tribes.

The bird, with its rapid motion and incomprehensible power of flight, appeared to the savage as a being of a higher order than himself, and its song the only hint of music with which he was familiar as something bordering upon the supernatural, the ability to understand which he had once possessed but had lost through the potency of some evil and unknown spell.

Some great sorcerer or medicine-man alone might break this spell, and this the shamans of the tribe sought assiduously to achieve, by means of close attention to the habits of birds, their motions and flights, and especially to their song. "The natives of Brazil regarded one bird in especial as of good augury," says Coreal, an early eighteenth-century traveler, in his "Voiages aux Indes Occidentals." He does not state to what bird he alludes, but proceeds to say that its mournful chant is heard by night rather than by day.

The savages say it is sent by their deceased friends to bring them news from the other world and to encourage them against their enemies. Here, it would seem, we have an example of bird-augury combined with divination by necromancy, and that the same held good in Mexico we know. Coreal probably alluded to the goat-sucker bird which, with the screaming vulture, some South American tribes the Guaycurus of Paraguay, for example suppose to act as messengers from the dead to their priests, between whom and the deceased persons of the tribe there is thought to be frequent communication.

A typical example of augury by bird-habit has come down to us in the account of the manner in which the Nahua of Mexico fixed upon the spot for the foundation of that city. Halting after years of travel at the Lake of Tezcuco, they observed perched on the stem of a cactus a great eagle with wings out- spread, holding in its talons a writhing serpent. Their augurs interpreted this as a good omen, as it had been previously announced by an oracle, and on the spot drove the first piles upon which was after-wards built the city of Mexico-Tenochtitlan. The legend of its foundation is still commemorated in the arms of the modern Republic of Mexico, and on its coinage and postal stamps.

The business of divination by means of dreams and visions, it is hardly necessary to say, was almost completely in the hands of the priestly class. In Mexico they were known as teopixqui or teotecuhtli, "masters of divine things," in Maya speech, cocome, "the listeners."

Nearly all messages supposed to be received from the supernatural came through the medium of dreams or visions, and those who possessed ability to read or interpret the dream were usually placed in a class by themselves.

The priests held it as an article of belief that the glimpse into futurity, with which visions or dreams provided them, was to be gained only by extreme privation and by purifying the vision through hunger or the use of drugs. To induce the ecstatic condition the Indians made use of many different mediums, such as want of sleep, seclusion, the pertinacious fixing of the mind upon one subject, the swallowing or inhalation of cerebral intoxicants such as tobacco, the maguey, coca, ololiuchqui, the peyotl.

From dreams during the puberty-fast a person's entire future was usually divined by the priests, his spiritual affinities fixed, and his life's course mapped out. The elaborate ceremonies known as "dances" were usually adumbrated to the priests through dreams, and the actual performance was made to follow carefully in detail the directions supposed to have been received in the dream or vision.

Many shrines and sacred places were also supposed to have been indicated to certain persons in dreams, and their contents presented to those persons by supernatural beings whilst they were in the visionary state. The periods for the performance of rites connected with a shrine, as well as other devotional observances, often depended on an intimation received in a dream.

"Visions" were also induced by winding the skin of a freshly killed animal around the neck until the pressure on the veins caused unconsciousness, and dreams resulted, possibly from an overflow of blood to the head. Some tribes believed that the vision came to the prophet or seer as a picture, or that acts were performed before him as in a play, whilst others held that the soul traveled through space and was able to see from afar those places and events of which it desired to have knowledge.

A legend which reveals the manner in which the Mexicans augured occurrences from dreams is that of the Princess Papantzin, the sister of Montezuma II., who returned from her tomb to prophesy to her royal brother concerning his doom and the fall of his empire at the hands of the Spaniards. On taking up the reins of government, Montezuma had married this lady to one of his most illustrious servants, the governor of Tlatelulco, and after his death it would appear that she continued to exercise her husband's almost vice-regal functions and to reside in his palace.

In course of time she died, and her obsequies were attended by the emperor in person, accompanied by the greatest personages of his court and kingdom. The body was interred in a subterranean vault of his own palace, in close proximity to the royal baths, which stood in a sequestered part of the extensive grounds surrounding the royal residence.

The entrance to the vault was secured by a stone slab of moderate weight, and when the numerous ceremonies prescribed for the interment of a royal personage had been completed the emperor and his suite retired. At daylight next morning one of the royal children, a little girl of some six years of age, having gone into the garden to seek her governess, espied the Princess Papan standing near the baths.

The princess, who was her aunt, called to her, and requested her to bring her governess to her. The child did as she was bid, but her governess, thinking that imagination had played her a trick, paid little attention to what she said. As the child persisted in her statement, the governess at last followed her into the garden, where she saw Papan sitting on one of the steps of the baths.

The sight of the supposed dead princess filled the woman with such terror that she fell down in a swoon. The child then went to her mother's apartment and detailed to her what had happened. She at once proceeded to the baths with two of her attendants, and at sight of Papan was also seized with affright. But the princess reassured her, and asked to be allowed to accompany her to her apartments, and that the entire affair should for the present be kept absolutely secret.

Later in the day she sent for Ticotzicatzin, her major-domo, and requested him to inform the emperor that she desired to speak with him immediately on matters of the greatest importance. The man, terrified, begged to be excused from the mission, and Papan then gave orders that her uncle Nezahualpilli, King of Tezcuco, should be communicated with.

That monarch, on receiving her request that he should come to her, hastened to the palace. The princess begged him to see the emperor without loss of time and to entreat him to come to her at once.

Montezuma heard his story with surprise mingled with doubt. Hastening to his sister, he cried as he approached her: "Is it indeed you, my sister, or some evil demon who has taken your likeness?"

"It is I indeed, your Majesty," she replied.

Montezuma and the exalted personages who accompanied him then seated themselves, and a hush of expectation fell upon all as they were addressed by the princess in the following words: "Listen attentively to what I am about to relate to you. You have seen me dead, buried, and now behold me alive again. By the authority of our ancestors, my brother, I am returned from the dwellings of the dead to prophesy to you certain things of prime importance.

"At the moment after death I found myself in a spacious valley, which appeared to have neither commencement nor end, and was surrounded by lofty mountains. Near the middle I came upon a road with many branching paths. By the side of the valley there flowed a river of considerable size, the waters of which ran with a loud noise. By the borders of this I saw a young man clothed in a long robe, fastened with a diamond, and shining like the sun, his visage bright as a star. On his forehead was a sign in the figure of a cross. He had wings, the feathers of which gave forth the most wonderful and glowing reflections and colors. His eyes were as emeralds, and his glance was modest. He was fair, of beautiful aspect and imposing presence. He took me by the hand and said: 'Come hither. It is not yet time for you to cross the river. You possess the love of God, which is greater than you know or can comprehend.'

"He then conducted me through the valley, where I espied many heads and bones of dead men. I then beheld a number of black folk, horned, and with the feet of deer. They were engaged in building a house, which was nearly completed. Turning toward the east for a space, I beheld on the waters of the river a vast number of ships manned by a great host of men dressed differently from ourselves. Their eyes were of a clear grey, their complexions ruddy; they carried banners and ensigns in their hands, and wore helmets on their heads. They called themselves 'Sons of the Sun.' The youth who conducted me and caused me to see all these things said that it was not yet the will of the gods that I should cross the river, but that I was to be reserved to behold the future with my own eyes and to enjoy the benefits of the faith which these strangers brought with them; that the bones I beheld on the plain were those of my countrymen who had died in ignorance of that faith, and had subsequently suffered great torments; that the house being builded by the black folk was an edifice prepared for those who would fall in battle with the seafaring strangers whom I had seen; and that I was destined to return to my compatriots to tell them of the 'true faith and to announce to them what I had seen that they might profit thereby."

Montezuma hearkened to these matters in silence and felt greatly troubled. He left his sister's presence without a word, and, regaining his own apartments, plunged into melancholy thoughts.

Papantzin's resurrection is one of the best authenticated incidents in Mexican history, and it is a curious fact that on the arrival of the Spanish Conquistadores one of the first persons to embrace Christianity and receive baptism at their hands was the Princess Papan.

AMULETS AND CHARMS

Amulets and charms were largely used among the Mexicans and Maya. As in other parts of America, the amulet was regarded in Mexico as a personal fetish. The wholesale manner in which everything pertaining to native worship or superstition was swept away by the Spanish Conquistadores renders a thorough knowledge of personal fetishism among the Nahua peoples impossible, but scanty notices in the writings of authors who lived in the generation immediately subsequent to the Conquest throw some light upon the description of charms and talismans in use among the Aztecs and kindred peoples. They appear to have been principally manufactured and sold by the priests of the various deities, in much the same manner as the medicine-men of the North American tribes make and sell such articles. The use of charms was chiefly notable in connection with the funerary customs of the Aztecs, as will be described later. In the Dresden Codex the pinturas represent the deceased on the road to Mictlan as wearing a wooden collar, probably an amulet, to show that he belongs to one or other of the Nahua deities.

For the same purpose, probably, he wears a plume on his head. The principal objects which have either come down to us or are known to have served the purpose of personal or household talismans to the Nahua peoples are: Death-masks. These were probably the skulls of ancestors and were kept in the houses of their descendants.

Some primitive peoples of Central America still keep the shrunken heads of their relatives. They consist of two classes: one in which the skull of the deceased person has been inlaid with mosaic, and the other in which a conventional image of the deceased has been manufactured by inlaying mosaic upon jade.

These death-masks are not to be confounded with the masks spoken of by many writers on Nahua custom as being used by the priests in religious ceremonial, or with those placed on the faces of the dead to ward off evil spirits. The mosaic work of which they are composed is often of a very great beauty, and excellent examples of it are to be seen in the American Room at the British Museum.

THE MAGIC AND MYSTERIES OF MEXICO

Specimens of such work are exceedingly rare, and are chiefly confined to those objects sent to Europe at a period immediately subsequent to the Conquest. Numerous small masks and heads which served as amulets have been discovered on the site of Mitla, the city of Mictlan, the god of the dead. Most of them are of terracotta and of good workmanship.

The tepitoton, or diminutive deities. These were small figures of the Lares and Penates type, but not, as has been thought, of the class of the Egyptian ushabtiu, or servant figurines. They were probably relics of a shamanistic form of worship, and nearer to the ancestor-idol type than the little fire-and-food gods of the Romans, though they possibly partook of the characteristics of both.

At the close of the great sun-cycle of fifty-two years, when the Nahua thought the universe was in danger of perishing, they broke those small figures in despair, believing they could no more seek aid from them. Travelers' staves are decorated with feathers and were carried by all merchants whilst on a journey, and show that they were under the protection of Quetzalcoatl, the culture-god of Mexico, or the great traveler.

Sahagun gives an interesting account of the worship of these stones by the Mexican itinerant merchants. On coming to their evening halting-place they tied their staves in a bundle and sprinkled them with blood taken from their ears, tongues, and arms. Incense was brought and burned before them, and food, flowers, and tobacco were offered to them. Although the name of the staff, coatl, means "serpent," it had, so far as its nomenclature was concerned, no connection with the god; and, indeed, when the staves were gathered together in a bundle the name they collectively bore was Yacatecutli, the name of the patron of merchants or pedlars.

Still, the staff was regarded as the invention of Quetzalcoatl, the culture-hero, and those using it practically placed themselves under his protection.

Amulets symbolic of the gods: These were numerous, but few are recorded. Chalchihuitlicue, the goddess of water, was worshipped under the likeness of a frog, carved from a single emerald or piece of jade, or sometimes in human form, but holding in her hand a lily-leaf ornamented with frogs.

In the Maya codices it appears as a symbol of water and rain. Images of it, cut from stone or made from clay, have been frequently discovered. They were kept by the post-Conquest Indians as talismans.

73

THE MAGIC AND MYSTERIES OF MEXICO

The symbol or crest of Uitzilopochtli, the Aztec war-god, was, as is implied by his name, a hummingbird.

This crest, the huitziton, was carried before his priests in battle, and it is probable that they and illustrious members of the warrior class wore the symbol as a talisman or decoration.

Flint talismans: As elsewhere, the thunderbolts thrown by the gods were supposed to be flint stones, and these were cherished as amulets of much virtue and as symbols of the fecundating rains. The Nava- hoes of New Mexico still use such stones as a charm for rain, and believe they fall from the clouds when it thunders.

The Chotas of Mexico continued until comparatively recent times the worship of their trinity the Dawn, the Stone, and the Serpent. Amulets depicted in the Mexican and Mayapinturas, or native MSS., give representations of what are obviously ornaments and personal decorations of the nature of amulets in great profusion, but, owing to the highly conventional drawing displayed in the Mexican pinturas, it is almost impossible to determine their exact nature.

The comparative clearness of outline in the Maya pinturas renders it much easier to speculate upon the nature of the objects represented therein. But it is only by induction that the character of these objects can be arrived at, the intolerance to which all native American objets d'art were subjected having long since destroyed their very names.

It will be well, then, to glance at the Maya MSS. while we attempt to discover what were the amulets worn by the figures depicted in them. We find that these objects are usually worn by figures representing gods, but it is well known that the symbol or ornament of the god usually becomes the symbol or ornament of his special worshippers the people of whom he is the tutelary deity.

In Egypt the ankh (the cruciform symbol of life carried by all the gods) was worn very generally, as was the uzat (the symbolic eye of Horus, which protected the wearer from the evil eye and against snake-bite), and the thet, the girdle-buckle of Isis.

In early Scandinavia the raven- wings of Odin adorned the helmet of the warrior; and, not to multiply instances, which are numerous, we have already seen that the Aztecs wore amulets depicting the frog-shaped rain-goddess Chalchihuitlicue. Hence there is no reason to suppose that the special worshippers of other Nahua deities did not wear amulets depicting either their tutelary deity or some ornament supposed to have been worn by himself, and perhaps representing one of his attributes like the staff of Quetzalcoatl, or the hummingbird of Uitzilopochtli.

An examination of the three Maya MSS. which we possess those of Dresden, Madrid, and Paris shows that most of the deities therein represented are accompanied by certain distinct and well-marked symbols which, it would seem, frequently decorate the figures of priests and people in the same MSS. As each god in the Maya MSS. is represented with his monthly sign it is not unlikely that his devotees would have worn these much in the same manner as persons in Europe wear amulet-rings in which are enclosed stones typifying the "virtues" of the several months.

The principal amulets worn by the chief Aztec gods occasionally resemble those of the Maya deities. Uitzilopochtli wears on his breast a white ring made from a mussel shell, which is described as "his breast-mirror," that is his scrying-glass, while, as we have seen, Tezcatlipoca wears a similar amulet, from which, indeed, he takes his name, and sometimes a white ring, resembling a large round eye, typical probably of his gift of prophetic vision. At the waist he sometimes has an ornament resembling the Maya Kin sign of the five points of the compass and painted blue.

Quetzalcoatl wears many amulets, a nape-appendage of grouse or crow feathers, the significance of which may be much the same as those feather-bunches worn by some of the North American Indians for protective purposes. He has white earrings of hook- like shape, a necklace of spirally voluted snail shells, and on the breast a large ornament sliced from a shell, the symbol of life. These ornaments are all of Maya origin and such have been taken from Maya graves, where they had been placed as symbols of resurrection.

He is frequently depicted as wearing a necklace of jaguar's teeth, the sign of the Maya balam or tiger-priesthood, and the tiger-skin hat of the same caste. Cinteotl, the young maize-god, wears a jadeite stone to symbolize the green shoots of the young plant over which he presides.

The goddess Xochiquetzal is seen in some MSS. wearing the wristlets or cuffs made of opossum skin which were put on the arms of women in labor to give them the courage of that animal in bringing forth. Tlaloc, the rain-god, wears the square ear-plug typical of the four quarters of the world, and bears a serpentine wand symbolic of water.

The magical amulets and spells employed at death are described by Clavigero, who alludes to the spells regarded as essential to the welfare of the spirit in the Otherworld as follows: "However superstitious the Mexicans were in other matters, in the rites which they observed at funerals they exceeded themselves. As soon as any person died, certain masters of funeral services were called who were generally men advanced in years. They cut a number of pieces of paper with which they dressed the dead body, and took a glass of water with which they sprinkled the head, saying that that was the water used in the time of their life. They then dressed it in a habit suitable to the rank, the wealth, and the circumstances attending the death of the party. If the deceased had been a warrior, they clothed him in the habit of Huitzilopochtli; if a merchant, in that of Jacatectli; if an artist, in that of the protecting god of his art or trade; one who had been drowned was dressed in the habit of Tlaloc; one who had been executed for adultery in that of Tlazolteotl; and a drunkard in the habit of Tezcatzoncatl, god of wine. In short, as Gomara has well observed, they wore more garments after they were dead than while they were living.

"With the habit they gave the dead a jug of water, which was to serve on the journey to the other world, and also at successive different times different pieces of paper, mentioning the use of each. On consigning the first piece to the dead they said: 'By means of this you will pass without danger between the two mountains which fight against each other. 'With the second they said: 'By means of this you will walk without obstruction along the road which is defended by the great serpent.' With the third: 'By this you will go securely through the place where there is the crocodile Xochitonal.'

"The fourth was a safe passport through the eight deserts, the fifth through the eight hills, and the sixth was given in order to pass without hurt through the sharp wind, for they pretended that it was necessary to pass a place called Itzehecajan where a wind blew so violently as to tear up rocks, and so sharp that it cut like a knife, on which account they burned all the habits which the deceased had worn during life, their arms, and some household goods in order that the heat of this fire might defend them from the cold of that terrible wind. One of the chief and most ridiculous ceremonies at funerals was the killing of a techichi, a domestic quadruped, resembling a little dog, to accompany the deceased in their journey to the other world. They fixed a string about its neck, believing that necessary to pass the deep river of Chiuhnahuapan or New Waters.

"They buried the techichi, or burned it along with the body of its master, according to the kind of death of which he died. While the masters of the ceremonies were lighting up the fire in which the body was to be burned the other priests kept singing in a melancholy strain. After burning the body, they gathered the ashes in an earthen pot, amongst which, according to the circumstances of the deceased, they put a gem of more or less value, which they said I would serve him in place of a heart in the other world. They buried this earthen pot in a deep ditch, and fourscore days after made oblations of bread and wine over it."

THE UNDERWORLD OF THE DEAD

The localities where the sorceries of the Mexican priests were held were usually caverns or the underground portions of the temples. Such a place at Mitla is described by Father Torquemada as follows: "When some monks of my order, the Franciscan, passed preaching and shriving through the province of Zapoteca, whose capital city is Tehuantepec, they came to a village which was called Mictlan that is Underworld (Hell). Besides mentioning the large number of people in the village they told of buildings which were prouder and more magnificent than any which they had hitherto seen in New Spain. Among them was a temple of the evil spirit and living-rooms for his demonical servants, and among other fine things there was a hall with ornamented panels, which were constructed of stone in a variety of arabesques and other very remarkable designs.

"There were doorways there, each one of which was built of but three stones, two upright at the sides and one across them, in such a manner that, although these doorways were very high and broad, the stones sufficed for their entire construction. They were so thick and broad that we were assured there were few like them. There was another hall in these buildings, or rectangular temples, which was erected entirely on round stone pillars, very high and very thick, so thick that two grown men could scarcely encircle them with their arms, nor could one of them reach the finger-tips of the other. These pillars were all in one piece, and, it was said, the whole shaft of a pillar measured five ells from top to bottom, and they were very much like those of the Church of Santa in Maria Maggiore in Rome, very skillfully made and polished."

Father Burgoa gives a more exact description. He says: "The Palace of the Living and of the Dead was built for the use of this person (the high priest of the Zapotecs). . . . They built this magnificent house or pantheon in the shape of a rectangle, with portions rising above the earth and portions built down into the earth, the latter in the hole or cavity which was found below the surface of the earth, and ingeniously made the chambers of equal size by the manner of joining them, leaving a spacious court in the middle; and in order to secure four equal chambers they accomplished what barbarian heathen (as they were) could only achieve by the powers and skill of an architect. It is not known in what stone-pit they quarried the pillars, which are so thick that two men can scarcely encircle them with their arms.

"There were four chambers above ground and four below. The latter were arranged according to their purpose in such a way that one front chamber served as chapel and sanctuary for the idols, which were placed on a great stone which served as an altar. And for the more important feasts which they celebrated with sacrifices, or at the burial of a king or great lord, the high priest instructed the lesser priests or the subordinate temple officials who served him to prepare the chapel and his vestments and a large quantity of the incense used by them. And then he descended with a great retinue, while none of the common people saw him or dared to look in his face, convinced that if they did so they would fall dead to the earth as a punishment for their boldness. And when he entered the chapel they put on him a long white cotton garment made like an alb, and over that a garment shaped like a dalmatic, which was embroidered with pictures of wild beasts and birds; and they put a cap on his head, and on his feet a kind of shoe woven of many-colored feathers.

"And when he had put on these garments he walked with solemn mien and measured step to the altar, bowed low before the idols, renewed the incense, and then in quite unintelligible murmurs he began to converse with these images, these depositories of infernal spirits, and continued in this sort of prayer with hideous grimaces and writhings, uttering inarticulate sounds, which led all present with fear and terror, till he came out of that diabolical trance and told those standing around the lies and fabrications which the spirit had imparted to him or which he had invented himself.

"When human beings were sacrificed the ceremonies were multiplied, and the assistants of the high priest stretched the victim out upon a large stone, baring his breast, which they tore open with a great stone knife, while the body writhed in fearful convulsions, and they laid the heart bare, ripping it out, and with it the soul, which the devil took, while they carried the heart to the high priest that he might offer it to the idols by holding it to their mouths, among other ceremonies; and the body was thrown into the burial-place of their 'blessed,' as they called them.

"The last (underground) chamber had a second door at the rear, which led to a dark and gruesome room. This was closed with a stone slab, which occupied the whole entrance. Through this door they threw the bodies of the victims and of the great lords and chieftains who had fallen in battle, and they brought them from the spot where they fell, even when it was very far off, to this burial-place; and so great was the barbarous infatuation of those Indians that, in the belief of the happy life which awaited them, many who were oppressed by diseases or hardships begged this infamous priest to accept them as living sacrifices and allow them to enter through that portal and roam about in the dark interior of the mountain, to seek the feasting-places of their forefathers. And when anyone obtained this favor the servants of the high priest led him thither with special ceremonies, and after they allowed him to enter through the small door they rolled the stone before it again and took leave of him, and the unhappy man, wandering in that abyss of darkness, died of hunger and thirst, beginning already in life the pain of his damnation, and on account of this horrible abyss they called this village Liyobaa.

"When later there fell upon these people the light of the Gospel, its servants took much trouble to instruct them, and to find out whether this error, common to all these nations, still prevailed; and they learned from the stories which had been handed down that all were convinced that this damp cavern extended more than thirty leagues underground, and that its roof was supported by pillars. And there were people, zealous prelates anxious for knowledge, who, in order to convince these ignorant people of their error, went into this cave accompanied by a large number of people bearing lighted torches and firebrands, and descended several large steps. And they soon came upon many great buttresses which formed a kind of street.

"They had prudently brought a quantity of rope with them to use as guiding-lines that they might not lose themselves in this confusing labyrinth. And the putrefaction and the bad odor and the dampness of the earth were very great, and there was also a great wind which blew out their torches. And after they had gone a short distance, fearing to be overpowered by the stench, or to step on poisonous reptiles, of which some had been seen, they resolved to go out again, and to completely wall up this back door of hell. The four buildings above ground were the only ones which still remained open, and they had a court and chambers like those underground; and the ruins of these have lasted even to the present day."

We must not close this chapter on Mexican magic without some reference to the physical apparatus of the Mexican magician. Perhaps the most striking emblem of his craft was the naualli or disguise, a cloak which gave him a resemblance to some animal and which was symbolical of shape-shifting. In certain Mexican manuscripts we find illustrations of these disguises, cloaks cut and painted to represent symbolically dragons, butterflies, bats, and jaguars, and most sorcerers probably owned several of these, using them in the belief that they actually transformed them into the animals or demons which they purported to represent. They appear to have been a "civilized version" of the beast-disguises employed by the ruder tribes of the prairies, bear-disguises, wolf-disguises and so forth, as used in tribal secret ceremonies by the medicine-men.

The magical wand or baton was an outstanding implement of the sorcerer, and Tezcatlipoca and other gods are represented as bearing it and are described as wielding it magically in the older Spanish writings and the chronicles written by Indian half-bloods, such as "The Annals of Quahutitlan." Quetzalcoatl also bears such a staff, an upright with several pierced cross-pieces, but it has a peculiar significance of its own. He used it chiefly to beat upon the soil to render it fruitful, and it has thus an analogy to those staves used for a similar purpose by the officiating priests of the Mysteries of Eleusis.

At other times he is seen holding a rattle-staff, the sound of which imitated the falling of the rain, thus inducing its presence by sympathetic magic. Human knuckle-bones were among the paraphernalia of the Mexican wizard. With these he cast lots, as with dice, and foretold "fortunes" and circumstances by the manner in which they fell when cast, as he did with beans and pebbles.

That the Mexican sorcerers also wore masks in the semblances of beasts and demons seems to be proved from illustrations in the manuscripts. The cloth or carpet was likewise an almost inseparable adjunct to minor sorcery, just as it is to legerdemain today.

CHAPTER V
THE DEMONOLOGY OF MEXICO

The demonhood of ancient Mexico was, perhaps, the most gruesome which ever haunted any race of men. It took many shapes, and varied somewhat with locality, and it scarcely resembles any recognizable system of demonology, European or Asiatic. Those demons most dreaded were the Tzitzimime, or "monsters descending from above," who were, indeed, the stars.

The interpreter of the "Codex Telleriano" says of them: "The proper signification of this name is the fall of the demons, who, they say, were stars; and even still there are stars in heaven called after their names, which are the following: Yzcatecaztli, Tlahvezcal-pantecuvtli, Ceyacatl, Achitumetl, Xacupancalqui, Mixauhmatl, Tezcatlipoca, and Contemoctli. These were their appellations as gods before they fell from heaven, but they are now named Tzitzimitli, which means something monstrous or dangerous."

Tezozomoc mentions them in his Cronica Mexicana in connection with the building of the great temple at Mexico. He states that their images were at one period still necessary for the completion of the building, and alludes to them as "angels of the air, holding up the sky," and "the gods of the air who draw down the rains, waters, clouds, thunders, and lightnings, and who are placed round Uitzilopochtli."

He further says that these "gods of the signs and planets" were brought to the sacred edifice and placed round the idol of Uitzilopochtli. They were thought of by the Mexicans in much the same manner as the mediaeval Christians regarded the fallen angels.

An ancient myth tells us that at one time they dwelt in heaven, but because of their sins were expelled from its delights. It was perhaps as the dwellings of the Tzitzimime rather than as those demons themselves that the stars were thought of, but their connection with the orbs of night is clear.

They are represented in the manuscripts as taking the shapes of noxious insects, spiders, scorpions, and so forth. One of the most terrifying figures in this stellar demonology is the goddess Itzpapalotl, who has the attributes both of the butterfly and the dragon a hideous mingling of the insect and the earth-monster. Another was Yacatecutli, a personification of the merchant's staff, to whom the peddlers of old Mexico offered nightly sacrifices of their own blood, drawn from their ears and noses, and smeared over a heap of the staves or bamboo walking-sticks which they generally carried.

These, in the exigencies of traveling, took the place of the idol of their patron deity. Once a year, too, they celebrated his festival with sanguinary rites in their own quarter of the city. At certain seasons of the year the natives were in the habit of sealing up every possible loophole in their houses, doors, windows, and chimneys, lest the baleful influence of the stellar demons should penetrate their dwellings and injure them or their children.

The beams of the stars were dreaded perhaps more than anything else, and even the gods themselves were not immune from baneful astrological influences. When night descended upon the pyramid-temples and market-places of Old Mexico, and the beneficent sun-god had betaken himself to the Underworld, it was a grim company indeed that came from the spirit- spheres to people the darkness.

TEZCATLIPOCA - DEMON OF THE NIGHT

The demonology of a Mexican midnight was eloquent of the harsh fatalism of a barbarian people who had but newly entered upon the possession of an ancient civilization. From sunset to sunrise Mexico of the marshes was a city of dreadful night indeed. Chief and most terrible of the tyrants of its dismal hours was Tezcatlipoca, "the Fiery Mirror," "He who Affrights the People," divine master of magicians, who took upon himself many fearful shapes and grisly disguises.

"These," says old Sahagun, one of the missionary fathers, "were masks which he took to terrify the folk, to have his sport with them." Perhaps the most menacing of the nocturnal disguises of this god, who wore the star of night upon his forehead, was the uactli bird, a species of hawk, whose cry of "yeccan, yeccan" boded a speedy death to him who heard it.

Another shape in which he haunted the woods was as the "axe of the night." As midnight approached, the watching acolytes in the temple precincts might hear a sound as of an axe being laid to the roots of a tree. Should the courageous wayfarer penetrate the wooded places whence the sound came, he was seized upon by Tezcatlipoca in the form of a headless corpse, in whose bony breast were "two little doors meeting in the centre."

It was the opening and closing of these, said the Aztecs, which simulated the sound of a woodcutter at work. A valiant man might plunge his hand into the grisly aperture, and if he could seize the heart within, might ask what ransom he chose from the demon. But the craven who encountered this awful phantom would speedily perish from fear. It is now believed that this peculiar sound is made by a certain nocturnal bird in the Mexican forests.

Hauntings of all kinds, indeed, were regarded as due to the agency of Tezcatlipoca. Especially feared were those forms of him, headless and without feet, which were said to roll along the ground, scattering maladies and diseases as they went.

These were believed to augur speedy death, either in battle or, still worse, by sickness, for a "straw death" was looked upon by the warlike Mexicans as a disgraceful end, unworthy of a soldier. But if the phantom was boldly grappled with and forced to purchase its release with a thorn of the maguey-plant, it was thought that the earnest thus secured would endow its owner with good fortune for the rest of his life.

Sometimes Tezcatlipoca would appear as a coyote, sometimes as a turkey-cock. " They sometimes painted him with cock's feet," says the priestly interpreter of one of the native manuscripts, "for they said at times only his feet were seen, and that at others he appeared sideways," alluding probably to the fact that fear-haunted wretches imagined they beheld him as they looked sideways out of the corners of their eyes.

It is strange to find the banshee in ancient Mexico, or at least a spirit which closely resembled her. The natives knew her as Cuitlapanton, and Sahagun says that she resembled "a little fairy." To see her, as in the case of her Irish congener, meant death or over-whelming misfortune. She had a short tail, long matted hair, which fell to her middle, and, like the banshee, she waddled like a duck, emitting a dolorous cry the while.

All attempts to seize her were vain, as she would vanish in one place and immediately reappear in another. Another grisly apparition of the Mexican night was a death's head which was in the habit of suddenly presenting itself to those bold enough to venture abroad after dark. It would dance in circles on the ground, making weird meanings. If one halted when pursued by this ghostly skull, its gyrations ceased.

Like the Cuitlapanton, it could not be grasped because of its protean habit of sudden disappearance, but it persisted in following the person who fled from it until he reached the door of his dwelling. If Europe can boast of its Blunderbores and its Famangomadans, its Skrymirs and other titans and jotuns, its Tom Thumbs, and its Alberichs, America has no reason to blush for her native giants and dwarfs. American Indian legend, indeed, swarms with figures monstrous and diminutive, the works of whose hands is still popularly supposed to be visible in the immense pyramids of Mexico and even in the mountains and valleys of the Western hemisphere, which, we are informed, were carved and shaped by their agency. The myth of Xelhua, one of the colossi of Mexico, bears a strange resemblance to the legend of Babel.

In the "Codex Vaticanus," that strange book written by Italian monks of the sixteenth century and illustrated by Aztec artists, his story is to be found in circumstances which, if they permit of the assumption of an ecclesiastical origin, still seem to indicate even more strongly the existence of a popular legend. We are informed that in the first age of Mexican mythical history giants dwelt in the land. Seven of the titan strain had escaped the Deluge, and, when the earth began to grow populous once more, one of these, Xelhua by name, betook himself to Cholula, and began to build the great pyramid which still stands in that place.

His intention in raising the huge mound or teocalli was to provide himself with a place of refuge should the waters once more seek to engulf the earth, but when it had reached a towering height, lightning from heaven fell and destroyed it. From the destructive bolt fell a precious stone in the shape of a toad, the symbol of a thunder-god, which spoke, reprimanding the builders, enquiring of them their reason for wishing to ascend into heaven, since it was sufficient for them to see what was on the Earth.

A fearsome monster now was that which plagued the Toltecs, the legendary people of Mexico, and helped to bring about their ultimate downfall. A great convention of wise men of the realm met at Teotihuacan, to find some means of appeasing the gods after a visitation of plague and war. During their conference a giant of immense proportions rushed into their midst, and, seizing them by the scores in his bony hands, hurled them to the earth, dashing their brains out.

The dwarf in American legend is equally ubiquitous with the giant. Among the Mexicans, the Tlaloque, the rain-makers, were regarded as dwarfish beings that lived in four chambers surrounding a great court, in which stood four immense water-casks containing the "good" and the "bad" rains. When commanded to distribute rain over a certain tract of country, they poured water from jars filled from the huge butts, and if these broke, thunder and lightning were sure to follow.

The "Dwarfs House" at Uxmal is the name of a small temple on the summit of an artificial hill, to which a charming legend is attached. An old woman, distressed by the loss of her family, found an egg, and wrapping it up in cotton cloth, placed it in a corner of her hut.

One day she noticed that the shell was broken, and soon after a tiny creature crawled forth. This Yucatecan Tom Thumb, like his English analogue, went to court, and challenged the King to a trial of strength. The monarch, amused, asked him to lift a stone weighing half a hundredweight, which he did, and in other contests of a similar kind defeated his antagonist. The King, enraged, told him that unless he built a palace loftier than any in the city, he should die. But his witch foster-mother came to his aid, and next morning the court awoke to discover, hard by, the palace or temple which still stands gleaming in all its carven glory on the summit of the mound.

In Yucatan dwarfs were sacred to the sun, and were occasionally sacrificed to that luminary, so that the pigmy in question was probably the Man of the Sun who emerges from the cosmic egg. America, like the Old World, carries its full quota of fairy folk, sprites, and goblins, but whether these have been created in an American environment or imported from the more venerable hemisphere, it is unnecessary to decide here.

THE REALM OF FAERIE

Quite a large proportion of American fairies appear to have a native "provenance," while others bear marks of importation visible to the student of folk-lore. The fairy and her kind were as familiar to the Red Man as to the White, for the excellent reason that throughout all his geographical ventures and peregrinations man has always been accompanied by these invisible playmates as well as by his gods and other more exalted tribal patrons.

From Hudson's Bay to Tierra del Fuego there exists a wealth of traditional material relating to little copper-colored fairy folk for the fairy invariably takes on the racial color of her environment. Nor is the lubber fiend, Puck or Robin Goodfellow, awanting.

In America, as in the Old World, the realm of Faerie implies a vast commonwealth of spiritual beings recruited from many classes gods degraded or half- forgotten, sorcerers, demons, and the souls of the human dead, in some instances associated with the Underworld, in others with the moon, that great reservoir of spiritual essence, where, it was thought, the souls of the dead awaited re-birth.

The Mexican goddess Xochiquetzal strikingly resembles the Morgan le Fay, Ursula, or "Venus" of the Teutonic and Celtic Underworlds, who, under one form or another, enticed Ogier the Dane, Tannhauser, and Thomas Rymour into her subterranean paradise. The American and European forms differ in that Xochiquetzal dwells on the summit of a lofty mountain rather than in its interior, but the general conditions are the same.

She is surrounded by minstrels, dwarfs, and dancing maidens, and boasts that no man is proof against her wiles; nor, once entrapped, may her victims escape from her blandishments. There is, indeed, a strong general similarity between y American and European fairy lore.

The Tepictoton were tiny Mexican spirits who seem to have assisted the agriculturist in his labors, coaxing the maize and agave plants to come to full growth and fruition. Occasionally, however, like all fays, they were mischievously disposed, and assumed the shape of spiders or scorpions. Other Mexican sprites, the Ciuateteo, were actually malignant, bringing strange diseases upon children, those time- honored victims of fairy spleen, epilepsy, and deformity. To behold them was to lose the sight of the offending eye.

They were, it was said, dead women or "witches," who mourned for their own children, and were vindictively disposed to the offspring of others. Like the fairies of Europe, they were associated with the moon, and an examination of their pranks throws a strong comparative light upon European fairyhood.

Among the Maya Indians of Guatemala the native fairy tales have been enwoven with Spanish stories of a similar character in a pattern at once most curious and instructive to the amateur of folk-belief. The story of "The Boy and the Sword," for example, preserves both the incidents of the slaying of the giants in "The Popol Vuh," a native book containing most ancient traditions, and the European folk-tale of the boy who sets out to seek his fortune.

The Maya still credit the existence of the Duenda, a capricious goblin, obviously of Castilian origin. Indeed, Guatemala and some other of the Spanish-American republics offer unrivalled fields for the accumulation of that traditional material which was quenched in Old Spain by the Inquisition, but still lingers in her ancient colonies.

There also exists in Guatemala an extraordinary mass of beast fairy lore, regarding the doings of such enchanted animals as the rabbit, the wolf, and the jaguar. We can even trace the origin of Shakespeare's Ariel to American folk-lore. Indeed, the whole of The Tempest is impregnated with American folklore, and it seems probable that Shakespeare was obliged for some of its incidents to contemporary books of travel.

D'Orbigny states that the Yurucares of Brazil fabled that at the beginning of things men were pegged Ariel-like in the knotty entrails of an enormous bole until the God Tiri, like Prospero, released them by cleaving it in twain. Nor does the American influence visible in Shakespeare's fairy play end here. The name Caliban is undoubtedly derived from the word Carib, often spelt Caribani and Calibani in older writers, and his "dam's god Setebos" was the supreme divinity of the Patagonians when first visited by Magellan, according to the Indian author Pigafetta.

A rich field of comparative inquiry lies open to the European investigator of fairy lore in America, by means of which he can test and not infrequently justify his conclusions regarding the Old World forms which crowd the lesser Olympus of Elfheim. The one drawback to such a work of collation is that American native folk-lore is scattered over a literature so vast and of such rapid and luxuriant growth as to daunt even the most courageous.

HERE THERE BE DRAGONS

But the Americanist, even more than the biologist, requires the courage of despair, that reckless bravado of the intellect, by dint of which new provinces of knowledge have so often been conquered. To squander precious time upon the comparison of American and European fairies may seem to many as wasteful and ridiculous excess and as indicating a sadly frivolous tendency; but the writer wishes with all his heart that grim circumstance did not stand between him and continued pilgrimage in these realms of old enchantment. And just as old Europe had her dragons, her phoenixes, and her basilisks, so the ancient world of America could boast of a mythical fauna equally weird and affrighting.

Differences of environment naturally dictated certain dissimilarity in the form and nature of the fabulous beasts of the New World from those of the Old, yet on the whole a close resemblance between the types is evident enough, and can only be accounted for by the spread of myth by migration. But whether America owes her mythical menagerie more to Europe or Asia is still obscure, though the probabilities lean to an Asiatic origin.

The dragon, along with the quite excessive burden of associated lore he carries on his scaly shoulders, was no stranger to the Columbian imagination. But the traditional form he takes in America is that of a great snake or serpent rather than the type familiar to us from Arthurian, Scandinavian or Chinese sources. In Mexico and Central America we find him taking on the local guise of a great bird-serpent, the "feathered snake," symbol of the rain and the accompanying trade-winds, and harbinger of the months of growth and fertility.

He was, indeed, a beneficent rather than an unfriendly monster, and had no such ravaging or maiden-snatching proclivities as made him the legitimate prey of champions in quest of high emprise. Indeed, when humanized, as he came to be, we rather find him in his man-like shape possessing all the attributes of the culture-hero. His vast serpentine form, with spreading flights of feather, not of scale, is a frequent motif on the walls of the ruined temples of Guatemala and Chiapas, and the Indians of those regions still see in the massed clouds which cluster round their hill-tops the winged snake of the rain, and murmur to one another that Quetzalcoatl is about to descend.

The Algonquins told a weird tale regarding a serpent-woman, half-snake, half-female, who, they told their Paleface hearers, was the grandmother of the human race. Closely resembling her was the Coatlicue of the Aztecs, half-woman, half-serpent, who was represented by them in her colossal statue, still preserved in the National Museum of Mexico, as a huge two-headed serpent with the breasts of a woman, attired in a robe of serpent skins, and having dragon's feet and claws.

Tradition spoke of her as the mother of the God of War, and still later legend as a "pious widow," beloved of the gods. It was to this fearsome figure that the Aztecs sacrificed thousands of war prisoners annually in order that the crops might flourish. She appears to have had many of the attributes of the Gorgons of classical story. Pek, the great lightning-dog of the Maya of Yucatan, descended from the heavens with open jaws and fiery tongue, a sufficiently horrible figure, recalling Cerberus. Possibly he was a relic of the time when dogs were sacrificed to the Fire-god.

He was the subject of many gruesome legends, which represented him in much the same guise as those ghostly canines which were formerly said to haunt certain localities in our island. Among the

Maya a belief was current that in certain remote and gloomy caverns there dwelt a huge and exceedingly bloodthirsty bat, called Camazotz, who swooped down upon and decapitated such venture some persons as chanced to disturb his dark domain.

Armed with enormous teeth and claws and a nose in the shape of a great flint knife, he pounced upon the interloper and with one blow of his razor-like snout severed head from body. In such a manner did he deal with one of the heavenly twins when they were imprisoned in his cavern by the Powers of Evil. But the survivor, catching a tortoise which chanced to be creeping past, clapped it to the bleeding trunk, which was magically accommodated with a new head.

In many drawings in the Aztec and Maya pictographs Camazotz is represented as a fiend, with outspread wings and Mephistophelean grin. Strange that the Old World never created a demon-figure from the bat, and that it was left to the genius of American art to conjure up a monster so entirely appropriate to an environment of gloom.

Indeed, the Maya Hades was peopled by demon creatures developed from the shape of bat and owl. That Camazotz was regarded by the Maya Indians with unconcealed terror is clear enough from the accounts of many travellers, who expressly state that no considerations of gain would tempt their native camp-followers to venture near the vicinity of one of his known haunts.

Fabulous birds also exercised the imagination of pre-Columbian Central America. Perhaps the most remarkable of these was the Moan bird of the Maya, a creature associated with the clouds, a species of cloud-spirit, somewhat resembling an owl, or, as some believe, a falcon. It is closely connected with the God of Death, and had an ominous and sinister significance.

To the Maya cloudland had a relationship with the Otherworld, and the Moan bird seems to have been regarded by them as the spirit of death, a fowl whose appearance and cry betokened dissolution to those it visited.

CHAPTER VI
WITCHCRAFT IN MEXICO

The cult of the witch appears to have been as general in ancient Mexico as it was in Europe and Asia, and in its American form it bore so startling a resemblance to the witchcraft of the Old World that it is difficult not to believe that both can be referred back to a common origin. Indeed, more than one of the zealous missionaries arrived at such a conclusion.

"These women," says one, writing of the Mexican sorceresses, "are such as we in Spain call witches." But, curiously enough, in Old Mexico, as in Burma, the Sabbath or convention of the witches was engaged in by the dead as well as the living, the evil ghosts who attended it being recruited from among those deceased women who had left young children behind them, and who, in consequence of their bereavement, were supposed to be particularly vindictive, wreaking their spite and disappointment on all who were so unlucky as to cross their path.

They are represented in the ancient paintings as wearing black skirts on which cross-bones were depicted, and round their heads a fillet or band of unspun cotton, the symbol of the earth-goddess. They carried the witch's broom of dried grass, and they are frequently accompanied by owls, snakes, and other creatures of ill-omen. Their faces were thickly powdered with white chalk, and sometimes the cheeks were painted with the figure of a butterfly, the emblem of the departed soul.

One of the most trustworthy observers of native customs says of them: "They vented their wrath on people and bewitched them. When anyone is possessed by the demons with a wry mouth and disturbed eyes . . . they say he has linked himself to a demon. The Ciuatete (Haunting Mothers), housed by the cross- ways, have taken his form."

The divine patroness of these witches, who flew through the air upon their broomsticks and met at cross-roads, was the earth-goddess

Tlazolteotl. The broom is her especial symbol, and in one of the native paintings she is depicted as the traditional witch, naked, wearing a peaked hat made of bark, and mounted upon a broomstick.

In other places she is seen standing at the door of a house accompanied by an owl, the whole representing the witch's dwelling, with medicinal herbs drying beneath the eaves. Thus the evidence that the Haunting Mothers and their patroness present an exact parallel with the witches of Europe seems complete, and should provide those who regard witchcraft as a thing essentially European with considerable food for thought.

The Mexican sorcery cult known as Nagualism was also permeated with practices similar to those of European witchcraft, and we read of its adherents smearing themselves with ointment resembling the "witch-butter" of the European hags, which was thought to aid flight through the air, engaging in wild orgies and dances, precisely as did the adherents of Vaulderie in Southern France, and casting spells on man and beast alike. But there is plenty of proof that living women desired to associate themselves with the Haunting Mothers. A monkish writer tells us that these betook themselves to cross-roads by night and, throwing aside their garments, drew blood from their tongues to sacrifice to the Father of Evil, leaving their clothes behind them as an offering.

Like their European sisters, the Mexican witches were in the habit of intoxicating themselves with some potent drug so that they might in spirit traverse great distances or prophesy coming events. Says Acosta: "To practice this art the witches, usually old women, shut themselves up in a house and intoxicate themselves to the verge of losing their reason. The next day they are ready to reply to questions. Some of them take any shape they choose, and fly through the air with wonderful rapidity and for long distances. They will tell what is taking place in remote localities long before the news could possibly arrive. The Spaniards have known them to report mutinies, battles, revolts, and deaths, occurring two hundred or three hundred leagues distant, on the very day they took place, or the day after."

The high priest who presided over the Mexican witches' revels at the cross-roads was the god Tezcatlipoca, a deity of ill-omen, who took the place of Satan in the European witch-Sabbath. He discoursed music for the sport of his devotees on a pipe made of the arm-bone of a deceased woman.

Sahagun says of the Ciuateteo: "The Ciuapipiltin, the noble women, were those who had died in childbed. They were supposed to wander through the air, descending when they wished to the earth to afflict children with paralysis and other maladies. They haunted cross-roads to practice their maleficent deeds, and they had temples built at these places, where bread offerings in the shape of butterflies were made to them, also the thunder-stones which fall from the sky. Their faces were white, and their arms, hands, and legs were covered with a white powder, ticitl (chalk). Their ears were gilded, and their hair done in the manner of the great ladies. Their clothes were striped with black, their skirts barred in different colors, and their sandals were white."

He further relates that when a woman who had died in her first childbed was buried in the temple-court of the Ciuateteo, her husband and his friends watched the body all night in case young braves or magicians should seek to obtain the hair or fingers as protective talismans. In some manuscripts the witches are represented as clad in the insignia of the goddess Tlazolteotl, the great mother-witch, with a fillet and ear-plug of unspun cotton, a golden crescent-shaped nasal ornament, empty eye-sockets, and the heron-feather head-dress of the warrior caste, for the woman who died in childbed was regarded as equally heroic with the man who perished in battle.

The upper parts of their bodies were nude, and round the hips they wore a skirt on which cross-bones were painted. They carried the witch's broom of malinalli grass, a symbol of death, and they were sometimes associated with the snake, screech-owl, and other animals of ill-omen. The face was thickly powdered with white chalk, and the region of the mouth, in some cases, decorated with the figure of a butterfly.

These furies were supposed to dwell in the region of the west, and as some compensation for their early detachment from the earth-life were permitted to accompany the sun in his course from noon to sunset, just as the dead warriors did from sunrise to noon. At night they left their occidental abode, the Cuitlampa, or "Place of Women," and revisited the glimpses of the moon in search of the feminine gear they had left behind them the spindles, work-baskets, and other articles used by Mexican women.

The Ciuateteo were especially potent for evil in the third quarter of the astrological year, and those who were so luckless as to meet them during that season became crippled or epileptic. The fingers and hands of women who had died in bringing forth were believed by magicians, soldiers, and thieves to have the property of crippling and paralyzing their enemies or those who sought to hinder their nefarious calling, precisely as Irish burglars formerly believed that the hand of a corpse grasping a candle, which they called the "hand of glory," could ensure sound sleep in the inmates of any house they might enter. Further proof is forthcoming that living women of evil reputation desired to associate themselves with the Ciuateteo.

Says the interpreter of "Codex Vaticanus A": "The first of the fourteen day-signs, the house, they considered unfortunate, because they said that demons came through the air on that sign in the figures of women, such as we designate witches, who usually went to the highways, where they met in the form of a cross, and to solitary places, and that when any bad woman wished to absolve herself of her sins she went alone by night to these places and took off her garments and sacrificed there with her tongue (that is, drew blood from her tongue), and left the clothes which she had carried and returned naked as the sign of the confession of her sins."

The temples or shrines of the Ciuateteo were situated at cross-roads, the centers of ill-omen throughout the world. That the Mexican witches had a connection with the lightning is shown by the fact that cakes in the shape of butterflies and "thunder-stones" were offered them. But they were also connected with baneful astral or astrological influences, and are several times alluded to in the Interpretative Codices in this connection.

The seasons at which they were most potent for evil were those connected with the western department of the tonalamatl, or "calendar." But we have further evidence that an entire college of witches existed in the Huaxtec region near the coast, and that it was sufficiently powerful to invade the Valley of Mexico in Toltec times.

These witches, who were also Amazons, appear to have succeeded in establishing a military superiority at Tollan, the capital, and in order to celebrate their triumph resolved to sacrifice a large number of prisoners to their patron goddess. Addressing their captives, they said: "We desire to drench the earth with you, to hold a feast with you, for till now no battle-offerings have been held with men."

The Huaxtec country, whence they came, was a rich and closely settled agricultural area, its people were of Maya or Central American stock, and its chief goddess, Tlazolteotl, whose priestesses these women were, represented the Earth-Mother, the bounteous giver of all fruits and grain. But they believed that this Mexican Ceres, worn out by the production of foodstuffs, required occasional refreshment. This had formerly been administered by pouring libations of the blood of animals on the hard, cracked tropical soil, which appeared to absorb them thirstily. But, flushed with triumph, these Amazons resolved to offer up a sacrifice which should out vie all former oblations. It is also clear from their menacing speech that the festival was intended to take the form of a cannibal feast, a thing until then unheard of in Mexico, as their own statement seems to make plain.

The native records insist upon the fact that the institution of ceremonial cannibalism was due to these witches, for such there is abundant evidence they were. Like the Hexen, or witches of ancient Germany, they seem to have had a penchant for human flesh, and further resembled that cult in their tendency to vampirism. The witch-cult in Mexico had thus a surprising resemblance to that of Europe. Indeed, such amazing parallels can be drawn betwixt the two systems that there can be little doubt regarding their common origin.

In both cases the chief minister was a great "black man" (in the Mexican case Tezcatlipoca, who appears as the witches' priest), the meetings were held at cross-roads or in desert places, the devotees of the cult flew through the air on broomsticks and employed magical unguents to enable them to do so; they wore peaked caps, and took as their common symbols the owl and the bunch of dried medicinal herbs.

They induced visions by drugs, and used dead men's flesh and bones as charms. What is lacking to prove the community of their origin? What was precisely the character of Tlazolteotl, their patroness? Will some consideration of her cultus assist us in discovering the underlying nature of Mexican witchcraft and indeed of witchcraft in general?

She is usually depicted as having her face smeared with white chalk, the upper part being surrounded by a yellow band, the color of the maize-plant. The space about her mouth is painted black, the symbol of sex. Sometimes she is clad in the skin of a sacrificial victim. On her head she wears a cotton fillet stuck full of spindles, emblematic of the woman's craft and business in life. She carries a broom made from stiff sharp-pointed grass.

So far as her emblematic side is concerned, she is assuredly the goddess of magic and of women, the bringer-forth in a dual aspect. That she had an aspect of variousness is clear from one of her names, Ixcuine, or "The Four-faced," that is, her idols were sometimes given four faces so that they might look upon every direction whence the rain might come. The witches who first made human sacrifices appear to have been called by this name. But I think we shall receive a more just impression of her actual nature from a consideration of her festival, the Ochpaniztli.

Dancing is one of the chief characteristics of this festival, dancing to the drum, and a particular kind of dancing, executed in silence and consisting mostly in movements of the arms. It was attended by "the medical women," that is the herbalists. A battle of flowers was associated with it. The victim sowed maize broadcast as she walked to the sacrifice. Her skin was worn by the priest, another priest wearing a mask made of it, along with a naualli, or disguise of feathers. He was covered in the morning with other feather-cloaks and bird-symbols.

Processions were marshaled, and more maize was sown. Also blood- stained brooms figure in the ceremonies. At the least, we can glean from the circumstances of this bizarre festival a number of those inalienably associated with the witch-cult as known both in Europe and America, such as dancing silently to the drum, herbalism, the sowing of seed.

THE SHAMAN'S ART

Do we find such allegory and ritual in any particular region whence they might have penetrated to Europe on the one hand and America on the other, or have acted as links between the analogous practices in those continents? We appear to do so in Siberia. The system of sorcery denominated Shamanism, which is widely prevalent among the tribes of the plains and tundras of the vast region known as Siberia appears to have a close resemblance to it.

Authorities are divided as to whether Shamanism is a form of primitive religion pure and simple or merely a survival of magical practices formerly connected with an ancient Asiatic faith, a species of necromancy practiced by a separate caste of priests whose duty it was to communicate with the world of spirits. The shaman is either a professional practitioner of his cult, or he may be a private individual whose addiction to the ritual is confined to the family circle.

Sometimes the office of shaman is hereditary, but in any case the gift of supernatural vision, of mediumship, so to speak, is an essential qualification for shamanhood. Strangely enough, nearly all the best Russian authorities on the subject agree that a neurotic condition in the shaman is necessary to success.

That condition is, of course, a well-known accompaniment of the gift of mediumship. The Siberian spiritualist is grave and reserved; he is, indeed, almost taboo to the people at large, whom he seldom addresses, but among whom he has great influence. Often among the civilized the nervous diathesis creates the recluse.

Many women adopt the shaman's art. These are not unusually persons of hysterical tendencies. "People who are about to become shamans," says Jochelson, "have fits of wild paroxysms, alternating with a condition of complete exhaustion. They will lie motionless for two or three days without partaking of food or drink. Finally they retire to the wilderness, where they spend their time enduring hunger and cold in order to prepare themselves for their calling."

When the shaman accepts the call he also accepts the guardianship of one or more spirits by whose means he enters into communication with the whole spirit world. But the shaman receives his call through the agency of some animal or plant or other natural object, which he encounters at the critical period when he is meditating on the life shamanic.

This is, of course, precisely what the Red Indian or Nagualist does when he goes to seek his totem, and it seems to me as if this analogy might throw a very considerable light upon the nature and origin of Totemism, regarding which there is at present great dubiety in scientific circles. Totemism, we know, has a root-connection with spiritism, and is also connected with ancestor- worship.

The spirit often appears and addresses the would-be shaman, precisely as does the totem among the American tribes. The training of a shaman usually lasts for two or three years, and is arduous in the extreme. The mental part of his graduation consists in getting into touch with the "right" spirits, that is, the guardian spirits who are to control the medium during his career.

"The process of gathering inspiration during the first stages," says Jochelson, "is so severe that a bloody sweat often issues on the forehead and temples. Every preparation of a shaman for a performance is considered a sort of repetition of the initiative process."

The physical training consists of singing, dancing and drum-playing. This latter business requires considerable skill, and a prolonged course of practice is essential to success in it. One shaman told Sternberg that before he entered upon his vocation he was exceedingly ill for two months, during which time he remained unconscious. In the night he heard himself singing shaman's songs. Then spirits appeared to him in the shape of birds, and one in human form, who commanded him to make a drum and the other apparatus of the art. Three kinds of spirits are associated with the Yakut shamans.

These are the amagyat, the yekua, and the kaliany. All shamans must possess the first. The second are more obscure, and appear to be what is known to students of folk-lore as spirits of the "Life-index" type, that is, souls closely associated with the welfare and continued existence of the individual. These are carefully concealed from the vulgar gaze.

"My yekua" said one shaman to Sieroszewski, "will not be found by anyone. It lies hidden far away in the mountains of Edjigan."

These yekua almost always take on an animal incarnation like the familiars of European witches, and the meaning of the word "animal-mother" seems to give them an affinity with the totemic spirits. If the yekua dies the shaman dies.

The kaliany are mere demons, obsessive or possessive. Among the Takuts a definite ceremony attends the consecration of a young shaman. One of the older among the brotherhood leads the youth about to be initiated to the top of a high mountain or into a clearing in a forest. Here he dresses the young man in ceremonial garments, gives him a shaman's rattle, and places on one side of him nine chaste youths and on the other nine chaste maidens. Then he commands him to repeat certain words.

He tells him that he must renounce all worldly things, and instructs him as to the dwelling-places of the various spirits to whom he is about to consecrate his life. An animal is then sacrificed, and the novice is sprinkled with its blood. This constitutes the primary ceremony, but there are nine in all, and of these only a small proportion of the brotherhood undergoes the whole.

Some of the later ceremonies are very involved, and have evidently the cumulative practice and ritual of many ages behind them. Among the northern Siberian tribes the shaman combines the offices of priest, medicine-man and prophet. In the south the shamanic brotherhood is divided into "black" and "white" shamans, the first class acting as the mouthpieces of the evil spirits, and the second as mediums between the beneficent spirits and mankind.

The white shamans take part in marriage ceremonies, fertilization rites and the curing of diseases, but the black are not necessarily malevolent, and frequently employ their powers for good. Again, all shamans are divided into "great," "middling," and "little," according to their powers.

Women among the southern Siberians are nearly always black shamans, the reason given for this being that their sex is more predisposed to the dark side of the occult arts. Shamanism is, then, a system of spiritism, but it embraces certain equivalents to witchcraft the use of the drum and dancing, herbalism, the cultivation of spiritual familiars.

So far we seem to have traced a connection between Asia and America. But whence came the broom, "the witch's palfry," to America, whence proceed the battle of flowers, the sowing of seed? The broom, in the ceremonies of the earth-goddess, was made of stiff malinalli or mountain-grass tied to a stick, and was the symbol of the spring florescence, the outbursting of nature.

It was splashed with the blood of the sacrificed victim, which, I consider, was thought to give it life, and I believe that thus splashed it was originally regarded as the emblem of nature revivified, and that the sweeping and cleansing process for which it was used in the temples was merely an afterthought.

Bathed in blood, it partook magically of the nature of life, was looked upon as a living thing, and together with the unguent of flight, which was rubbed on the body, came to be thought of as a magical agent of levitation. Perhaps, by the law of sympathetic magic, the heights whence its material was gathered, conferred on it the ability to raise one in the air, the idea of lofty motion.

The strange thing is that in America, a continent where no horse or other animal suitable for riding was known in pre-Columbian times, the notion of riding on the broom is found, and this certainly looks as if the idea had been imported. I believe it to have been so in what are known to students of Pre-history as Azilian times.

In a rock- shelter at the village of Cogul near Lerida in Spain some curious paintings have been discovered portraying the rites of early witchcraft among the Azilian population which flourished in that area more than ten thousand years ago. One of these depicts a number of women wearing skirts and peaked hats precisely like those of the witches of later times, dancing round a black man, doubtless the priest or "Great Black Man" of later witch-tradition.

It is known, too, that mummy-flesh or dead men's flesh was employed for magical purposes by the witches of both Europe and America. Throughout the witch-literature of Europe the mummy is constantly alluded to as part of the magical apparatus of the witch. When she failed to obtain it she had recourse to using earth taken from a newly-made grave as a substitute.

So far as I am aware, we do not find this practice in Eastern Asia, but that it was in vogue in America is substantiated by more than one instance. Allusion has already been made to the magical employment of the hands and fingers of dead women in Mexico, and Dawson, in his "Rites and Observations on the Kwakiootl People of Vancouver," alludes to an interesting case of it in that part of America. He says that when a Kwakiootl wizard desired to bewitch anyone, he tried to procure a lock of his hair, or a part of his clothing.

"These are placed with a small piece of the skin and flesh of a dead man, dried and roasted before the fire, and rubbed and pounded together. The mixture is then tied up in a piece of skin or cloth, which is covered over with spruce gum. The little package is next placed in a human bone, which is broken for the purpose and afterwards carefully tied together and put within a human skull. This again is placed in a box, which is tied up and gummed over and then buried in the ground in such a way as to be barely covered. . . .This is done at night or the early morning and in secret, and is frequently repeated until the enemy dies."

The drying of the human remains over a fire shows quite clearly that what was desired was a piece of flesh capable of desiccation and admixture with other elements, as in the operations of European witches. Benzoni tells us that the medicine-men among the Borenquenos of the West Indies took some small bones and a little flesh and powdered them together as a purgative for the sick.

My impression is, then, that the witchcraft of Mexico drew its origin from two different areas: the Azilian area of Spain, which, by the way, was the chief home of the broom-riding witch-cult in the Europe of the late Middle Ages, and the Shamanism of Siberia. From the former area it may have penetrated by way of one of the land-bridges which until recently, spanned the Atlantic, whilst it would draw elements from the latter by way of Kamschatka and the Aleutian Islands.

I am not at all sure; however, that Mexico, or at least some part of America, did not receive very considerable religious and cultural gifts from Druidic Britain, although I advance the suggestion with the greatest possible reserve and as a suggestion merely. The British peoples of the first Christian century were capable of building ships much larger and more seaworthy than those of the Romans, so Caesar tells us, and that both British and Irish Druids were addicted to levitation and believed themselves capable of flying through the air is clearly demonstrated by legend.

There is, indeed, nothing in Mexican witchcraft which might not well have emanated from early Britain. May not Quetzalcoatl have been a Druid priest? It would be comparatively easy to bring a vast amount of evidence to prove that he was, but that evidence would lack the certainty of historical corroboration and could rest on analogy only.

CHAPTER VII
MEXICAN ASTROLOGY

The Mexican system of Astrology, although it has considerable resemblances with those of Europe and Asia, is really a system of native growth and origin, and must be studied separately from all others. It is based on what is known as the tonalamatl, or so-called "calendar" of the Aztecs. But I will deal with it here very practically, in order that students of other astrologies may compare it with the system they study, and because it is certainly time that this particular American system should be presented to students of the occult in a plain and understandable manner.

A thorough knowledge of the tonalamatl is essential in order to grasp the fundamentals of Mexican religion, but its significance has perhaps been heightened by the difficulties which certainly attend its consideration. I have endeavored to present the subject here as simply as possible, and to keep all distracting side-issues for later consideration and away from the main proof.

Most of these, indeed, have been created by writers who have too closely identified the tonalamatl with the solar calendar, and have added to the obscurity of the subject by the introduction of abstruse astronomical hypotheses which have only a problematical connection with it.

The word tonalamatl means "Book of the Good and Bad Days," and it is primarily a "Book of Fate," from which the destiny of children born on such and such a day, or the result of any course to be taken or any venture made on any given day, was forecasted by divinatory methods, similar to those which have been employed by astrologers in many parts of the world in all epochs.

The tonalamatl, was, therefore, in no sense a time-count or calendar proper, to which purpose it was not well suited; but it was capable of being adapted to the solar calendar. It is equally incorrect to speak of the tonalamatl as a "ritual calendar." It has nothing to do directly with ritual or religious ceremonial, and although certain representations on some tonalamatls depict ritual acts, no details or directions for their operation are supplied. The original tonalamatl was probably a day-count based on a lunar reckoning. The symbols appear to have been those of the gods or other mythological figures.

Thus cipactli was merely the earth-monster, quauhtli the eagle, a surrogate for the Sun-god, and So on. Later the tonalamatl lost its significance as a time-count when it was superseded as such by the solar calendar. It then took on the complexion of a book of augury, so that the temporal connection it had with the gods was altered to a purely augural one.

The various days thus became significant for good or evil according to the nature of the gods who presided over them, or over the precise hour in which a subject was born or any act done; As in astrology, a kind of balance was held between good and evil, so that if the god presiding over the day was inauspicious, his influence might, in some measure, be counteracted by that of the deity who presided over the hour in which a child first saw the light or an event occurred.

The tonalamatl was composed of 20 day-signs or hieroglyphs repeated 13 times, or 260 day-signs in all. These 260 days were usually divided into 20 groups of 13 days each, sometimes called "weeks."

To effect this division the numbers 1 to 13 were added to the 20 day-signs in continuous series as follow:

No.	Name	Sign	No.	Name	Sign
1	cipactli	crocodile (good)	11	ozomatli	monkey (uncertain)
2	eecatl	wind (uncertain)	12	malinalli	grass (unlucky)
3	calli	house (uncertain)	13	acatl	reed (uncertain)
4	cuetzpallin	lizard (good)	1	ocelotl	ocelot (bad)
5	coatl	serpent (bad)	2	quauhtli	eagle (lucky)
6	miquiztli	death's-head (unlucky)	3	cozcaqu-auhtli	vulture (bad)
7	mazatl	deer (unlucky)	4	ollin	motion (uncertain)
8	tochtli	rabbit (good)	5	tecpatl	flint knife (bad)
9	atl	water (bad)	6	quiauitl	rain (unlucky)

10	itzcuintli dog (lucky)	7	xochitl	flower (good)

It will be seen from this list that the fourteenth day-sign takes the number 1 again. Each of the day-signs under this arrangement has a number that does not recur in connection with that sign for a space of 260 days, as is proved by the circumstance that the numbers of the day-signs and figures (20 and 13), if multiplied together, give as a product 260, the exact number of days in the tonalamatl.

The combination of signs and figures thus provided each day in the tonalamatl with an entirely distinct description. For example: the first day, cipactli, was in its first occurrence 1 cipactli; in its second 8 cipactli; in its third 2 cipactli; in its fourth 9 cipactli, and so on.

No day in the tonalamatl was simply described as cipactli, coatl, or calli, and before its name was complete it was necessary to prefix to it one of the numbers 1 to 13 as its incidence chanced to fall. Thus it was designated as ce cipactli (one crocodile) or ome coatl (two snake) as the case might be.

Each of the 20 groups of 13 days (which are sometimes called "weeks") was known as a division by the name of the first day of the group, as ce cipactli (one crocodile), ce ocelotl (one ocelot), ce mazatl (one deer), and so on. Each of the day-signs of the tonalamatl was presided over by a god who was supposed to exercise a special influence over it.

These patron gods were as follow: Day-sign Patron god Day-sign Patron god Cipactli Tonacatecutli Miquiztli Tecciztecatl Eecatl Quetzalcoatl Mazatl Tlaloc Calli Tepeyollotl Tochtli Mayauel Cuetzpallin Ueuecoyotl Atl Xiuhtecutli Coatl Chalchihuit- Itzcuintli Mictlantecutli licue Ozomatli Xochipilli Cozcaqu- Itzpapalotl auhtli Malinalli Patecatl Olin Xolotl Acatl Texcatlipoca Tecpatl Tezcatlipoca (or variant) (or variant) Ocelotl Tlazolteotl Quiauitl Chantico Quauhtli Xipe Xochitl Xochiquetzal.

There are slight divergences from the standard list in some of the codices, but such are usually accounted for by the interpolation of variant phases of the deities given. Each of the 20 tonalamatl divisions, or "weeks" of 13 days each, as they are sometimes erroneously but usefully designated, had also a patron god of its own which ruled over its fortunes. The initial days of these "weeks" gave the name to the entire "week," therefore the designation of the 20 weeks was the same as that of the 20 day-signs; but the "weeks," or rather the week-names, did not follow each other in the same incidence as the days, as will be seen from the foregoing table.

The list of gods of the "weeks" would thus be as follows: Tonacatecutli Quetzalcoatl Tepeyollotl Ueuecoyotl Chalchihuitlicue Tecciztecatl Tlaloc Mayauel Xiuhtecutli Mictlantecutli Patecatl Itzlacoliuhqui Tlazolteotl Xipe Totec Itzpapalotl Xolotl Chalchiuhtotollin Chantico Xochiquetzal Xiuhtecutli and Itztli.

Apart from the signs of the days themselves, the presiding deities of the weeks and the gods of the individual dates, the numerical signs also possessed a lucky or unlucky significance. Three and four were 1 Ce cipactli . 2 Ce ocelotl . 3 Ce mazatl t 4 Ce xochitl , 5 Ce acatl (6 Ce miquiztli 7 Ce quiauitl . 8 Ce malinalli 9 Ce coatl t 10 Ce tecpatl . 11 Ce ozomatli 12 Ce quetzpallin 13 Ce ollin p 14 Ce itzcuintli 15 Ce calli t 16 Ce cozcaquauhtli 17 Ce atl . . 18 Ce eecatl t 19 Ce quauhtli . 20 Ce tochtli.

Lucky numbers, five and six were generally ominous, seven was invariably good, eight and nine bad, ten, eleven, twelve, and thirteen good. The diviner took into account all these possible influences in considering the fortune attached to a particular day.

Besides the patron gods of the days and the weeks there were nine "Lords of the Night" which, I am inclined to think with Seler, were not "lords" or governors of nine consecutive nights, but of the nine hours of each night. We know the names of these gods from the first interpreter of "Codex Vaticanus A," who gives them as follows, with their influences : 1 Xiuhtecutli . . Good 2 Itztli . . . Bad 3 Piltzintecutli . . Good 4 Centeotl . . . Indifferent 5 Mictlantecutli . . Bad 6 Chalchihuitlicue . . Indifferent 7 Tlazolteotl . . Bad 8 Tepeyollotl . . Good 9 Tlaloc . . . Indifferent.

Gama describes these nine gods as Acompanados (Companions) and as Senores de la Noche (Lords of the Night) and from his obscure rendering of Cristoval de Castillo, as well as from the "Manuel de Ministros de Indios" of Jacinto de la Serna, we gather that they held sway over the night hours from sunset to sun- rise.

The Mexicans divided the night into nine hours, and it is obvious from the astrological point of view that the Mexican soothsayers who used the tonalamatl must have found it necessary to estimate not only the "fate" of the several days, but also that of the several hours and times of the day and night. This of course applies with equal force to the thirteen so-called "Lords of the Day," who almost certainly acted as gods of the thirteen hours of the day.

They were: 1 Xiuhtecutli 8 Tlaloc 2 Tlaltecutli 9 Quetzalcoatl 3 Chalchihuitlicue 10 Tezcatlipoca 4 Tonatiuh 11 Mictlantecutli 5 Tlazolteotl 12 Tlauizcalpantecutli 6 Teoyaomiqui 13 Ilamatecutli 7 Xochipilli Seler, in his "Commentary on the Aubin Tonalamatl," gives the following table of the gods of the night and day hours: (Noon) 7. Xochipilli-Cinteotl 6. Teoyaomiqui 8. Tlaloc 5. Tlazolteotl 9. Quetzalcoatl 4. Tonatiuh 10. Tezcatlipoca 3. Chalchihuitlicue 11. Mictlantecutli 2. Tlaltecutli 12. Tlauizcalpantecutli 1. Xiuhtecutli (Day) 13. Ilamatecutli IX. Tlaloc I. Xiuhtecutli VIII. Tepeyollotl II. Itztli VII. Tlazolteotl III. Piltzintecutli-Tonatiuh VI. Chalchihuitlicue IV. Cinteotl V. Mictlantecutli (Midnight).

This casts light on the method of augury of the priests. Thus the hour of noon was auspicious because it was connected with the mystic number 7, and 9 was a number of good augury with sorcerers because it gave the number of the underworlds and of the night-hours.

Recapitulating we find: 1. That the tonalamatl was a "Book of Fate," and not in itself a calendar or time-count. 2. That it was composed of 20 day-signs, repeated 13 times, or 260 day-signs in all. 3. That these were usually divided into 20 groups of 13 days each, erroneously but usefully called "weeks." The initial day of these "weeks" gave the name to the entire "week." 4. To effect this division the numbers 1 to 13 were added to the 20 day-signs in continuous series. 5. That by this arrangement each day-sign had a number that did not recur in connection with that sign for a space of 260 days. 6. That the name of a day-sign in the tonalamatl was not complete without its accompanying number. 7. Each of the day-signs of the tonalamatl was presided over by a god who was supposed to exercise a special influence over it. (See list.) 8. Besides the patron gods of the days and "weeks" there were: (a) Nine "lords" or patron gods of the night- hours. (b) Thirteen "lords" of the day-hours. Now we have seen that the day-gods each possessed a special sign, and that some wielded a good and others an evil influence.

The like holds true of the gods of the weeks, the day and night hours. In the balance and repercussion of their signs with and on one another lay the whole art of Mexican "astrology," just as in the consideration of the evil and good influence of the planets at a certain time the astrologers of Europe and Asia were able to predict certain occurrences and issues.

We know what certain of the signs portended for the Mexicans. For instance, Sahagun says of the sign Ce ail (one water) that the great lords and rich merchants at the birth of one of their children "paid the greatest attention to this sign," and the day and hour at which the child was born.

"They at once inquired of the astrologers what fortune the child might expect to encounter, and if the sign were propitious they had the infant baptized without delay, whereas if it were the opposite they waited until the nearest day which had a propitious sign."

It was believed that the "week" sign Ce quiauitl (one rain) was especially ominous, because at this season the dead witches, the Ciuateted, descended and inflicted maladies upon the people, distorting their limbs and causing epilepsy, especially among women and children. On this occasion they sacrificed malefactors to these evil spirits. The same held good of the "week" sign ce ozomatli (one monkey).

The sign ce acatl (one cane) was propitious and denominated the star of Quetzalcoatl, the light of the world, as were the thirteen days commenced by Malinalli, the symbol of grass, presided over by Patecatl, the drink-god. Of persons born on the day five cipactli (crocodile) they said "that the men would all be rogues and the women prostitutes."

Men born on thirteen quauhtli (eagles) would be valiant in war, but those who saw the light under ollin (motion) would be rascals and tale-bearers, this sign having a protean character.

If a person were born under the sign six eecatl (winds) he would be rich and prudent, but those who came under seven quauhtli would suffer from incurable diseases of the heart, the eagle sign probably inferring height and therefore dizziness.

A man born under the symbol of one wind would be healthy in his nativity, but did he fall into ill-health would suffer from severe pains in the side and cancer. The day of nine dogs applied to magicians, possibly because of its arcane number, and especially to those sorcerers who transformed themselves into beasts or serpents.

The people in general therefore feared this day exceedingly, and shut themselves up in their houses in order that they might not witness any magical metamorphoses. The same applied to the sign ollin. Men born in the sign of one flower would be musicians, physicians or weavers.

This sign was presided over by Xochiquetzal, the Mexican Venus or Titania, and was especially of good omen. The sign of seven serpents was especially fortunate for everything, but particularly for marriages that would last a long time and bear plenty of male children, and the symbol two canes indicated long life. But the first sign of the serpent was evil for it signified the loss of a limb.

Expert huntsmen were those born under one flint, and the fifth of the flint series portended that a person born under it would be a jester. If anyone had his nativity beneath the signs ruled by Tezcatlipoca let him beware, for all were unlucky, and false evidence given on these days it was impossible to rebut. It was also of evil omen in war.

The sign one house was unlucky and was under the influence of the dead witches. Spies and impostors were born under some of the signs of air, indeed there is a great sameness in the fortunes of many of the signs, of which it is impossible to give an entire list as many of the significances of the series of 260 are irretrievably lost. Each sign was held as applying to a certain part of the body and as having dominance over it.

Says the interpreter of the "Codex Vaticanus": "The sign of the wind was assigned to the liver, the rose to the breast, the earthquake to the tongue, the eagle to the right arm, the vulture to the right ear, the rabbit to the left ear, the flint to the teeth, the air to the breath, the monkey to the left arm, the cane to the heart, the herb to the bowels, the lizard to the womb of women, the tiger to the left foot, the serpent to the male organ of generation, as that from which their diseases proceeded in their commencement, for in this manner they considered the serpent wherever it occurred as the most ominous of all their signs. Even still physicians continue to use this figure when they perform cures; and according to the sign and hour in which the patient becomes ill they examined whether the disease corresponded with the ruling sign, from which it is plain that this nation is not as brutal as some persons pretend, since they observed so much method and order in these affairs, and employed the same means as our astrologers and physicians use, as this figure still obtains amongst them, and may be found in their repertories."

It is in such passages as that found in the Cronica Mexicana of Tezozomoc that we find the connection between Aztec "astrology" as observed in the tonalamatl or "calendar" and stellar astrology proper.

In Chapter 82 of that marvelous book is to be found an account of the formalities observed at the election of the Emperor Montezuma, a record of the duties required from him in his royal position. Among other things he was "especially to make it his duty to rise at midnight (and to look at the stars): at yohualitqul mamalhuaztli, as they call 'the keys of Saint Peter ' among the stars in the firmament, at the citlaltlachtli, the north and its wheel, at the tianquiztli, the Pleiades, and at the colotl ixayac, the constellation of the Scorpion, which mark the four cardinal points in the sky.

"Toward morning he must also carefully observe the constellation xonecuilli, the 'cross of Saint Jacob,' which appears in the southern sky in the direction of India and China; and he must carefully observe the morning star, which appears at dawn and is called tlauizcalpan teuctli."

These words outline the scope of Mexican astronomical knowledge and are corroborated in the seventh book of the original Mexican text of Sahagun's great work, "*Historia General*," preserved in the Palace Library, Madrid, in which the constellations are represented by pictures, and among other stars, the planet Venus, which had especial associations for the Mexicans, who kept an unerring record of the days when it appeared and disappeared.

They regarded the morning star as connected with Quetzalcoatl, the father of all magic, and believed it to have a special magical significance. When he left Mexico, according to one legend, he immolated himself by fire, and his heart, flying upward out of the ashes, became the star Citlalpol, or the planet Venus.

In his form as that planet the god was known as Tlauizcalpan tecutli. On all days connected with the signs of the alligator, jaguar, snake, water, reed, stag, and movement the planet Venus had a dubious significance, usually uncanny.

Regarding its action on some of these days an ancient story tells us: "And as they (the ancients, the forefathers) learned. When it appears (rises). According to the sign in which it (rises). It strikes different classes of people with its rays. Shoots them, casts its light upon them. When it appears in the (first) sign, '1 alligator,' It shoots the old men and women. Also in the (second) sign, ' 1 jaguar,' In the (third) sign, ' 1 stag,' In the (fourth) sign, ' 1 flower,' It shoots the little children. And in the (fifth) sign, ' 1 reed,' It shoots the kings. Also in the (sixth) sign, ' 1 death,' And in the (seventh) sign, ' 1 rain,' It shoots the rain, It will not rain; And in the (thirteenth) sign, ' 1 movement,' It shoots the youths and maidens; And in the (seventeenth) sign, ' 1 water, 5 There is universal drought."

In the *Vatican and Borgian* Codices especially we see representatives of these various classes of people struck by the evil spear of the planetary god. Seler says on this point: "It is possible that we have on these pages simply an astrological speculation arising from superstitious fear of the influence of the light of this powerful planet. By natural association of ideas the rays of light emitted by the sun or other luminous bodies are imagined to be darts or arrows which are shot in all directions by the luminous body. The more the rays are perceived to be productive of discomfort or injury, so much the more fittingly does this apply. In this way the abstract noun miotl or meyotli with the meaning c ray of light 'is derived from the Mexican word mill, 'arrow' . . . thus miotli is the arrow which belongs by nature to a body sending forth arrows, a luminous body. . . .When the planet appeared anew in the heavens, smoke-vents and chimneys were stopped up lest the light should penetrate into the house. ... It is hardly possible to see anything else in these figures struck by the spear than augural speculations regarding the influence of the light from the planet suggested by the initial signs of the period."

This, then, seems to furnish us with direct proof that at least one planet was regarded as controlling human affairs, and in all likelihood the twenty day-signs are capable of being collated with various planets or stars, although this has not yet been affected. Their early calendric associations seem, indeed, to point to such a conclusion.

The fact that early Mexican myth lent to the stars a demonic significance scarcely militates against this view. Indeed, Tezozomoc says of the Tzitzimime demons that these were "gods of the signs and planets," that is of the tonalamatl in its astrological sense. That the several planets had ominous and usually disastrous effects upon humanity is clear.

Thus the Abbe Clavigero tells us that at the festival of Ome acatl, or "two reeds," that of the sun-god, the people remained in the utmost suspense and solicitude, hoping on the one hand to find from the new fire a new century granted to mankind, and fearing on the other hand the total destruction of mankind if the fire by divine interference should not be permitted to kindle.

Husbands covered the faces of their pregnant wives with the leaves of the aloe, and shut them up in granaries, because they were afraid that they would be converted into wild beasts and would devour them. They also covered the faces of children in that way, and did not allow them to sleep, to prevent their being transformed into mice.

The moon, Metztli, on the other hand, was regarded as an active and malevolent wizard dwelling in an incandescent cavern. His influence upon mankind was occasionally benevolent, as in the case of birth, but on the whole was significant of evil humors and emanations.

Associated with the calendar was the system by which the Aztecs regarded the several points of the compass, or world-directions, as having a bearing on their "astrological" ideas. The east was known as Tlapcopa, the north Mictlampa, the west Ciuatlampa, and the south Uitzlampa.

To these a central or sometimes an up-and-down or "above-below" point was added. With the east were associated all the years which took in the cycle-sequence the primary date acatl (reed). With the north the tecpatl (stone knife) years, with the west the calli (house), and with the south the tochtli (rabbit) years. The gods and colors governing these were respectively Tonatiuh, the sun-god and yellow; Mictlantecutli, the death-god and red; the corn-goddess and blue; and the water-god Tlaloc and white, while Xiuhtecutli, the god of the hearth-fire, governed the central point.

The day-signs were divided as follows, according to the compass directions: East cipactli, acatl, coatl, ollin, otl. North ocelotl, miquiztli, tecpatl, itzcuintli, eecatl. West mazatl, quiauitl, ozomatli, calli, quauhtli. South xochitl, malinalli, quetzpalin, cozcaqu- auhtli, tochtli.

The eastern years were supposed to be fertile, the north variable, the west good for man but evil for vegetation, and the south years hot and waterless. In Mexican ritual and divination the greatest attention was paid to the compass directions.

DAY SIGNS OF THE MEXICAN CALENDAR

CHAPTER VIII
THE MYSTERIES OF NAGUALISM

The breakdown of the Maya and Mexican faiths was followed by a phenomenon so curious that it is well worth the attention of those students of history and comparative religion who are looking for an illustration of what humanly follows when an ancient faith is debarred from popular practice and thrust into the background.

In the case of the Maya this resulted in the formation of a vast secret society known as that of the Naguales, in which the more popular and primitive forms of native religion took the place of the loftier tenets of the priesthood. In short, the idea of magic of the lower cultus took the place of the higher wisdom-religion formerly in vogue, and those traditional notions born of totemism and the concept of the beast-guardian which had been suppressed by the enlightenment of the priestly caste came once more into practice, accompanied by all the horrors of black magic.

The general conception underlying this return to primitive beliefs is well, if simply, outlined by Herrera in his *"General History"* which dates from 1530. He writes: "The Devil deluded them, appearing in the shape of a lion, or a tiger, or a coyote, a beast like a wolf, or in the shape of an alligator, a snake, or a bird, which they called naguales, signifying keepers or guardians, and when the bird died the Indian who was in league with him died also, which often happened and was looked upon as infallible.

"The manner of contracting this alliance was thus: the Indian repaired to the river, wood, hill, or most obscure place, where he called upon the devils by such names as he thought fit, talked to the rivers, rocks or woods, said he went to weep that he might have the same his predecessors had, carrying a cock or dog to sacrifice. In that melancholy fit he fell asleep, and either in a dream or waking saw some one of the aforesaid birds or other creatures, whom he entreated to grant him profit in salt, cacao, or any other commodity, drawing blood from his own tongue, ears, and other parts of his body, making his contract at the same time with the said creature, the which, either in a dream or waking, told him, 'Such a day you shall go abroad a-sporting, and I will be the first bird or other animal you shall meet, and will be your nagual and companion at all times.' Whereupon such friendship was contracted between them that when one of them died the other did not survive, and they fancied that he who had no nagual could not be rich."

This, of course, is the concept of the guardian spirit, as found widely distributed throughout North America. The circumstances and ritual connected with the cultus normally show a period of isolation at puberty, a long ceremonial purification, and intentness upon supernatural communication and "the acquisition of the name and power and song of the guardian spirit in a vision." In fact, all the phenomena of the early stages of initiation into the mysteries as found in the Old World, but here commingled with individual totemism, the cult of the animal protector or genius.

The cult of Nagualism, according to Brinton, still "prevails widely today in Mexico and Central America, men and women join in the dances in a state of nudity, and the Christian priests claim with probability that those rites terminate in wild debauches."

Women were preeminent in the worship of the cult. In the chronicles of Mexican Nagualism it is recorded that the marvelous power of the adepts in transforming themselves into the brute form of their guardian spirit (tonal) was first taught them by a mighty enchantress, who herself could assume at will any one of four forms.

This explains why in the later revolts of these tribes, even down to that in Guatemala in 1885, we find so often that the moving spirit, the prompter and leader of the rebellion is some warrior woman, driven by a divine energy to seek the independence of her tribe from the hated yoke of the whites.

Such was Maria Candelaria, the heroine of the Tzental insurrection of 1712, a girl of twenty summers, but fired by an eloquence and a resolution that summoned to her banners fifteen thousand fighting men, and for many months bade defiance to the arms of Spain. Nor would she then have failed had it not been for cowardice and treachery in her own camp.

A popular illustration of Nagualism is that afforded by Francisco Fuentes y Guzman. In his "*History of Guatemala*," written about 1690, the author gives some information regarding a sorcerer who on arrest was examined as to the manner of assigning the proper nagual to a child.

When informed of the day of its birth he presented himself at the house of the parents, and taking the child outside, invoked the demon. He then produced a little calendar which had against each day a picture of a certain animal or object.

Thus in the Nagualist calendar for January the first day of the month was represented by a lion, the second by a snake, the eighth by a rabbit, the fourteenth by a toad, the nineteenth by a jaguar, and so on. The invocation over, the nagual of the child would appear under the form of the animal or object set opposite its birthday in the calendar.

The sorcerer then addressed certain prayers to the nagual, requesting it to protect the child, and told the mother to take it daily to the same spot, where its nagual would appear to it, and would finally accompany it through life. Some of the worshippers of this cult had the power of transforming themselves into the nagual.

Thomas Gage, an English Catholic who acted as priest among the Maya of Guatemala about 1630, describes in his "New Survey of the West Indies" the supposed metamorphosis of two chiefs of neighboring tribes, and the mortal combat in which they engaged, which resulted in the death of one of them. But Nagualist power was by no means confined to a single transformation, and was capable of taking on many and varied shapes.

Speaking of one of the great musician-kings of the Quiche of Guatemala, the "Popol Vuh," a native book, states that Gucumatz, the sorcerer-monarch in question, could transform himself into a serpent, an eagle, a tiger, and even into lower forms of life. Many of the confessions of the natives to the Catholic priests remind one forcibly of those which were discovered by the European witch trials of the sixteenth and seventeenth centuries.

Thus an old man in his dying confession declared that by diabolical art he had transformed himself into his nagual, and a young girl of twelve confessed that the Nagualists had transformed her into a bird, and that in one of her nocturnal flights she had rested on the roof of the very house in which the parish priest resided. All Christian ceremonies celebrated by the friars were at once annulled by the Nagualist priesthood. If a child were baptized with the holy water it was immediately carried to the cave or secret meeting-place of the Nagualists, where the rite was "reversed" by the aid of black magic.

This was effected by endowing the child with a nagual or animal guardian, a totem protector, which was regarded as its spiritual guide and mentor, to whom in all the difficulties and perplexities of it must turn for advice and instruction. But shape-shifting and witchcraft were not the only magical resources of the Nagualists. Their arts were manifold. They could render themselves invisible and walk unseen among their enemies.

They could transport themselves to distant places, and returning, report what they had witnessed. Like the fakirs of India, they could create before the eyes of the spectator rivers, trees, houses, animals, and other objects. They would, to all appearance, rip themselves open, cut a limb from the body of another person and replace it, and pierce themselves with knives without bleeding.

They could handle venomous serpents without being bitten, as can their representatives among the Zuni Indians of Arizona to-day, cause mysterious sounds in the air, hypnotize both men and animals, and invoke spirits who would instantly appear. Of these things the missionary friars believed them fully capable.

What wonder, then, that they were regarded by the natives with a mixture of terror and respect? Does Nagualism survive in Mexico and Central America today?

No reasonable doubt can be entertained that it does. I give here in the form of a story an account of an occurrence which took place in a certain remote Mexican locality not very many years ago. Naturally, I have had to alter the names of persons and places. Browning lounged on the verandah, the last long drink of the stifling day untouched at his elbow.

Conscience was having its way with him. Beatrice would sail from Southampton in a week, and he had not yet told Jacinta that she must go. He had thought that when the time came it would be easy enough. Such things were done every day in Soconusco. But what would have been easy to many men in the Tropics he was finding horribly difficult.

Scruples rarely attacked him before the event, but, later, crowded and battened upon him, finding congenial soil in his rash sentimental heart. Yes, it would be the deuce to do this thing after two years. He cursed weakly and looked drearily over the coffee slopes where the trade-wind rains had made the dull green of the hardwood trees glisten like the plumage of rare birds in the yellow of the tropic sundown.

If he fondly believed that the woman was all unconscious of his intention he was badly at fault. Vaguely brown young women with gazelle eyes and the lithe grace of panthers are rather more amenable to instinct than their white sisters.

There had been a thousand intimations of mood and manner on his part, and a sneering hint from the major-domo. At first she had accepted the news in the fatalistic spirit of her race. Who could expect the love of a god with chestnut hair and eyes like the noon sky to last for ever? She had been blessed with two years of him. It was strange that hope should have visited her at all.

Something more tenacious than is usually encountered in brown minds urged her not only to hope but to act. And that is why, on the very evening that Browning sat with distorted forehead on his verandah, she drifted like a spirit in her white cotton nequen through the thin woods which curtained the Hacienda Mozara to the hut of Canek - the ah-kin or medicine-man.

Central America has long been the home of two religions, one official and white, the other quite unorthodox and brown, but none the less very much alive. The few who know anything about it call it Nagualism.

After being baptized by the padre the brown baby is carried to the ah-kin or native priest, who, by some sleight of devildom, nullifies the sacred power of the holy water and bestows on the child a nagual or beast-guardian, a spiritual guide and mentor in animal shape, who accompanies him through life, and in whose shape he can disguise himself.

Jacinta had so far been without this dark benefit. Her parents had been pious followers of the white man's faith, for her father had strenuously believed himself to be white, and cherished certain proofs that he was not mistaken. But in his daughter the mother-race was triumphant. Can-ek was at home. He had known for some time that Jacinta would come to him and he was prepared.

He was very dirty, and his bee-hive hut was the last thing in native squalor. The pungent smell of fresh peyotl arose from the wooden bowls, and strings of dried herbs, alligators' tongues, and stuffed vampire bats lent that professional touch of mystery on which practitioners in all times and climes have relied to impress the lay mind.

Can-ek did not believe in these, but he knew his clients did. He listened to what Jacinta had to say with all the immobility of the specialist.

"You have not been of us," he said when she had done at last, " yet you desire me to help you. You know well that we help only those who believe in us."

"Would I have come to you did I not believe? Jacinta asked.

"That is a woman's answer," grunted Can-ek.

"Do not make me such replies. If you believe, you must prove it. You must become one of us."

"And if I do so, Ah-kin?"

"Then help will be forthcoming. But first the water of the white priests that was shed on your face must be washed away, and you must be made one with the nagual."

"It is enough," said Jacinta, "I agree."

I cannot say precisely what happened in the beehive hut because I do not know. No white man knows. But when Jacinta left it half an hour later her gazelle eyes seemed to have grown larger, and she glanced furtively among the tree-trunks where the night had now drooped in blue shadow.

Once or twice she cowered in the rank undergrowth and moaned. And she hugged something in the bosom of her dress. Three days later Browning was aware of an unusual flavor in his morning coffee.

Being a good judge of coffee, he sniffed it, and told the boy to take it away and bring some more. And Jacinta, hanging upon him that evening, was uneasily aware by his clouded brow and moody looks that the love-philtre of the ah-kin had not proved efficacious. Her heart sank, and she muttered the strange words Can-ek had taught her.

There was a rustling sound in the tall grass beneath the eucalyptus trees, and Browning started.

"Cougar!" he whispered, pulling out his gun.

"Fancy him venturing this length. Brute must be hungry."

"Don't shoot!" almost screamed Jacinta.

"Oh, Mother of God, Don Jorge, don't shoot!"

"What on earth for?" he asked almost sulkily.

"Some of your beastly superstitions, I suppose. Think if I shoot the beast I'll kill someone's double, you little fool?"

She clutched at his arm, pulling down the menacing barrel, and unclasped his fingers from the stock. The rustling sound passed like a breeze among the grass.

"Lord, child, you're almost white," he laughed uneasily.

"If I hadn't known you were a Christiano I'd have thought you were one of those what d'ye call them...it's some meztizo name for devilry, anyhow. Come on into the house. You and I have got to talk to-night, Jacinta. Now, don't cut up rough. It's all over, but I'll let you down easy as easy. You'll see . . ."

The incident had stirred him to the necessity for a prompt straightening out of this entanglement. Half an hour later the words of doom had been spoken.

It had been settled that she was to go in the morning not unprovided for, but go she must. Browning had anticipated a scene. But she took the verdict quietly very quietly. Next day she went, as had been ordained. There was a loose handshake, a perfunctory peck on the warm brown cheek, and that was all.

She had told him that she would go to her sister in San Thomas. But only half a mile down the narrow white road she turned abruptly and dived like a wild thing into the woods. And as she waded through the tall grass something unseen rustled cat-like not far off, keeping pace with her steps.

About a month later he met Beatrice at Vera Cruz, married her there at the British Consul's, and took her home to Tampila. All traces of Jacinta had carefully been removed, indeed the memory of her had faded out of Browning's mind nearly a fortnight before, which goes to show that people who feel very keenly do not, as a rule, suffer very long.

Beatrice had made up her mind to like Tampila, and she succeeded. At first, doubtless, she felt cut off from her kind, caught very definitely in an environment of utter strangeness. It was all so unlike what she had expected it to be.

She had thought of Soconusco in terms of Malay, where a married sister had settled. The life was idle and she enjoyed it, the fierce dry days, the enveloping odor of coffee-dust, the long rides with her husband through the rich plantations and the encircling woods with their frequent vestiges of a ruined past, crumbling temples and carven pillars, a memory of civilizations eaten up with tropical luxuriance.

Then, as she came to know the country around Tampila, Beatrice insensibly formed the habit of taking long lonely rides in the vicinity. At home she had almost lived in the saddle, and her free life in lonely Westmoreland had made her contemptuous of the dangers which might lurk in such solitary canters.

As the weeks passed her excursions took a larger compass. The unfamiliar and extraordinary environment in which she found herself tempted the spirit of exploration which had always stirred her, and which she had hitherto found no way of satisfying. The white winding roads, the dark avenues of the forest fringes, the dry, keen turf at the base of the foot-hills, the warm still fragrance of the tropic afternoons, jeweled with tiny, brilliant birds, painted butterflies, and the wonder of exotic flowers made it impossible for her to remain in the stuffy air of the hacienda living-room.

At first Browning had gravely warned her of the risks she ran. Jaguars and cougars, he told her, were not infrequent in the neighborhood, and poisonous plants which cast deadly pollen took toll of many native lives. A local banditti made occasional and half-hearted efforts at a hold-up. But Beatrice seemed to care for none of these things. Besides, was she not armed?

In vain her husband pointed out that a revolver which might well have been purchased at a Bond Street jeweler's could scarcely be regarded as an effective weapon. At last, really alarmed at the wide circuits she made, he suggested that one of the peons should accompany her, and to his insistence on this she had no option but to agree.

Pedro, a nephew of the major-domo, was told off as a mounted bodyguard. Beatrice did her best to ignore his presence, but had to admit that on more than one occasion it had been very welcome. Of late she had been dimly conscious of a feeling that she was overlooked, spied upon, and followed.

Had she been a native of the region she would have told herself that she was being stalked. There was always the sensation of nearness, that inexplicable instinct which registers human or animal proximity so unerringly.

At times this sense was accompanied by more material manifestations by sounds like the passing of the breeze among the long grass, or the patter of stealthy steps on the dry soil. Even on the verges of the foot-hills where there were few trees to conceal man or beast it could at times be heard.

When Beatrice drew rein and allowed her mount to proceed at a walk it died down to the shadow of a sound. And once and again there was sight of a long yellow body dappled with black stars passing at dusk between the slender trunks of the hardwood trees in the clearing near the hacienda.

Beatrice had heard that certain wild animals frequently stalked their prey for days before making the final spring, as conscientiously and scientifically indeed as a rhino hunter takes pains to make himself acquainted with the habits of his quarry before seizing the opportune moment for its dispatch. But she was not greatly concerned, for had Pedro not his rifle, and had she not her silver-mounted pop-gun?

As most very British people would have done, she simply refused to let the matter get on her nerves, and ignored it with all the sang-froid of her island. Whether Pedro had noticed it or not, she disdained to inquire and he disdained to mention. We are not the only self-contained people on this queer star.

Nevertheless the rides continued. There certainly was misgiving, but Beatrice held on. She would not speak of her private fears to Browning her training did not allow of that. So she cantered out every afternoon with Pedro a lazy second, brushing the verge of the woods and galloping the long stretches of the foot-hill slopes.

On the day it happened at last she had ridden even farther than usual and had gone on at a bridle-pace to a little old hacienda in the hills, where she had tea and exchanged her text-book Castilian for the quick-fire Spanish of a humorous but stately Senora of eighty years, who had regarded her much as she might have regarded a wonlan from Mars, so alien were her ideas to those of eight decades of seclusion. Two hours of this strange intercourse brought evening, and in some haste at the thought of the brief Soconuscan twilight Beatrice remounted and galloped off as quickly as her English saddle would allow her.

So fast did she ride that she was almost home before she noticed that Pedro did not follow. It was on the fringe of woodland not half a mile from the hacienda that the beast sprang at last, a yellow streak of vindictive fury in the dingy gold of sunset sprang high over the horse's withers at her throat.

Even so she was prepared, the tiny revolver spat straight into the grinning open jaws, and the mottled shape fell noiselessly back into the long grass. With a fierce thrust of the spur Beatrice drove her mount forward. Now that all was over she was panic-stricken, and galloped wildly as if pursued.

As she rushed the bend she was aware of a horseman coming swiftly towards her. It was her husband.

"Hallo!" he cried, "I've had the wind up properly. Where on earth have you been? Was that your shot just now?"

Then, as he saw her face in the gathering darkness, "My God, child, what's wrong?"

"Yes," she was breathing hard, "a jaguar, I shot it, and killed it, I think. But I was frightened and simply couldn't stay to make sure."

"I should think not," he laughed, relieved. "Get in at once, I'll ride on a bit and see if you bagged it. Take your time. No danger now."

She trotted steadily away into the eucalyptus shadows, and Browning hastened forward. It was almost dark now, and he could just see Pedro, who had suddenly appeared as if from nowhere, bending over something which lay in the long grass.

As Browning came up with the meztizo the man drew himself erect, but said nothing. "Is it a jaguar, Pedro?" he asked casually as he dismounted. But Pedro did not reply. Browning peered through the darkness, where a crumpled shape made a vague white patch among the green. Then he stumbled backwards with a cry like a wounded man, for he had looked upon the dead face of Jacinta!

CHAPTER IX
THE MAGICAL BOOKS OF THE AZTECS

When the rainbow-colored records of aboriginal America were given to that fire which was no brighter than themselves, when the flame-like manuscripts of Mexico dissolved in living flame, an art and tradition fantastically and remotely beautiful were consumed on the pyre of human superstition and intolerance. Mystical secrets, occult wisdom expired in the smoke of that holocaust, along with a delicate elfin graciousness, a rich and grotesque imagery, and a kaleidoscopic page of history was deliberately torn out of human record and almost irretrievably lost.

Fantasy was conquered by fanaticism, the bizarre by bigotry, for the glowing chronicles in which the Aztecs had for generations taken a strange and mystical delight were to the conquering Spaniards only "the picture-books of the devil." But a civilization as brilliant and complex as that of Tropical America was not without its resources, and as displaying a salient and peculiar phase of human development its literature might not so easily be quenched.

When Archbishop Zumarraga decreed the wholesale destruction of its chronicles and sacred writings he could, of course, apply his ukase only to the royal libraries and to such collections as his agents were able to seize upon. Many examples of Aztec literary art survived. But for generations these were carefully concealed by their pious owners, or else discovered and collected by more enlightened Europeans, who carried them westward to enrich the libraries of the Old World.

Of these poor waifs and strays some forty odd survive, lying like dead flowers on the borders of the world's garden of literature, unheeded, save by eyes sympathetic to their plaintive loveliness. The history and adventures of many of these strange books, whose writers were also painters, are among the greatest romances of literature.

It was frequently their fate to fall into the hands of those who, utterly ignorant of their origin and significance, took them for nursery books, the painted fables of fairy-tale. Others rotted in Continental libraries until, through the action of damp or the attacks of vermin, only their broader details might be descried unless by the most painstaking scholarship.

But, little by little, and after centuries of application almost unexampled in the records of research, their ultimate secrets have been probed and they are no longer regarded as meaningless daubs of barbaric eccentricity, but have come into their own as among the most precious and significant of those documents which illustrate the development of literary processes. In general appearance these Aztec manuscripts are far removed from the European idea of the book, or even from that of the Oriental manuscript.

They consist of symbolic paintings executed upon agave paper, leather or cotton, and are usually folded in "pages" which open out on the principle of a screen. Taking that which is, perhaps, most typical of all as a general example, the "Codex Fejervary-Mayer," we find its length to be about sixteen feet and its breadth about seven inches. The general effect is that of a dwarf fire-screen, somewhat extended, perhaps, painted in the brilliant colors of the setting sun, as behooves a manuscript of the West, and displaying a seemingly inextricable symbolism.

At first sight the pages present such a riot of colored confusion that it is only after considerable practice and acquaintance that the emblems which they contain can be separated visually and reduced to individual coherence. The Mexican manuscripts, or "papyri," as some writers have named them, although the words pintura and lienza are more frequently used by experts to describe them.

I have divided into two classes: those which deal with mythological and astrological matters, and those which represent either historical narratives or fictional writings. The first class I have again subdivided into "Interpretative" Codices, the "Codex Borgia" group, and a third group which I have labeled "Unclassified."

The Interpretative Codices are those which were painted either by native scribes under the superintendence of Spanish priests of experience in Mexican affairs or by such priests themselves who appended to them the lengthy interpretations from which they take their name. The Borgia group is made up of a number of codices painted by native scribes, and the several manuscripts composing it obviously possessed a common area of origin.

The Unclassified Codices hail from various Mexican areas and their contents differ considerably from those of the other groups. The manner in which these manuscripts reached Europe is obscure, but some of them have passed through extraordinary vicissitudes since their arrival in the Old World.

None of them, perhaps, has survived circumstances of such imminent peril as the "Codex Borgia," by far the most important of them all. It was bequeathed by the nephew of Cardinal Borgia to the Library of the Congregation of Propaganda at Rome, in the Ethnographical Section of which it is still preserved. Formerly it belonged to the Giustiniani family of Venice, to whom, probably, it was handed down by some seafaring ancestor. But it was so greatly neglected that it fell into the hands of the children of some of their household servants, who, as children will, after deriving all the amusement they could out of it as a nursery book, made several attempts to burn it.

But the tough deer-skin on which it is painted withstood the fire, the marks of which, however, remain on its edges. It was rescued by someone who seems to have had an inkling of its value, and soon afterwards passed into the possession of the Borgias, who, as literary cognoscenti, would naturally appreciate its true significance.

If we examine this magnificent codex, by far the finest example of native Aztec work extant, we find that the first few sheets contain the astrological calendar divided into groups of days by the simple device of using the symbol of a black footprint as a point or colon. The various days are represented by such symbols as a monkey's head, a jaguar, a flower, and so forth, as explained in the chapter on Astrology.

Of these there are twenty, for the Aztec ritual month consisted of twenty days, the period betwixt the waxing and waning of the moon. These signs were repeated thirteen times, to make up the content of the 260 days of the tonalamatl, or Book of Fate, and were again subdivided into weeks of thirteen days each.

Some of the signs were auspicious, others were distinctly unlucky, and the tonalamatl or calendar was thus capable of being used as a book of astrology, or rather of augury, from which the fortunes of a person born on any given day, or the success of an act performed on that date, might be augured. But the "Codex Borgia" is principally concerned with the gods, their attributes, costume, and significance.

In its pages we encounter the terrible Tezcatlipoca, the deity of sacrifice and justice, the dread recorder and chastiser of sin, the beautiful sun-god Tonatiuh, with the painted myth of his passage through the heavens from morning to night, the pious magician and priest Quetzalcoatl, the fertile maize-goddess, and the myth of the planet Venus, which occupies seventeen vignettes, and illustrates the magical dangers to which both kings and commonalty are liable at the hands of this vindictive genius, who, in Mexican mythology, is a male.

Four folios are devoted to the loves of the luxurious Xochiquetzal, who may be called the Fairy Queen of Mexico, and the "book" concludes with pages dedicated to the gods of pleasure and procreation and the hovering and ever-watchful deities of death and sacrifice. In many cases it has been only after long consideration and comparison with native-written accounts and by dint of the most ingenious and involved reasoning that the weird and uncanny gestures and actions of the deities represented have been duly explained and the intricate symbolism which surrounds them unriddled.

Indeed, this task alone has certainly equaled in difficulty and perplexity that presented by the solution of the hieroglyphic systems of Egypt. But whereas Egyptology had its Rosetta Stone, Mexican scholars were without such an aid to enlightenment, so far as these manuscripts were concerned. And are they accompanied by anything in the nature of actual script? They are. Here and there are to be found in their pages symbols which, when read together in the manner of a rebus, supply us with names. But these are far more frequently encountered in such of the paintings as deal with tribute or legal conveyances of land.

The name of King Ixcoatl, for instance, is represented by the picture of a serpent (coatl), pierced by flint knives (iztli) ; and that of Motequauhzoma (Montezuma) by a mouse-trap (montli), an eagle (quauhtli), a lancet (zo), and a hand (maitl).

The phonetic values employed by the scribes varied exceedingly, and they certainly conveyed their ideas more by sketch than sound. A piece of Nahua literature, the disappearance of which is surrounded by circumstances of the deepest mystery, is the Teo-Amoxtll, or "Divine Book," which is alleged by certain chroniclers to be the work of the ancient Toltecs.

Ixtlilxochitl, a native Mexican author, states that it was written by a Tezcucan wise man or wizard, one Huematzin, or "Lord of the Great Hand," about the end of the seventh century, and that it described the pilgrimage of the Aztecs from Asia, their laws, manners, customs, religion, arts, and magic.

In 1838 the Baron de Waldeck stated in his *Voyage Pittoresque* that he had it in his possession, and the Abbe Brasseur de Bourbourg identified it with the "Maya Dresden Codex" and other native manuscripts. Bustamante also states that the native chroniclers had a copy in their possession at the time of the fall of Mexico. But these appear to be mere surmises, and it seems unlikely that the Teo-Amoxtli was ever seen by a European. The "Codex Fejervary-Mayer," or at least one side of it, is known to Mexican specialists as "the Wizards' Manual." Its origin is unknown, and it is the property of the Liverpool Public Museums, to which it was bequeathed by a Mr. Joseph Mayer in 1867.

One side of this manuscript is generally alluded to as the "day" or "priests'" side, and the other as the "night" or "wizards'" side, as it deals with the lore of darkness, sorcery, and the occult. The whole is divided into forty-four sheets.

Let us examine these passages devoted to arcane matters: Sheet 1 represents the five regions of the world and their presiding deities, and the four quarters of the tonalamatl, or "Book of Fate" as well as the nine lords of the night, in a direction opposite to their usual sequence.

The gods governing the five regions in this sheet are: Centre Xiuhtecutli, the fire-god. East Mixcoatl, god of the chase; Tlaloc, the rain-god. North Itztli, the stone-knife god; Xochipilli, god of flowers and games. West Iztac Tezcatlipoca (the white or fruitful Tezcatlipoca); Quetzalcoatl, the wind-god. South Macuilxochitl, god of pleasure; Xipe, god of sacrifice.

Sheets 2-4 deal with the nine lords of the night hours. In these sheets are depicted the gods of the five regions in a different sequence from that shown in sheet 1, that is, the deities represented pose as patrons of the reversal of things, otherwise of the Black Art. They are: Centre Tezcatlipoca; Iztac Mixcoatl. South Xopilli; Xochiquetzal. West Tlaltecutli; Chantico. North Centeotl; Xolotl. East Tlauizcalpantecutli; Patecatl.

These gods introduce a series of pages (sheets 15-18) which deal with sorcery and occult lore, especially with the subject of death by magic. A tonalamatl resembling that just described is shown, and in each picture the earth-demon with a head like that of a badger is depicted. The sequence is probably East, North, West, South, According to Seler, these show the four forms of the god of the planet Venus in his relation to the cardinal points.

In the eastern section the bat-god is depicted; in the northern, Mixcoatl; in the western, Xochipilli; and in the southern and last, the eagle. Sheet 43 once more depicts the five regions of the universe, which here take the form of a crossway showing the cardinal points and a double manual indicator for the Above and Below regions.

Sheet 44 represents Tezcatlipoca as a wizard, surrounded by the twenty "weeks" of the tonalamatl. If we seek light on these magical pages we find that Sheet 1 depicts the influence of the nine lords of the night or the five quarters of the world. Xuihtecutli, lord of fire, rules the centre that is the hearth of the world, for the hearth in Mexico usually occupied the centre of the native dwelling.

Mixcoatl, god of the chase, rules the east, the direction of the rising sun. He was s the Toltec Abraham, or patriarch, and symbolized wisdom and knowledge. Tlaloc, the rain-god, accompanies him, bringing the beneficent showers which caused growth and prosperity.

These gods are of good omen. But from the dreadful north, the House of Fear in Mexico, descend Itztli, god of death and the stone knife of sacrifice. As a mitigating influence he is accompanied by Xochipilli, the god of pleasure, so that this world-direction was not regarded as altogether ominous of evil.

The west quarter takes Tezcatlipoca, in his white or fruitful form, a beneficent side of him, and Quetzalcoatl, always a good sign. The south holds the picture of Macuilxochitl, a pleasure deity, but is darkened by the figure of the ghastly Xipe, Lord of Sacrifice, in his dress of human skins.

These beings ruled the fortunes of the several earth-regions or compass-directions over which they presided. The Lords of the Night Hours who appear in sheets 2-4 have been dealt with in the chapter on Astrology.

In sheets 5-14 the gods of the five regions are shown in reversed sequence. Thus in the centre region stand Tezcatlipoca, the god of vengeance, showing that here he governs the heart of things. With him is Mixcoatl in his "white" character as a mitigating influence. The South is ruled by Xopilli and Xochiquetzal, both gods of pleasure, so that it is especially of good omen in this place.

The West, with Tlaltecutli and Chantico, is not particularly fortunate, as being under the influence of rain in the evil sense, the deluge of fire which fell from heaven at the end of the water-sun age. Chantico, moreover, represents the volcanic fire imprisoned in the centre of the earth, so that he has a plutonic and therefore a sinister significance as a tonalamatl figure.

As the North is governed by Centeotl and Xolotl, it is favourable and fruitful of good. The East has Tlaaizcalpantecutli, a sacrificial god, and Patecatl, a drink deity, usually an unfortunate symbol, therefore it can scarcely be said to be of happy auspices. It is likely that this sequence represents the five regions as used astrologically for the night hours, whereas the former were similarly employed by the augurs during the day.

Sheets 41-42 hold the bad influence of the bat-god, which is, however, mitigated by the cheerful presence of the god of sport and by the wisdom of Mixcoatl. Sheet 43 is indicative of the witches' meeting-place, the cross-roads of the terrible Ciuateteo, and shows the downward terrestrial influence in conjunction with that from the above-world.

There is no question that the "books" of ancient Mexico which dealt with sorcery were quite as much in demand by the naualli or wizard class as were the grimoires of the Middle Ages by the sorcerers of that era. But they were more mnemonic than explanatory; that is, they held only the hints and outlines of magical knowledge and procedure rather than a full exposition of them.

It could scarcely be expected that such a system of writing and symbolism as the Mexicans possessed could have achieved more than such a sketch of any department of knowledge, and the fanaticism of the Spanish conquerors has spared us merely a fraction of that. Before undertaking a magical act the naualli consulted his tonalamatl and satisfied himself that the astrological omens were favorable.

He then applied himself to the study of the ritual procedure, as illustrated by pictures in such a book as the "Codex Bologna"," the only surviving manuscript which gives us a hint that such books actually existed. These preliminary steps accomplished, he next betook himself to a desert place, and called upon one or other of the presiding deities of magic, and possibly the god of the hour, for assistance in his task.

If he had been "retained" by a client to employ magical power upon a third party, he did so by means of intense concentration. Sitting in his cavern or on some wild hill-side, he brought all his mental powers to bear on the idea of the person whom it was desired to influence either for good or evil. Instances are on record of Mexican wizards who pitted their wills and magical influences against one another.

Says Brinton: "In these strange duels a Voutrance, one would be seated opposite his antagonist, surrounded with the mysterious emblems of his craft, and call upon his gods, one after another, to strike his enemy dead. Sometimes one, 'gathering his medicine,' as it was termed, feeling within himself that hidden force of will which makes itself acknowledged even without words, would rise in his might, and in a loud and severe voice command his opponent to die! Straightway the latter would drop dead or yielding in craven fear to a superior volition, forsake the implements of his art and with an awful terror at his heart, creep to his lodge, refuse all nourishment, and presently perish."

CHAPTER X
THE MAYA PEOPLE

It is, indeed, deplorable that the study of the rich and mysterious civilization of the Maya Indians of Central America should not more generally commend itself to British archaeologists. Thousands of people in Great Britain would, if they could, peruse the wondrous story of those silent isthmian temples with the delight of greater children for a grown-up fairy-tale. But they can scarcely be expected to burrow among the bulletins of the United States Bureau of Ethnology, even if they ever heard of that surprisingly efficient, if rather dreary institution, and no modern book in English gives an account at once adequate and attractive of the marvelous panorama of Maya progress.

What is really required is a volume neither of the etiolated proportions of the modern textbook, nor on the other hand over portly, written out of sound knowledge and setting forth in the manner of a Prescott or a Layard the wondrous tale of Maya history. It should tell in chapters of enthrallment, provided with good illustrations, of the deserted temples of Guatemala and Yucatan, and provide a picturesque account of what is known of the mythology and religious customs of the Maya race. Nor should such a volume be without a description of the strange systems of writing and arithmetic employed by this gifted people, or of their extremely beautiful and individual art and intricate symbolism.

A brief summary of the results of recent research in the study of Maya antiquity is all that can be attempted here in the hope that it may attract a larger number of interested readers to such works as presently await their attention. The Maya appear to have emerged from barbarism during the first or second century of the Christian era. Their earliest dated monuments cannot with safety be ascribed to a more remote period.

No sooner had Maya civilization been fairly set upon its feet than it began to progress with extraordinary rapidity. Regarding the precise place of its origin authoritative opinion is practically agreed. The general character of the architectural remains in the region lying between the Bay of Tabasco and the foot of the Cordilleras and watered by the river Usumacinta and the Rio de la Pasion in the modern state of Chiapas, points conclusively to this district as the first settlement of Central American civilization, and the relatively archaic type of the hieroglyphs found upon its monuments as well as the early dates these contain give to this theory something of finality.

The oldest centers of Maya life are probably Tikal and Peten in Eastern Guatemala. It is believed that the development of the southern Maya states continued for nearly four hundred years, or until the close of the sixth century A.D., about which time disaster seems to have come upon them with tragic suddenness. We do not know the cause of the downfall of what must have been a complex and highly-developed civili- zation.

Possibly a horde of barbarians from the north swept down upon its settled communities. But even today its gorgeous temples and palaces show no signs of deliberate destruction such as would surely have been evident had they fallen into the hands of savage marauders. More probably these cities were emptied of their inhabitants by one of the migratory impulses which reappear so frequently in American native history.

This theory is rendered possible by the fact that the period of their desertion synchronizes with that of the discovery by the Maya of Yucatan, a region whose wealth in stone probably attracted a nation of builders. But Yucatan is, on the whole, an arid country, and it is still more likely that the retreat of the Maya thence was dictated by the imperative reason of self-preservation or by the command of the tribal gods.

The most important of the older city-states were Palenque, Piedras Negras, Ocosingo, Tikal, Yaxchilan, and Quirigua, sites which are scattered over Southern Mexico and Guatemala, while Copan, per- haps the most important of all, is situated in Honduras, the southern limit of Maya culture, so far as is presently known. Of the later sites in Yucatan, Chichen-Itza was by far the most famous, Mayapan, Uxmal, and Labna barely approaching it in celebrity.

With the discovery of Yucatan a new era opened up for Maya art and social activity. At first the struggle for bare existence on the inhospitable and poorly-irrigated plateau was probably intense. But the ingenious immigrants triumphed over conditions of the unhealthiest kind, and by degrees improved their agricultural knowledge and astronomical science, fixing the revolutionary periods of the planets with accuracy and developing the solar calendar. The Maya Renaissance was fully under way by the end of the tenth century and edifices which recall the palmy days of Palenque and Copan were once more rising all over Yucatan.

About the year A.D. 1000 Chichen-Itza, Uxmal, and Mayapan formed a political confederacy and under the pacific conditions which followed the institution of this league art and science blossomed forth anew. Cities multiplied with astonishing rapidity and the art of sculpture, which had now become merely an adjunct to architecture, achieved an elaboration and intricacy of design unsurpassed, perhaps, by any people in any age.

With the disruption of what may be called the Triple Alliance about the year 1200, an event precipitated by the conspiracy of the ruler of Chichen-Itza against his colleague of Mayapan, a series of disastrous wars ensued which lasted until the country was discovered by the Spaniards. These endless internecine struggles led to the employment of mercenaries from the ruder tribes of Mexico, the presence of whom set an indelible stamp upon Maya art and manners, and we find the graceful Maya sculptors forced to carry out the designs, and even accompanying them with the completely different hieroglyphical inscriptions, of a Mexican military aristocracy.

Had they placed side by side with these the equivalent Maya characters, modern science would have been provided with an American Rosetta stone, as the Mexican glyphs, unlike those of the Maya, can now be deciphered with a reasonable degree of exactitude. This brings us to the problem of Maya writing, which is still almost entirely a closed book to investigators. For the pursuit of this quest a far greater degree of industry and ingenuity has been needful than for the decipherment of the ancient writings of Egypt or Sumeria.

Certain of the "calculiform" or pebble-shaped characters have been unriddled, especially those which apply to the sun, moon, and planets, those for "beginning," "ending," the symbols for the year, "night," and the glyphs for the "months" and "days."

The glyphs appear as a number of small squares rounded at the corners and representing human faces and other objects highly conventionalized by generations of artistic usage. They are arranged as a rule in two parallel columns and are read two columns at a time, from left to right and top to bottom.

Formerly it was believed that the work of Landa, Bishop of Yucatan, written in 1565, contained the "key" to the script. But it is now known that the natives, exasperated at his destruction of their manuscripts, deliberately deceived him, and that with the exception of the symbols for the days and "months" his "key" is quite misleading.

Much difference of opinion exists as to whether the system is phonetic or ideographic in character. It is probably both phonetic and pictorial to some extent, but for the most part it appears to be of the nature of rebus writing, in which the characters do not indicate the meaning of the objects which they portray, but only the sounds of their names.

Thus, if English were written in this manner, the picture of a human eye might stand for the first personal pronoun, a drawing of a bee for the verb "to be," and so forth. But it seems probable that an ever-increasing number of phonetic elements will be identified, though the idea of a glyph will always be found to overshadow its phonetic value.

Through generations of use the system came to possess a significance entirely ideographic, and would not necessitate any such effort of mental translation as a people unused to rebus writing would have to make in order to comprehend it readily. The manner in which the arithmetical system and dating of the Maya was discovered by Emile Forstemann of Berlin is decidedly the greatest triumph of American archaeology within recent years.

A dot stood for 1 and a bar or line for 5. By various combinations of these the Maya expressed all the numerals from 1 to 19 inclusive. Twenty was denoted by the moon, as indicating the number of days in which the moon waxes and wanes. But the manner in which the higher mathematics of the Maya was evolved is much too intricate a process to be described here.

Each of the periods of time in use among the Maya was based on the period of revolution of one or other of the heavenly bodies and was represented by an appropriate hieroglyph, and when a date was sculptured on a monument the number of periods it contained, years, "months," and days, was set forth in the glyphs which denoted them. These dates can be collated with European chronology through the agency of manuscripts known as the Books of Chilan Balam, "The Tiger Priesthood," native annals of the priestly hierarchy of Yucatan, in which the ancient system of chronology is preserved.

The annals in question were fortunately continued into the post-Conquest period, so that some of the events they date in the native manner have known European equivalents. If we count backwards from these and reduce the Maya system of computing time to the terms of our own, it becomes possible to interpret the dates on the monuments with a fair likelihood of correctness. Thus the period of the foundation of the city of Palenque has been fixed at 15 B.C., that ofYaxchilan at 75 B.C., Copan A.D. 34, Piedras Negras A.D. 109, and the abandonment of Copan and Quirigua at A.D. 231 and A.D. 292 respectively.

Perhaps no sphere of archaeology still offers such vistas of conquest as that of Central America, and the mysterious interest which cleaves to the antiquities of the isthmus is by no means yet dissipated by the searchlight of discovery. The architecture of the Maya was their greatest artistic and human triumph.

The wonderful structures which have aroused the admiration of generations of archaeologists, like the temples and pyramids of Egypt or the palaces of Babylon, still occupy their ancient sites and are better capable than any other manifestation of Maya life of illuminating our ideas on the subject of the civilization of Central America. For the most part they are buried in dark and mysterious forests, although certain of them stand open on the arid plains of Yucatan, where the native genius which raised them arrived at its apogee.

The majority of these buildings were either raised for the specific purposes of religion or royal occupation. Few old domestic dwellings survive in the Maya area, these having been for the most part either constructed of adobe, or merely of reeds, like the houses of the Maya peasantry of the present day. But the greater Maya buildings were usually erected upon a mound or ku, either natural or artificial, as were some of the Mexican religious edifices.

The most general foundation of the Maya temple was a series of earth-terraces arranged in exact parallel order, the buildings them-selves forming part of a square. They were constructed from the hard sandstone of the country. But the Maya were surprisingly ignorant of some of what we would call the first principles of architecture. For example, they were totally ignorant of the principles upon which the arch is constructed.

This difficulty they overcame by making each course of masonry overhang the one beneath it, after the method employed by a boy with a box of bricks, who finds that he can only make "doorways" by this means, or by the simple expedient also employed by the Maya of placing a slab horizontally upon two upright pillars. In consequence it will readily be seen that the superimposition of a second story upon such an insecure foundation was scarcely to be thought of, and that such support for the roof as towered above the doorway would necessarily require to be of the most substantial description. Indeed, this portion of the building often appears to be more than half the size of the rest of the edifice. This space gave the Maya builders a splendid chance for mural decoration, and it must be said they readily seized it and made the most of it, ornamented facades being perhaps the most typical features in the relics of Maya architecture.

Apart from this, the Maya practiced a pyramidal type of architecture of which many good and even perfect examples remain. A first story was built in the usual manner, and the second rose above it by making a mound at the back of the edifice until it was on a level with the roof, and then building upon it. But length usually took the place of height in Maya architecture. Survey, design, previous calculation, all entered into the considerations of the Maya architects.

The manner in which the carved stones fitted into each other shows that they had previously been worked apart. In certain localities we discover various methods. In Chiapas we find the bas-relief in stone or stucco almost universally employed. In Honduras the stiffness of design apparent implies an older type of architecture, along with caryatids and pillars in human form.

In Guatemala there are traces of the use of wood, especially in the lintels of doorways. In the modern state of Chiapas are situated the remains of the city of Palenque, one of the most celebrated and imposing of the Maya communities, nestling on the lower slopes of the Cordilleras and built in the form of an amphitheatre. If one takes his stand on the central ku or pyramid, he finds himself surrounded by a circle of ruined palaces and temples raised upon artificial terraces.

The principal and most imposing is the Palace, a building reared upon a single platform, and in the shape of a quadrilateral surrounding a minor structure. On the walls of some of the buildings are sculptures of the Feathered Serpent, Kukulkan, or Quetzalcoatl.

The Temple of Inscriptions, perched on an eminence some 40 feet high, is the largest edifice in Palenque. It has a facade 74 feet long by 25 feet deep, composed of a great gallery which runs along the entire front of the fane.

The building has been named from the inscriptions with which certain flagstones in the central apartments are covered. Three other temples occupy a piece of rising ground close by. These are the Temple of the Sun, closely akin in type to many Japanese temple buildings; the Temple of the Cross, in which a wonderful altar-piece was discovered; and the Temple of the Cross No. II.

In the Temple of the Cross the inscribed altar gave its name to the building. In the central slab is a cross of the American pattern, its roots springing from the hideous head of the Earth-mother. Its branches stretch to where on the right and left stand two figures, evidently those of a priest and an acolyte, performing some mysterious rite.

On the apex of the tree is placed the sacred turkey, or "Emerald Fowl," to which offerings of maize paste are made. The whole is surrounded by inscriptions.

Ake, thirty miles east of Merida, is chiefly famous for its pyramids, hockey or tlachtli courts, and the gigantic pillars which once supported immense galleries. One of its principal buildings is traditionally known as "The House of Darkness," as it can boast not a single window, the light filtering in from the doorway alone.

The "Palace of Owls" is noteworthy for its diamond-shaped frieze, the work of the earliest Maya builders in Yucatan. Chichen-Itza, one of the most venerable of the ruined cities of Yucatan, is chiefly remarkable for its great pyramid-temple, known as El Castillo, which stands on a mound whence temples and palaces radiate in a circular plan.

Its so-called "Nunnery" is one of the most famous examples of Maya architecture, and here dwelt the sacred women, dedicated to the god Kulkucan. On the walls of the contiguous building called "El Castillo" are base-reliefs representing Kukulkan and his priesthood. But it is impossible in a work dealing with the occult sciences of these countries to afford more than passing mention to their architecture, absorbing though it be, and we must turn to Maya history.

This commences about the beginning of the Christian era and in the area of Palenque, Piedras Negras, and Ocosingo in Chiapas. Regarding the earlier centuries we know little or nothing, and light first shines for us about the sixth century, when the Maya of Guatemala deserted their cities, and answering some unknown impulse decided to immigrate into Yucatan.

It is possible that they were forced to do so by a Nahua invasion, traces of which are to be found in a Kuikatec manuscript of early origin, but it is equally likely that, as had happened before in their history, and as is evident from the pages of "The Popol Vuh," which supplies a precedent, that they left their settlements in the south because of some religious summons sent by the gods through their priests. But not all of the Maya race deserted their cities. Many remained, and a cleavage between the customs of the Maya of the south and those of Yucatan is hence-forward to be remarked.

Everything points to a late occupation of Yucatan by the Maya, and architectural effort exhibits deterioration, evidenced in a high conventionality of design and excess of ornamentation. Evidences of

Nahua influence also are not wanting, a fact which is eloquent of the later period of contact which is known to have occurred between the peoples, and which alone is almost sufficient to fix the date of the settlement of the Maya in Yucatan.

It must not be thought that the Maya in Yucatan formed one homogeneous state recognizing a central authority. On the contrary, as is often the case with colonists, the several Maya bands of immigrants formed themselves into different states or kingdoms, each having its own separate traditions.

It is thus a matter of the greatest difficulty to so collate and criticize these traditions as to construct a history of the Maya race in Yucatan. As may be supposed, we find the various city-sites founded by divine beings who play a more or less important part in the Maya pantheon. Kukulkan, for example, is the first king of Mayapan, whilst Itzamna figures as the founder of the state of Itzamal.

The founders of the northern city of Itzamal soon formed a powerful state on a religious or priestly basis, whereas those who settled in Chichen-Itza, further to the south, were of more warlike disposition. About the year 1000 a triple alliance was entered into by Chichen-Itza, Uxmal and Mayapan, as has been said, and this lasted for about 200 years.

The people of Chichen-Itza, who were ruled by an aristocracy known as the Tutul Xius, came into conflict with the Cocomes or Nahua aristocracy of Mayapan, who, after a struggle of nearly 120 years' duration, overthrew them and made Chichen-Itza a dependency. The ruling caste, the Tutul Xius, fled southward, and settled in Potonchan, where they reigned for nearly 300 years.

They took into their service a large number of Aztec and other Nahua mercenary troops, and commenced a campaign of northward military extension, ultimately reconquering the territory they had lost to the Cocomes. Like the Romans, they made excellent roads, and wherever they made a conquest they founded a city.

This, indeed, was the period of the full blossoming of Maya art, architectural and otherwise, and from the shrines of Chichen and the island of Cozumel great highways radiated in every direction for the convenience of pilgrims. But the rule of the Mexican Cocomes still flourished and eventually became a tyranny.

The other Maya states existed in a condition of comparative helotage to them, and even the Tutul Xius had to pay a crushing tribute for the lands they held. The Cocome aristocracy, secure in its armed might, permitted itself every possible luxury and excess, morality ceased to be regarded as a virtue among them, and popular discontent was rife. The dissolute habits of the alien Cocomes at length aroused general disgust and a revolutionary feeling gained ground.

The Cocomes on their part now engaged fresh mercenaries from Mexico, and when revolt at last ensued, these stemmed the tide for some time. The Tutul Xius were forced from their possessions and settled in the city of Mani. The Cocome ruler of Mayapan, Hunac Eel, was of sterner make than his degenerate nobles.

Although tyrannical, he possessed statesmanship and experience, and resolved to attack the head and front of the rebellious states, the city of Chichen-Itza. At the head of a great host he marched against it and succeeded in inflicting a severe defeat on the Itzaes. But he had shortly to face revolution at home, and the defeated Itzaes had now joined forces with his other enemies, the Tutul Xius.

A terrific onslaught was launched against the Cocomes, and in 1436 they and their city were destroyed. They fled to Zotuta, a region in the centre of Yucatan, sur- rounded by almost impenetrable forests. But in crushing the Cocomes, the rulers of Chichen-Itza had almost crushed themselves.

Gradually their city crumbled into ruin, political and physical, and its aristocracy left it at last to seek the cradle of the Maya race in Guatemala, or so tradition says. The Maya people of Guatemala, the Quiches and Kakchiquels, have a separate history of their own, which is preserved for us in the pages of "The Popol Vuh," their sacred book, a part of which the reader will find outlined in the section which deals with the arcane writings of the Maya.

As with the earlier dynasties of Egypt, considerable doubt surrounds the history of the early Quiche monarchs. Indeed, a period of such uncertainty occurs that even the number of kings who reigned is lost in the hopeless confusion of varying estimates. From this chaos emerge the facts that the Quiche monarchs held the supreme power among the peoples of Guatemala, that they were the contemporaries of the rulers of Mexico City, and that they were often elected from among the princes of the subject-states.

Acxopil, the successor of Nima-Quiche, invested his second son with the government of the Kakchiquels, and placed his youngest son over the Tzutuhils, whilst to his eldest son he left the throne of the Quiches. Icutemal, his eldest son, on succeeding his father, gifted the kingdom of Kakchiquel to his eldest son, displacing his own brother and thus mortally affronting him.

The struggle which ensued lasted for generations, embittered the relations between these two branches of the Maya in Guatemala, and undermined their joint strength. Nahua mercenaries were employed in the struggle on both sides, and these introduced many of the crudities of Nahua life into Maya existence. This condition of things lasted up to the time of the coming of the Spaniards.

The Kakchiquels dated the commencement of a new chronology from the episode of the defeat of Cay Hun-Apu by them in 1492. They may have saved themselves the trouble; for the time was at hand when the calendars of their race were to be closed, and its records written in another script by another people. One by one, and chiefly by reason of their insane policy of allying themselves with the invader against their own kin, the old kingdoms of Guatemala fell as spoil to the daring Conquistadores.

Magic and divination played an extraordinary part in the policy and administration of the Maya states. No ruler would act without the advice of his soothsayers, and it may well be said that seldom has a state of fairly advanced human society acted so much in accordance with the systems and dictates of the arcane sciences.

This does not in any way imply that its downfall was due to the acceptance of such wisdom, for it was only upon the lack of observance of the mystical rule which the wise priesthood of the Maya applied that the city-states of Yucatan crashed into ruin. Had the nobility pursued the custom of its predecessors and hearkened to the divine voices which formerly dictated their policy their fall would have been averted, but, like many another aristocracy, they forsook a well-devised theocracy for an insensate luxury and the degradations of profligate pleasure.

CHAPTER XI
MAYA RELIGION

The most intensive examination of the gods of the Maya people of Central America and Yucatan has so far been directed to those pictures of them which appear in the three principal Maya manuscripts remaining to us, the Dresden, Paris, and Tro-Cortesianus Codices, and not to the sculptured representations of divine forms on the surviving monuments of that marvelous people.

The pictured forms of personages in the manuscripts are, indeed, so obviously those of divinities that we are justified in attempting to collate them with the various members of the Maya pantheon alluded to in literary sources, in the "Books of Chilan Balam," "The Popol Vuh," "The Book of the Cakchiquels" and elsewhere. But the same can scarcely be said of the sculptured figures which appear on the temple walls and stelae of Central America.

Certain of these, indeed, are as manifestly divine as any of the forms depicted in the manuscripts, and are capable of being compared if not identified with them, but others, again, are as obviously representations, either modeled from the life, or post-mortem sculptures, of great leaders or hierophants.

Nor is it always possible, in view of our present poverty of data and knowledge, to discriminate between these figures which had a human and a divine significance. The hieroglyphs which in almost every instance accompany these pictures and sculptures in human form still remain undeciphered, and until these yield their secret it will be impossible to identify the gods or personages they name with any degree of certainty.

For nearly a generation the painted representations of gods in the Maya manuscripts have been for the sake of convenience described by the letters of the alphabet from A to P, a method which has been found much more satisfactory than any dogmatic system of nomenclature which might have affixed to them the names of divine beings in Maya myth without the absolute assurance that they actually applied to the painted representations whose accompanying hieroglyphic titles we cannot yet decipher.

The first student of Maya antiquities to apply this provisional and truly scientific system of nomenclature was Dr. Paul Schellhas, who, so long ago as 1897, introduced it to the notice of Americanists in his "*Representations of Deities in the Maya Manuscripts*" as "a purely inductive natural science method," essentially amounting to " that which in ordinary life we call 'memory of persons.'

By an intensive examination of the pictures of gods in the manuscripts he learned gradually to recognize them promptly by the characteristic impressions they made as a whole. He was aided in this not only by dissimilarities in face and figure, but by such details as the constant occurrence in the case of each god of some outstanding hieroglyph, ornament, or other symbol.

He dealt with the figures in the manuscripts alone, and almost entirely avoided hypotheses and deductions. The present writer, following in his path, has, however, not refrained from application to those other sources of information which he ignored, and by degrees has been enabled to arrive at a rather fuller comprehension of that extensive Maya godhead for whose worship the gorgeous temples of tropical America were erected.

Schellhas candidly admitted his lack of knowledge of the places of origin of the three invaluable manuscripts which preserve for us those graceful and delicate representations of a forgotten Olympus. But Dr. H. J. Spinden, of the American Museum of Natural History, in his monumental work on "*Maya Art*," has, by a careful comparison of the art-forms of those wonderful aboriginal paintings, dissipated nearly all existing doubts on the question.

The "Codex Dresden" he assigns to the region south of Uxmal in Yucatan. In the "Codex Peresianus" he finds marked similarities to the art of the ruined cities of Naranho, Quirigua, and Piedras Negras in Peten, a district immediately to the south of the Yucatan peninsula.

As for the "Codex Tro-Cortesianus," he believes it to have been the work of a painter living in the northern district of Yucatan. It is, of course, manifest that all of these must be copies of much older manuscripts, and Spinden is of opinion that the last-mentioned may be dated not much later than A.D. 1200.

This means that all three originated in those districts which had been colonized by the Maya after they had left their original settlements in Guatemala and had been driven northward into Yucatan by racial pressure or other causes, and it is clear that all have reference to the same deities and arose out of one and the same religious impulse. It is possible, however, within reasonable limits, to attempt to collate many of these drawings with the gods of Maya myth. The figures appear again and again, and there is in the manner of their representation a constancy and similarity of form and attitude which justify the inference that it is possible, as Schellhas thought, to verify a god from his general appearance and his accompanying symbols.

The god first encountered in this alphabetic sequence, God A, as he is generally described, is without doubt that grisly genius who in all mythologies presides over the realm of the departed. He is readily to be recognized by his skull-like countenance and bony spine, and the large black spots, denoting corruption, which covers the emaciated body. He wears as a collar the ruff of the vulture, the bird of death, and a symbol which usually accompanies him, but which Schellhas was unable to decipher, undoubtedly represents the maggot, evidently a kind of hieroglyph for death. But the distinguishing glyph for this god is a human head with eyes closed in death, before which stands the stone knife of sacrifice.

In one part of the "Codex Dresden" God A is shown with the head of an owl, the bird of ill-omen, his almost constant attendant, and this recalls to us a passage in the "Popol Vuh," a religious book of the Maya, which states that the rulers of Xibalba, the Underworld, "were owls," the inhabitants of a dark and cavernous place.

I believe Schellhas's God A to be Ah-puch, the death-spirit mentioned by Father Hernandez. His name means "the Undoer" or "Spoiler," and he was also known as Chamay Bac or Zac, that is "white teeth and bones."

In some of his portraits he is decorated with a feather, on which are seen the conventional markings of the symbol of the flint knife, and I have deduced from this that the glyph for "feather" was synonymous with that for "knife," a notion which I have substantiated from the fact that in Maya the first wing feather of a bird was called "a knife."

The personality of God B is a much debated one. He has a long proboscis and tusk-like fangs, and certain writers on American antiquities have called him "the elephant-headed god." Apart from these peculiarities, his eye has a characteristic rim, and he is easily recognized by the strange head-dress he wears, which I take to be a bundle of "medicine" or magical appliances.

And here it may be as well to say that I believe the head-dresses of these gods represent the earliest symbols by which they were known to their priests and worshippers in the period before writing was invented or hieroglyphs came into use. They would thus rank as hieroglyphs, as something to be immediately recognized or "read," and probably acted as a definite step in the invention of written symbols. But their earliest use seems to have been as personal signs by which the gods could be readily identified.

That God B has an affinity with water is plainly evident. He is seen walking on its surface, standing in rain, fishing, paddling a canoe, and even enthroned on the clouds. He is connected with the serpent, which is, in America, the water-animal par excellence.

In some places, indeed, his head surmounts a serpentine body, and, like the priests of the modern Zufii Indians of Arizona, he is represented as clutching tame serpents in his hands. Like the old British god Kai the "Sir Kai the Seneschal" of Malory he is seen in some parts of the manuscript carrying flaming torches. Kai was a god of the waters; so, in some measure, is God B.

The "elephantine" aspect of this god is accounted for by his wearing the mask of the medicine-man or priest during the religious ceremony. Indeed, in one statue of his analogous Mexican form we see him in the very act of removing this mask.

In Mexico the mask resembles the beak of a bird; in Central America it is more like a snout whether that of an elephant, tapir, or other animal I do not possess sufficient data to form an opinion. God B is, indeed, none other than Kukulkan, "The Feathered Serpent," the Maya name for the Quetzalcoatl, the god of the rain-bearing trade-wind.

But in Central America proper, whence he originally hailed, he is more intimately connected with water than with wind, and the learned priests of his cult explained him to the Spanish conquerors as "the ripple wind makes on water," the ruffled feathers on the serpentine stream. But in later times he came to be regarded as the priest who conjured down the rain by magic, and his possession of the caluac, or rain-maker's wand, places his position in this respect beyond all question.

Coming to the third letter of our alphabet of gods we find God C simple of explanation. At first sight his outward semblance may seem puzzling. His face is framed by the painted border seen on the xamach or flat dish on which the Maya baked their tortillas or maize pancakes.

But xamach also means "north," so that in this instance we have an example of that rebus-writing on which the Maya hieroglyphical system was undoubtedly based. There was, we know from tradition, a god called Xamanek, who represented the pole star, and that God C is identical with this deity scarcely admits of any doubt.

In the "Codex Cortesianus" we see his head surrounded by a nimbus of rays which can symbolize only stellar emanations, and in the same manuscript we find him hanging from the sky in the noose of a rope. Elsewhere he is accompanied by familiar planetary signs.

In D we have a god of night and the moon. He is represented as an aged man with toothless jaws, and is indicated by the hieroglyph akbal, "night." His head, in the reduced cursive writing of the texts, stands for the sign of the moon, and is frequently accompanied by the snail, the emblem of birth, over which function the moon had planetary jurisdiction.

Among the Maya deities D is the only one who can boast of a beard, a certain sign in the case of the neighboring Mexican pantheon that a god possesses a planetary significance, and for this reason, no less than because of his venerable appearance, I would collate him with Tonaca tecutli, the Mexican creative deity, father of the gods, the Saturn of their Olympus.

This figure was known to the Maya of Guatemala as Xpiyacoc, but can scarcely be collated with Hunab Ku, "The Great Hand," the " god behind the gods," invisible, impalpable, of whom we are assured that he was represented in neither painting nor sculpture.

In God E we have such a definite picture of a divinity connected with the maize-plant that we have no difficulty in identifying him as Ghanan, the traditional Maya god of the maize, whose other name was Yum Kaax, "Lord of the Harvest Fields." He bears the maize-plant on his head, and this, becoming in course of time the conventionalized form of an ear of maize with leaves, composed his hieroglyph. His face-paint, too, frequently bears the symbol of fertility, and the rain-vase is depicted as an ornament above his ear.

God F, in his insignia, is reminiscent of the Mexican harvest-god Xipe, whose annual festival brought forth such grisly horrors of human sacrifice. He has the same distinguishing vertical face-mark, implying "war," for plenteous harvests were only to be secured by drenching the soil with the blood of prisoners taken in battle. He is, indeed, a war-god, and is occasionally represented in full war-paint, with flint knife and blazing torch, setting fire to tents or huts. In some places he is pictured underneath a stone axe in the shape of a hand, with thumb turned upwards, which probably had an inauspicious significance.

God G is not often represented in the manuscripts. He appears to be a sun-god, and his hieroglyph, a circle enclosing four teeth, is believed by some authorities to symbolize the "biting" nature of tropical heat. His own teeth are filed to a sharp point. His head-dress recalls that of the priesthood of Yucatan, and in some of his representations has a certain resemblance to the Egyptian wig. There is, indeed, no question that it is a wig. He frequently holds the flower symbolic of a life rendered to him in sacrifice, and is occasionally depicted standing amid tongues of solar flame, a central eye blazing upon his forehead.

That he is Kinich Ahau, the sun-god, is scarcely open to dispute. Another of his hieroglyphs consists of a composite picture, including a solar disk, the sign been, which means "straw-thatch," and the sign ik, which in this connection is to be translated "fire which strikes upon the roof," in allusion to the frequency with which the thatched roofs of the Maya were ignited by the fierce rays of the sun of Yucatan.

The distinguishing characteristic of God H consists in what is known as the chiccan or serpent-spot appearing on his brow. He has practically no other distinctive marks, and that he has some relation to the serpent is clear. With I we come to the first of the two goddesses represented in the list a divinity of water.

She is scarcely prepossessing, and has claws in place of feet. She wears on her head a knotted serpent, and seems to pour the flooding rains from a large vessel. But she is evidently not a beneficent deity, for her face is distorted by an expression of angry menace, and it is obvious that she personifies water in its more harmful guise the baneful flood rather than the grain-bringing rain. In some of the representations of her water belches from her mouth, breasts, and armpits, and she wields the rattle of the thunderstorm.

Such data as we possess regarding the deity indicated by the letter K is not of a kind that would permit us to arrive at any very definite conclusions regarding him. He closely resembles B, and has even been confounded with him by some authorities. He is frequently represented on the walls of the temples of Copan and Palenque, so it follows that he must have been a divinity who ranked high in the galaxy of gods.

He has the same description of mask, with elongated snout, as B, but his hieroglyph differs very markedly from the symbol of that god, representing as it does an almost ape-like head with a peculiar foliation in the region of the forehead a constant feature in his pictures. From his position as lord of the calendar years which belong to the east, Professor Seler believes him to be Ah-Bolon Tzacab, "Lord of the Nine Generations."

In my view he is a variant of B. The two most famous deities among the Maya, Kukulkan, and Itzamna, were undoubtedly one and the same in origin and essence, although in later times they came to be regarded as rivals and as swaying the fortune of opposing cities, and I believe K represents Itzamna, as B is unquestionably Kukulkan. A deity of darksome hue appears in God L, known as "The Old Black God." In some of the pictures in the "Codex Dresden" his face is entirely black, but in the other manuscripts only the upper part of it is so painted.

From the insignia which accompany him I have been led to the provisional conclusion that he is in some manner connected with the synodical appearances of the planet Venus, which bulked largely in the Maya chronology as the basis of a time-count for the calendar. He is also the fire-maker, who kindles the new flame with the fire-drill on the recurrence of the time-cycle.

In God M we have an even duskier deity, a patron of the native porters or coolies, and, like them, well- nigh black through constant exposure to the tropical sun. He has, in fact, an appearance almost negroid, thick red lips, the lower drooping pendulously. He bears on his head a bale of merchandise secured by thick ropes.

Occasionally he is drawn with the skeleton-like frame of the death-god, and this, and the circumstance that he usually carries arms, inclines me to the belief that he is symbolical of the great risks run by the itinerant merchants of Mexico and Yucatan, who frequently acted as spies upon neighboring tribes or as the advance-guard of an invading army. He is, indeed, the god Ek Ahau, or Ek Chuah, "The Black Lord," a cruel and rapacious deity, whose general character reflects none too amiably upon the methods of Maya commercial activity.

God N, another aged divinity, is the god of the end of the year, and his head-dress contains the sign for the year of 360 days. O is the only other goddess of the group, and her picture does not appear elsewhere than in the "Madrid Codex." She is also depicted as advanced in years, and is usually represented as sitting at a loom. P, the last of the series, is easily to be recognized as the Maya frog-god, whose head-dress, like that of God N, contains the sign for the year.

It is then possible to identify with reasonable likelihood six out of these sixteen figures, to label them with the traditional names they bore, and to fix the nature and characteristics of some of them. We now come to those pictured representations of divinities who are not included in the alphabetical series of Schellhas.

The Bacabs are deities of the four points of the compass, and are represented in the Dresden manuscript, especially in the familiar pages 25 to 28, where they are coordinated with the signs for the compass points. The Maya of Yucatan believed that these Bacabs were four brothers whom the gods had placed at the four corners of the world to support the heavens and keep them from falling. Landa says that their collective names were Uayayab, "they by whom the year is poisoned," and prefaces to this the personal names Kan, Chac, Zac, and Ek, but these titles merely imply "yellow," "red," "white," and "black," and signify the colors associated with the south, east, north, and west respectively.

The Bacabs had also a funerary significance, and their heads in stone occasionally appear as the lids of "Canopic jars" found in Maya tombs. In the "Popol Vuh," the sacred book of the Maya-Quiche, these Bacabs are alluded to by the generic name of Balan, and are associated with the four winds.

Shooting stars are the burning stumps of gigantic cigars which they fling down from heaven. When it thunders and lightens they were said to be striking fire to light their cigars. The god Chac is sometimes alluded to as if he were a personification of the Bacabs collectively, and seems to be the same as Schellhas's GodB.

Zotz, the bat-god, appears to have been the deity of the Ah-Zotzil, or bat-folk, a tribe long settled in the vicinity of San Cristobal de Chiapas, as well as of another clan, part of the Kakchiquels of southern Guatemala. In the "Popal Vuh" the god of the Kakchiquel is called Zotziha Chimalcan, and after him the two royal lines of the Kakchiquel tribe were named. He is a god of caverns, and had a twofold form as well as a twofold name, which seems to signify "Bat's House-Serpent Shield."

Perhaps the name might be read "Serpent Shield (or pond) in the Place of Darkness," and may refer to these cenotes or subterranean wells which are so frequently encountered in Yucatan, because of the constant connection of the serpent with water by the Maya. In any case, Zotz appears to have been connected with a cult whose worship was carried on in caverns, like that of the Nagualists.

The Maya designated the twenty-day period Zotz, after this god, and his glyph is frequently encountered on the Copan reliefs. On one of the temples of Copan is a relief depicting a combat between this god and Kukulkan, perhaps an allegory of the strife between light and darkness.

In the Dresden manuscript a deity is represented whose face appears to have animal characteristics. His glyph contains an element which occurs in the glyph of a god with a deer's head also to be found in the Dresden manuscript and in the "Codex Tro-Cortesianus in a glyph denoting weaving or embroidery.

The goddess who acts as regent of the Second Period in the Dresden manuscript, does not seem to be met with elsewhere in the manuscripts, and is not mentioned in Schellhas's list. Seler believes her to represent the planet Venus. Her body is painted red, and on the front of the trunk are the vertebrae and ribs of a skeleton. The nose curves down like that of God B, but she has not the long, crooked teeth and the flourish on the bridge of the nose. A string of precious stones, hanging over in front from the head-dress, has attached to it by a bow the glyph of the planet Venus.

Seler also alludes to a deity who figures as regent of the Fourth Period in the Dresden manuscript. He says, "He is obviously a war-like divinity. A jaguar-skin is wrapped around his hips, and he wears on his breast a disk apparently bordered with jaguar-skin. As head-dress he wears the conventionalized head of a bird having a crest. An entire bird is worn as an ear-peg, with the head stuck toward the front through the much enlarged hole in the lobe of the ear. There is a serpent's head before his mouth (as a nose-peg?), and the head of a bird projects over his forehead. The face painting strikingly recalls that of the Mexican Tezcatlipoca. . .There is, in front, the element which in the hieroglyph of the jaguar is combined with the abbreviated jaguar head, and in other places is associated with the cardinal point east, probably denoting a color (red). It is not difficult to recognize the element kin, sun, at the right, and in the centre a head with a bleeding, empty eye-socket. All these are elements which imply that he is a war-god."

If we now look for any of these gods on the monuments of Central America or Yucatan, we shall find that little has been done to locate them there, or collate them in any way with the figures of the manuscripts. Indeed, this is a department of Maya archaeology which calls loudly for research.

Dr. Spinden writes sanely on this subject and on the methods of collating and recognizing deities in his excellent monograph on Maya art. He says, "Because of the natural exuberance of Maya art, identification, even of gods, is far from easy. Fewkes declares that in any attempt to classify the Maya deities the character of the head must be taken as the basis. This statement is true within certain limits, simply because characterization is more easily expressed in the head than elsewhere, especially when the figures are largely anthropomorphic. But in many cases the character and decoration of the body are also significant and should be examined."

He proceeds to compare certain sculptures with God B, whom he collates with a long-nosed manikin god, as found in sculptures at

Quirigua, and sees his surrogate, God K, on a vase in the American Museum of Natural History, the representation on which, however, might perhaps equally well apply to the bat-god. But there are clearer indications of his presence in details from Copan and Yaxchilan. God D, too, he finds in two sculptures at Yaxchilan, in the form of the earth-dragon.

"On Stela I, at that city," says Dr. Spinden, "there is a bust of a human being or of a god directly over the center of the planet strip that forms the body of the two-headed monster, and its resemblance to God D of the codices is evident at the first glance. The Roman nose, the open mouth with the lips drawn back, the wrinkles on the cheek, the peculiar tooth projecting outward, the ornamented eye and the flowing hair and beard are all features that occur in the Codices in connection with God D. The air of old age is admirably characterized."

Spinden, too, sees another manifestation of God D in the face-form of the glyph known to Mayologists as Kin, which represents a single day, and he adduces sculptures from Copan, Yaxchilan, Chichen-Itza, and Palenque to prove his contention. He finds, too, further representations of this god in a sculptured block from Copan and a detail from Piedras Negras, on a pottery flask from the Uloa Valley, as well as in the Atlantean figures that support the altar at Palenque.

He has seen, too, anthropomorphic figures of the bat-god at Copan, and has identified his glyph on the back of Stela D at that city. God A and his attributes appear in connection with many conceptions to be found on the monuments, especially at Chichen-Itza, Copan, Tikal, and Palenque, a distribution which bears witness to a far-flung worship of this divinity.

Regarding the maize-god, E, Spinden says: "On the monuments the representation of this god may be discerned in the youthful figure with a leafy head-dress. It occupies a secondary position on the monuments, but the characters are constant and are, moreover, consistent with those appearing on the figures in the Codices. On Stela H at Copan, several small human beings of this type . . . may be seen climbing round and over the interwoven bodies of serpents. At Quirigua the occurrence is similar . . . while at Tikal the head . . . thrusts itself out of the eye of a richly embellished serpent head, the upturned nose of which is shaped into the face of the Roman-nosed god (D)."

In all these drawings the determining feature is the bunches of circles enclosed in leaf-like objects that may represent the ear of maize or bursting seed-pods. In an interesting stucco decoration in the Palace at Palenque . . . are shown comparable circular details as well as maize-ears rather realistically drawn, while the god himself appears at the top of the design. Details which seem to represent ears of maize or bursting pods are recorded in a drawing by Waldeck of one of the now lost tablets of Palenque. The maize-ears in this instance seem to depend from the inverted head of the long-nosed god. The form of the maize-god in all these instances is distinctly human and in marked contrast to the other deities so far considered.

The beautiful sculpture from the facade of Temple 22 at Copan, which Maudslay calls a "singing girl," may represent the youthful maize-god. Other comparable figures from the same building are in the Peabody Museum. . . . The head-dress resembles that of this deity as given in the Codices. There is clear enough evidence that the faces and figures of the long-nosed god (B), the Roman-nosed god (D), and the death-god (A) were used to decorate the facades of temples in this city, and the usage may have included other deities as well.

Two sculptured stones from the terrace east of the Great Plaza at Copan doubtless bear representations of the maize-god. The face of God C has also been found on the Hieroglyphic Stairway at Copan, part of which is now in the Peabody Museum and in inscriptions at Palenque and Copan.

Gods F and H have so far not been clearly identified in the sculptures, nor have L, O, or P, as yet, been encountered on stela or temple wall. The penetrative work of Spinden, notwithstanding the great need of the further collation of the manuscript form, of the gods with those depicted on the monuments, not only in major form, as found, but in lesser detail and grotesquerie, is obvious.

Can we now relate these forms, pictured and sculptured, to what is known of Maya religious tradition, and try to gather not only a clearer notion of the identity of the deities in question, but some knowledge of their functions and worship? Unfortunately, the early contemporary notices of Maya religion are extraordinarily scanty. They consist almost entirely of the "Historia del Cielo y de la Tierra" of Pedro de Aguilar, the "Historia de Yucatan" of Fray Diego Lopez, the account, in Las Casas' "Historia de las Indias," of Francisco Hernandez, the "Relacion de las cosas de Yucatan" of Diego de Landa, and the "Constituciones Diocesianus" of Nunez de la Vega, as well as the "Documentos Ineditos," published at Madrid, and containing fugitive and sometimes anonymous notices of native beliefs and customs.

From these it is only a fragmentary account of the Maya pantheon which we can glean. The religion of the Maya seems to have possessed few divine figures of note, as Hernandez remarks, and he adds that the "principal lords" alone were acquainted with the history of the gods, their myths and allegories. The spirit of the religion appears to have been dualistic. We witness, indeed, a dualism almost as complete as that of ancient Persia the conflict between light and darkness. Opposing each other we behold on the one hand the deities of the sun, the gods of warmth and light, of civilization and the joy of life, and on the other the deities of darksome death, of night, gloom, and fear.

From these primal conceptions of light and darkness all the mythological forms of the Maya are evolved. When we catch the first recorded glimpses of Maya belief we recognize that at the period when it came under the purview of Europeans the gods of darkness were in the ascendant and a deep pessimism had spread over Maya thought and theology.

Its joyful side was subordinated to the worship of gloomy beings, the deities of death and hell, and if the cult of light was attended with such touching fidelity, it was because the benign agencies who were worshipped in connection with it had promised not to desert mankind altogether, but to return at some future indefinite period and resume their sway of radiance and peace.

The heavenly bodies had important representation in the Maya pantheon. In Yucatan the sun-god was known as Kinichahau (Lord of the Face of the Sun). He was identified with the Fire-bird, or arara, and was thus called Kinich-Kakmo (Fire-bird; lit. Sun-bird). He was also the presiding genius of the north. Sacrifices to him were made at midday, when it was believed that the deity descended in the shape of the arara or macaw.

Such ceremonies were especially performed in times of pestilence or destruction of the crops by locusts. But this god was probably much less prominent in the public mind than the greater solar deities, and his attributes were occasionally assigned to Itzamna. He is certainly God G.

Itzamna, one of the most important of the Maya deities, was a deity of moisture, the father of gods and men. In him was typified the decay and recurrence of life in nature. His name was derived from the words he was supposed to have given to men regarding himself: "Itz en caan, itz en muyal" ("I am the dew of the heaven; I am the dew of the clouds"). He was tutelar deity of the west.

Itzamna may indeed be regarded as the chief of the Maya pantheon. "He received," says Brinton, "the name Lakin chan, the Serpent of the East, under which he seems to have been popularly known. As light is synonymous with both life and knowledge, he was said to have been the creator of men, animals, and plants, and was the founder of the culture of the Mayas. He was the first priest of their religion, and invented writing and books; he gave the names to the various localities in Yucatan, and divided the land among the people; as a physician he was famous, knowing not only the magic herbs, but possessing the power of healing by touch, whence his name Kabil, 'the skilful hand,' under which he was worshipped in Chichen-Itza. For his wisdom he was spoken of as Yax coc ahmut, 'the royal or noble master of knowledge.' He was, indeed, the son of Hunab-Ku, the great and unseen divine spirit behind the pantheon of the Maya."

The centre of his cult was the city of Izamal, to which pilgrimage was made from all parts of Yucatan. As has been said, he is probably God K, although some students of the Codices identify him with God D.

Ekchuah was the god of travelers, to whom they burned copal. He is certainly God M. He is painted the color of cocoa, the merchant's staple of exchange.

There were quite a number of war-gods, and it is difficult to know which of them should be identified with God F of the Codices; whether Uac Lorn Chaam, "He whose teeth are six lances," worshipped at Merida, Ahulane "the Archer," depicted as holding an arrow, whose shrine was on the island of Cozumel, Pakoc, "the Frightener," or Hex Chun Chan, " The Dangerous One."

The last two were especially gods of the Itzaes of Yucatan. Kac-u-pacat, "Fiery Face," carried in battle a shield of fire, Ah Chuy Kak, "Fiery Destroyer," Ah Cun Can, "The Serpent Charmer," and Hun Pic Tok, "He of 8000 lances," were all divinities of war.

Now God F is pictured much more frequently in the "Codex Peresianus" than elsewhere and, as we have seen, that manuscript probably came from the district of Peten, immediately to the south of the Yucatec peninsula. We may then dismiss the idea that he is closely associated with the war-gods of Northern Yucatan, who were nothing if not distinctly tribal. In all probability he is a much older warrior deity of the people of the settled district of Peten.

It is, however, not a little strange that his body-paint closely resembles that of the Nahua war-god Uitzilopochtli. Xamanek, the North Star, has already been identified with God C, and A with Ahpuch, the death-god. D is evidently a lunar deity. But although we find a moon goddess in Maya myth, Ix-hunye, there seems to be no record of a male lunar-god.

God E, as has been said, is the maize-god, Yum Kaax, "Lord of Harvests." God H is rather puzzling. He is certainly a deity of serpentine character, but that is to be inferred from the serpent-skin mark upon his forehead. I believe him to be a variant or surrogate of Itzamna, one of whose minor names was Lakin Chan, "the Serpent of the East," by which he seems to have been popularly known.

All this goes to show that while we can safely identify several of the gods of Schellhas's list with the known figures of the Maya pantheon; others cannot be equated at present with any known Maya divine figure. A (Ahpuch), B (Kukulkan), C (Xamanek), E (Yum-Kaax), G (Kinich-ahau), K (Itzamna), and M (Ekchuah), can reasonably be regarded as identified with the names bracketed. The rest remain uncertain or unknown.

It is not that the Maya pantheon has not many other deities besides these embraced by the alphabetic gods of the manuscripts. The names of many other Maya gods are known to us, only we are either unaware of their outward appearance, or the circumstances of their descriptions do not tally with the pictorial forms of the gods in the three Maya manuscripts.

Of Ixtab, the goddess of suicides, we know that she was also a goddess of ropes and snares for wild animals, and therefore probably had a textile significance originally. She seems to be pictured in some of the manuscripts. Cum Ahau, "Lord of the Vase," or of the Rains, we may, perhaps, identify as a phase of Itzamna. Zuhuy Kak, "Virgin Fire," appears as a patroness of infants, and Zuhuy Dzip, is a species of Maya Diana, a divine huntress of the woods.

Ah Kak Nech was the deity of the domestic hearth, and Ah Ppua and Ah Dziz were divinities of fishermen. Lesser departmental deities and caste gods abounded. Acan was the god of intoxication, resembling the pulque gods of Mexico.

Ix Tub Tun, "She who spits out Precious Stones," was the goddess of workers in jade and amethyst, and bears a marked likeness to a Japanese goddess who similarly ejects precious stones. Cit Bolon Turn was a god of medi- cines, and Xoc Bitum a god of song.

The Maya, to their honor, had also a god of poetry, Ab Kin Xoc or Ppiz Hiu Tec, and Ix Chebel Yax was the first inventress of colored designs on woven stuffs. We labor, then, under the dual disability of a lack, almost unparalleled, of early descriptive sources and the impossibility in many cases of collating Maya divine figures as described in myth with the pictured and sculptured representatives of the pantheon.

This would seem to imply that Maya mythology, as we know it, belonged to a different age from the manuscripts. The sculptured representations of the gods, too, may represent a period apart from either. We can, by means of the dates which usually accompany them, fix approximately the period of the sculptured forms which, so far as Guatemala is concerned, are obviously older than the manuscripts or myths, dating roughly as they do from about A.D. 330 to 600.

It would then seem to be indicated that we should take as a basis these sculptured forms, conscientiously collect and collate both those of Guatemala and Yucatan, and fix their dates as far as possible, grouping them in chronological order. This task accomplished, a careful comparison of their forms should be made with those in the manuscripts, a process which should result in the approximate fixation of the dates of these paintings, and enlighten us more convincingly regarding their spheres of provenance. Then, with increased confidence, it might be possible to apply the mythic descriptions to this better charted and chronologically fixed picture-gallery of the Maya gods.

In some such system of examination and research, in the writer's estimate, resides the best hope for an increased knowledge of the Maya pantheon. Until further research of this nature has been given to the subject, it will, however, be wise to retain Schellhas's alphabetical nomenclature, which our present knowledge and data have by no means outgrown.

THE DEMON OF PLANET VENUS SPEARING A GODDESS

CHAPTER XII
THE MAGIC OF THE MAYA

By far the most striking passage in the literature dealing with the Maya which refers to magic is that to be found in the "Constituciones Diocesianos de Chiapas" of Nunez de la Vega, Bishop of Chiapas, relating to a book in the Quiche tongue, said to have been written by Votan or Quetzalcoatl, which the Bishop made use of in his work, but ultimately destroyed in his holocaust of native manuscripts at Heuheutlan in 1691. One, Ordonez de Aguilar, had, however, made a copy of it before its destruction, and incorporated it in his "Historia de Cielo" MS. In this work Votan declared himself "a snake," a descendant of Imos, of the line of Chan, of the race of Chivim.

Taking Aguilar's account along with that of Nunez de la Vega, as both rely upon the same authority, we find that Votan proceeded to America by divine command, his mission being to lay the foundation of civilization. With this object in view he departed from Valum Chivim, passing "the dwelling of the thirteen snakes," and arrived in Valum Votan, whence, with some members of his family, he set out to form a settlement, ascending the Usumacinta River and ultimately founding Palenque.

By reason of their peculiar dress the Tzendal Indians called them TzequitUs, or "men with shirts," but consented to amalgamate with them. Ordonez states that when Votan had established himself at Palenque he made several visits to his original home. On one of these he came to a tower which had been intended to reach the heavens, a project which had been brought to naught by the linguistic confusion of those who conceived it. Finally, he was permitted to reach "the rock of heaven" by a subterranean passage.

Returning to Palenque, he found that others of his race had arrived there, and with them he made a friendly pact. He built a temple by the Heuheutan River, known, from its subterranean chambers as "the House of Darkness," and here he deposited the national records under the charge of certain old men called tlapianes, or guardians, and an order of priestesses. Here also were kept a number of tapirs.

A quotation of the passage dealing with this temple may be made from Nunez de la Vega: "Votan is the third heathen in the calendar (that is the deity who is ascribed to the Third Division of the calendar), and in the little history written in the Indian language all the provinces and cities in which he tarried were mentioned; and to this day there is always a clan in the city of Teopisa that they call the Votans. It is also said that he is the lord of the hollow wooden instrument which they call tepanaguaste (that is, the Mexican drum or teponaztli); that he saw the great wall, namely, the Tower of Babel, which was built from earth to heaven at the bidding of his grand- father, Noah; and that he was the first man whom God sent to divide and apportion this country of India, and that there, where he saw the great wall, he gave to every nation its special language. It is related that he tarried in Huehueta (which is a city in Soconusco), and that there he placed a tapir and a great treasure in a slippery (damp, dark, subterranean) house, which he built by the breath of his nostrils, and he appointed a woman as chieftain, with tapianes (that is, Mexican tlapiani, "keepers") to guard her. This treasure consisted of jars, which were closed with covers of the same clay, and of a room in which the pictures of the ancient heathens who are in the calendar were engraved in stone, together with chalchiuites (which are small, heavy, green stones) and other superstitious images; and the chieftainess herself and the tapianes, her guardians, surrendered all these things, which were publicly burned in the market-place of Huehueta when we inspected the aforesaid province in 1691. All the Indians greatly revered this Votan, and in a certain province they call him 'heart of the cities' (Corazon de los pueblos)."

This account gives us a general impression of the arcane nature of Maya magic. It reveals that it was practiced by a separate caste and in secret, and that Quetzalcoatl or Kukulkan was its founder. Side by side with the official priesthood existed a class devoted to the study of sorcery, known as ah-cuyah and ah-tun, or ah-tzyacyah, with whom may be associated those called pulahoobs, or practices of divination.

According to Landa, a high priest of the Maya of Yucatan was called Abkin Mai, whose office was hereditary. We also find a class of priests known as the Chilan, or "tigers," who appear to have been chiefly devoted to oracular pursuits and studies. They announced the will of the gods, whose mouthpieces they were, and uttered prophecies.

Says Daniel Garrison Brinton in his pamphlet on "*The Books of Chilan Balam*," the Tiger Priesthood: "There are not wanting actual prophecies of a striking character. These were attributed to the ancient priests and to a date long preceding the advent of Christianity. Some of them have been printed in translations in the 'Historias' of Lizana and Cogolludo, and of some the originals were published by the late Abbe Brasseur de Bourbourg, in the second volume of the reports of the 'Mission Scientifique au Mexique et dans l Amerique Centrale.' Their authenticity has been met with considerable skepticism by Waitz and others, particularly as they seem to predict the arrival of the Christians from the East and the introduction of the worship of the cross.

"It appears to me that this incredulity is uncalled for. It is known that at the close of each of their larger divisions of time (the so-called 'katuns'), a 'chilan,' or inspired diviner, uttered a prediction of the character of the year or epoch which was about to begin. Like other would-be prophets, he had doubtless learned that it is wiser to predict evil than good, inasmuch as the probabilities of evil in this worried world of ours outweigh those of good; and when the evil comes his words are remembered to his credit, while, if, perchance, his gloomy forecasts are not realized no one will bear him a grudge that he has been at fault. The temper of this people was, moreover, gloomy, and it suited them to hear of threatened danger and destruction by foreign foes.

"Here is one of the prophecies in question: 'What time the sun shall brightest shine, Tearful will be the eyes of the king. Four ages yet shall be inscribed, and then shall come the holy priest, the holy god. With grief I speak what now I see. Watch well the road, ye dwellers in Itza. The master of the earth shall come to us. Thus prophesies Nahau Pech, the seer, in the days of the fourth age, at the time of its beginning.'"

Father Lizana has much to say regarding the oracles of the Maya city of Itzamal, in his tract on "*Our Lady of Itzamal*," published in 1663. He tells us that in the days of Maya paganism the numerous kus, or pyramids, which are to be found in Yucatan, were the seats of deities who spoke in frequent oracular utterance to the priests. Their horoscopes were cast. In Itzamal was an idol known as Itzmatul, "that which holds the substance of heaven," that is, the rain.

Itzmatul, or Itzamna, once a living king, when dead became an oracle, and people from far and near crowded to his pyramid to consult his spirit, chiefly about things to come. The dead were also frequently carried thence in the hope that they might be restored to life, and the sick that health might be bestowed upon them. For this particular purpose a second ku, or temple, was raised to Itzamna in his form of

Kab-ul, or "the Magic Hand," the hand which could, with a touch, bestow life. Here offerings of the richest kind were made.

Pilgrims came to the shrine by way of four roads set in the directions of the four winds, which extended to the extremities of the country. The god was supposed to descend upon his altar at midday, and the priests then acquainted the devotees with the answer he gave to their petitions.

These priests were the Ah-kin, or prophets. The astrological system of the Maya closely resembled that of the Mexicans, but was of much more ancient origin and had reached a higher level of development though it did not occupy so prominent a place in Maya ritual. Its significance and the duration of its tonalamatl, or "calendar," were identical with the Mexican, and its ritual "week" of thirteen days was divided into four quarters, each of which was under the auspices of a different quarter of the heavens, and a particular deity.

So far as augural purposes were concerned it had no connection with the calendar proper or the time-counts alluded to in the chapter on Maya civilization. Indeed, we are not here concerned with the question of time, but with that of Maya occult lore, so cannot enter into a discussion of the large question of Maya chronology.

THE MAYA DAY-SIGNS

From the account of Nunez de la Vega, as from that of Francisco Fernandez, it appears that each of the twenty days of the week was dedicated to a governing deity. They supply, however, no precise list of these, and it is due to the industry of Professor Paul Schellhas and Dr. Forstemann that we are enabled to furnish an approximation to such a list.

Day-sign 1. Kan (Maize). 2. Chiccan (Serpent) 3. Cimi (Death). 4. Manik (Deer?) 5. Laraat (planting?) 6. Muluc (cloud). 7. Oc (dog?) 8. Chuen (monkey) 9. Eb (grass) 10. Ben (reed) 11. Ix (jaguar) 12. Men (moan bird) 13. Cib (vulture). 14. Caban (earth). 15. Ezanab (knife) 16. Cauac (rain) 17. Ahau (god Ahau) 18. Imix (honey). 19. Ik (air). 20. Akbal (darkness) Presiding god GodE GodH God A GodF Grain-god (?) GodK Lightning-god GodC A goddess Chahalhuc (?) Jaguar-god God G (?) The vulture-being The Four Bacabs, or deities of the four quarters God I (?) Tortoise-god God D, or Ahau Honey-god God B (Kukulkan) GodL.

The means by which these signs, and these of the "months" were used for divinatory purposes were the same as in the case of the Mexican system, that is, the auspicious were weighed against the evil, and thus a balance was struck. We can now proceed to discuss the magical significance of the various periods of time, but here there is no need to treat of them as chronological units.

As we have seen, the Bacabs presided over the points of the compass. These were thought of as being beset by demons called Uayeyab, who were driven out by magical ceremonies. Great statues of stone representing the Bacabs were placed on the several roads converging on a village, and at the end of the year pottery figures of the fertility god were placed so as to influence them.

The priests, accompanied by the people, gathered together and offered incense to the idols of the Bacabs, sacrificing fowls in front of them, then they placed the image dedicated to the year on a litter and carried it to the house of the chief, where presents were placed before it, and sacrifices made to it by drawing blood from the ears. The statue was permitted to remain in position until the five unlucky days at the end of the year were over, when the Uayeyab was supposed to have been scared away and the new year to have begun auspiciously.

The four Bacabs had each a year in which they were thus chosen as guardians and were opposed by different Uayeyabs, which took the names of the four different colours of the compass. As regards the significance of the months of the Maya year and their days, Pop, the first month, was regarded with much solemnity.

It was essentially a time of purification, when houses were cleaned and ashpits emptied, nor must one take condiments with his food during its course. During the month Uo the priests, mediciners, and sorcerers held a festival for the hunters and fishers, invoking the aid of Itzamna, and examining in their sacred books the omens for the year.

They accordingly took precautions against evil happenings. In the month Zip the sorcerers gathered in their quarters along with their wives for the worship of the Gods of Medicine, Itzamna, Cit-Bolan-Tun, and Ahau-Chamahez, and the Goddess of Medicine, Ixchak, and danced symbolical and magical dances.

In the month Yax the prognostications of the Bacabs were made. In the month known as Mac a strange magical allegory was celebrated. Wild animals were assembled in the court of the temple of the Rain-gods, and a priest carrying a vase of water presided. He set fire to a heap of dry wood. He then took the hearts from the captive wild beasts and cast them into the flames, and as regards such animals as were not available, their hearts were modeled in incense gum and thrown into the blaze. Then he extinguished the embers of the flame with the water he carried. The intention was to secure an abundance of water for the grain during the year, and the magical significance of the rite was the metamorphosis of blood into rain, the fierce blood of the forest animals being regarded as more intense in its action than any other.

From these notices it is clear that few of the mensual festivals had a magical significance. Of the astrological qualities of the several days of the year or months we are ignorant, but it is most probable that in this respect they were similar in their influence to those in the Aztec tonalamatl.

The Venus period was also regarded by the Maya as a season of magical influence. In the Dresden manuscript we see a god casting his spear at the "various classes of people," as we are told was the case in Mexico. These are the same as in the Aztec MSS., but the Maya deities who cast the missiles differ from the Aztec.

In the first place it is God K, in the second the God Chac, in the third God E, whilst the remaining two are obscure; but Seler believes these figures to represent planetary conjunctions having a special astrological and magical significance. He says: "It is hardly possible to see anything else in these figures struck by the spear than augural speculations regarding the influence of the light from the planet, suggested by the initial signs of the periods. We shall have to accept this as true, but not only for the representations of the Borgian Codex group (Mexican), but also for the pictorial representations and the hieroglyphic text of the Dresden manuscript" (Maya).

Augury was also influenced by the Bacabs, or deities of the four quarters. These were called Kan, Muluc, Ix, and Cauac, and represented the east, north, west, and south respectively. Their symbolic colours were yellow, white, black, and red. They had an influence upon certain years in the calendar.

The "astrology" of the Maya is unfortunately most obscure owing to the paucity of the data concerning it and the necessity for much further study of the glyphs and calendar-system, which is by no means so far advanced as that of the Mexican tonalamatl. The superstitions of the Maya are likewise difficult to come at.

During the five days at the end of the year people in Mexico were careful not to fall asleep during the day, nor to quarrel or trip in walking, because they believed that what they then did "they would continue to do for evermore."

We find the same notion in Yucatan. On these days men left the house as seldom as possible, did not wash or comb themselves, and took special care not to undertake any menial or difficult task, doubtless because they were convinced that they would be forced to do this kind of work throughout the whole ensuing year.

The Mexicans were more passive in regard to these days, inasmuch as they merely took care to avoid conjuring up mischief for the coming year, while the Maya did things more thoroughly, as we have seen when dealing with the Uayayeb festival. Maya demonology is obscure. A sinister figure, the prince of the Maya legions of darkness, is the bat-god, Zotzilaha Chimalman, who dwelt in the "House of Bats," a gruesome cavern on the way to the abodes of darkness and death. He is undoubtedly a relic of cave- worship pure and simple.

"The Maya," says an old chronicler, "have an immoderate fear of death, and they seem to have given it a figure peculiarly repulsive."

We shall find this deity alluded to in the "Popol Vuh," under the name Camazotz, in close proximity to the Lords of Death and Hell, attempting to bar the journey of the hero-gods across these dreary realms. He is frequently met with on the Copan reliefs, and a Maya clan, the Ah-zotzils, were called by his name.

They were of Kakchiquel origin, and he was probably their totem. Indeed, more than one Maya tribe was called after him, and he was evidently a "nagual" or tribal animal-sorcerer and guardian. The fact that he is called "this Xibalba" in the "Popol Vuh" shows that he is of plutonic nature, a deity of the Underworld. He is also the vampire-beast of darkness that combats the sun-god and swallows his light.

The dog, pek, was the symbol of the death-god and the bearer of the lightning. But he has also a stellar significance, and probably represents some star or constellation as at times he is dotted with spots to represent stars. We see him also playing on the medicine drum.

Another horrible figure associated with the death-god is the moan bird, a noxious cloud- spirit, represented in the manuscripts by a bird of the falcon species. We can glean much regarding the magical propensities of the Maya priesthood from a study of the customs of the related Zapotec priests of southern Mexico, whose religion was of Maya origin.

Their high priests were known as Uija-tao, or "great seer," and their chief function was evidently to consult the gods in important matters relating either to the community or to individuals. We have already seen in Burgoa's account of Mitla how the high priest conferred with the deities on the occasion of a human sacrifice, placing himself in an ecstatic state, and how they were regarded as the living images of Quetzalcoatl or Kukulkan.

That they employed stones for scrying or visionary purposes is clear from the following passage from Seler's essay on "*The Deities and Religious Conceptions of the Zapotecs.*" "As Yoopaa, or Mictlan, was the holy city of the Zapotecs, so Nuundecu, or Achiotlan, was the holy city of the Mixtecs, where the high priest had his abode and where there was a far-famed oracle, which indeed King Motecuhzoma is said to have consulted when he was disturbed by the news of the landing of Cortes. The chief sanctuary was situated on the highest peak of a mountain. Here, as Father Burgoa relates, there was among other altars one of an idol which they called the heart of the place or of the country and which received great honor.

"The material was of marvelous value, for it was an emerald of the size of a thick pepper pod (capsicum), upon which a small bird was engraved with the greatest skill, and, with the same skill, a small serpent coiled ready to strike. The stone was so transparent that it shone from its interior with the brightness of a candle flame. It was a very old jewel, and there is no tradition extant concerning the origin of its veneration and worship."

The first missionary of Achiotlan, Fray Benito, afterward visited this place of worship and succeeded in persuading the Indians to surrender the idol to him. He had the stone ground up, although a Spaniard offered three thousand ducats for it, stirred the powder in water, and poured it upon the earth and trod upon it in order at the same time to destroy the heathen abomination entirely and to demonstrate in the sight of all the impotence of the idol.

Burgoa says, writing of an oracle in the Laguna de San Dionisio near Tehuantepec, that on an island there "was a deep and extensive cave, where the Zapotecs had one of their most important and most revered idols, and they called it 'soul and heart of the kingdom' (Alma y Corazon del Reyno), because these barbarians were persuaded that this fabulous deity was Atlas, upon whom the land rested and who bore it on his shoulders, and when he moved his shoulders the earth was shaken with unwonted tremblings; and from his favor came the victories which they won and the fruitful years which yielded them the means of living."

There was an oracle connected also with this temple, and the last king of Tehuantepec, Cocijo-Pij, is said to have received here from the god the information that the rule of the Mexicans was at an end and that it was not possible to withstand the Spaniards. When the baptized king was later seized and imprisoned on account of his falling back into idolatry the vicar of Tehuantepec, Fray Bernardo de Santa Maria, sought out the island, forced his way into the cave, and found there a large quadrangular chamber, carefully swept, with altar-like structures around on the sides, and on them many incense vessels, rich and costly offerings of valuable materials, gorgeous feathers, and disks and necklaces of gold, most of them sprinkled with freshly drawn blood.

From what has gone before, it is clear that our knowledge of Maya magic and all that it implies is certainly not on a level with that relating to Mexican occult science. This owes chiefly to the paucity of the records left us by the Spanish priesthood, and by their endeavors to stamp out the memory of all native culture and thought. We must also bear in mind that Maya origins and the ancient history of the country, which greatly pre-dates that of Mexico, have not as yet been thoroughly explored.

Yet a general conclusion may be reached. In all likelihood the arcane knowledge of the Maya resembled that of Mexico, which indeed had its roots in Maya practice, and like it was founded on an alimentary basis. The food supply was regarded in Guatemala and Yucatan as the direct gift of the gods, maize, honey, and all food products being regarded as the donations of deities.

HUMAN SACRIFICE AND BLOOD

If we do not find human sacrifice among the Maya so rampant as in Mexico it is simply because the practice in the more southern sphere remained, as in early Mexico, on a lesser scale owing to the non-adoption by the Maya of the awful conclusion arrived at by the Aztecs that the more blood shed the more rain would be likely to descend. There is good evidence, too, that at a certain period in their history the Maya, in some instances at least, substituted human sacrifice by the use of paste images of human beings, little cakes of maize paste made in the shapes of distorted dwarfs.

The dwarf, we know, was in Mexico an especial sacrifice to the rain-gods, probably because he was thought to resemble the Tlaloque, or small gods who poured down the rain. The more dwarfs dispatched to help them in this task, the more rain, argued the Mexicans. This substitution seems to have been general among the Maya, and to have supplanted human sacrifice to a great extent. But the gods who sent the people food must them-selves be kept in life, and for this purpose the

Maya appear to have employed magical formulse rather than sacrificial means.

They certainly gave blood drawn from the tongue and thighs, as some of their wall-carvings show, and this substitution of the part for the whole exhibits a higher degree of civilized thought than that obtaining in Mexico. But this was not all. Their festivals, from what we know of them, seem to have resembled the external shows of the Egyptian Mysteries in enacting the myths of the gods of growth, and thus they helped by sympathetic magic to induce the gods themselves to enact the drama of growth with benefit to humanity. In their religion the deities of fruitfulness played a most important part, and are adorned with symbols relating to agriculture.

Indeed, it would seem that the elements current in their hieroglyphic script were borrowed from agricultural implements. Maya religion may, indeed, be summed up in the expression "sun-worship."

In an illuminating passage Dr. Haebler writes: "The varied representations of the gods in the monuments and in manuscripts were certainly to some extent only different forms of one and the same divine power. The missionaries were able to describe this consciousness of an underlying unity in the case of the god Hunabku, who was invisible and supreme; naturally their zealous orthodoxy saw here some fragmentary knowledge of the one God.

"Hunabku does not appear very prominently in the Maya worship or mythology; of this the sun is undoubtedly the central point. Kukulcan and Guku-matz probably in his essence Itzamna also are only variant names, originating in difference of race, for the power of the sun that warms, lights and pours blessings upon the earth. As the sun rises in the east out of the sea, so the corresponding divinity of the traditions comes over the water from the east to the Maya, and is the bringer of all good things, of all blessings to body and soul, of fruitfulness and learning.

"In the last character the divinity is fully incarnated. He appears as an aged greybeard in white flowing robes; as Votan he divides the land among the peoples and gives the settlements their names; as Kabil, the Red Hand, he discovers writing, teaches the art of building, and arranges the marvelous perfection of the calendar.

"This part of the myth has undoubtedly a historical connection with the sun-myth, the real center of all these religious conceptions, and is further evidence of the powers of the priesthood and of the fact that their influence was exercised to advance the progress of civilization. Fully realistic is a conception of that particular deity which is represented in the Maya art by the widely prevailing symbol of the feathered snake. This is also a branch of the sun-worship.

"In the tropical districts for a great part of the year the sun each day, at noon, draws up the clouds around himself; hence, with lightning and thunder, the symbols of power, comes down the fruitful rain in thunderstorms upon the thirsty land. Thus the feathered snake, perhaps even a symbol of the thunder, appears among the Maya, on the highland of Central America, among the Pueblo Indians, and also among some Indian races of the North American lowland. It represents the warm fruitful power of the heavens, which is invariably personified in the chief luminary, the sun. The symbols of the snake and of Quetzal, the sacred bird with highly colored plumage, are attributes of more than one Maya divinity."

Under different shapes in the Tzendal district, in Yucatan to a large extent, and particularly in Chichen-Itza, they have so colored the religious and the artistic conceptions of the Maya that we meet with traces of this symbolism in almost every monument and every decoration. The dualism of the Maya Olympus also originates in a mythological interpretation of natural phenomena.

The representatives of the sun light and life are opposed to those of the night darkness and death; both have nearly equal powers and are in continual conflict for the lordship of the earth and of mankind. Moreover, the good gods have been obliged to abandon man after expending all their benefits upon him, and have made him promise of a future return, to support him in the struggle, and to assure him of victory at the last.

Around these central mythological conceptions, which in different forms are practically common property among most early peoples, are grouped in the case of the Maya, a large number of individual characteristics, each diversely developed. Not only was human life subject to the power of the gods in a large and general way, since the gods had created and formed it, but also religion or, to be more exact, the Maya priesthood had contrived a special system whereby a man's life was ostensibly under the permanent influence of the gods, even in the most unimportant trifles.

Upon this subject the quarters of the heavens and the constellations were of decisive importance; careful and keen observation, lasting apparently over a great period of time, had put the Maya priesthood in possession of an astronomical knowledge to which no other people upon a corresponding plane of civilization has ever attained. This is, of course, reflected in the Solar Calendar and the Maya tonalamatl.

The solar year was considered in relation to all other annual calculations, and on it the priestly caste established a code of astronomical laws. The ritual year of twenty weeks, each of thirteen days, was of equal importance.

Here the four quarters of the heavens played an important part, since to each of them a quarter of the ritual year belonged. But in all this diversity the consciousness of a higher unity clearly existed; evidence for this is the special symbol of the four quarters of the heavens the cross which the Spaniards were highly astonished to find everywhere in the Maya temples as an object of particular veneration. Moreover, an influence upon the motions of the earth was certainly attributed to the morning and evening stars and to the Pleiades. Perhaps also the periods of revolution for Venus, Mercury, and Mars were approximately known and employed in calculation.

The knowledge of these minute astronomical calculations was the exclusive possession of the highest priesthood, though at the same time they exercised a certain influence upon the whole national life. Upon these calculations the priests arranged the worship of the gods.

The principal Maya manuscripts which have escaped the ravages of time are the Codices in the libraries of Dresden, Paris, and Madrid. These are known as the "Codex Perezianus," preserved in the Bibliotheque Nationale at Paris, the "Dresden Codex," long regarded as an Aztec manuscript, and the "Troano Codex," so called from one of its owners, Senor Tro y Ortolano, found at Madrid in 1865.

These manuscripts deal principally with Maya mythology, but as they cannot be deciphered with any degree of accuracy, they do not greatly assist our knowledge of the subject. As has been said, these manuscripts have mostly an astrological significance, but little if anything can be gleaned from them which might be described as of the nature of magic proper.

"Those who would follow Forstemann's (and my own) views in understanding the codices," says Dr. Brinton, "must accustom themselves to look upon the animals, plants, objects, and transactions they depict as largely symbolical, representing the movements of the celestial bodies, the changes of the seasons, the meteorological variations, the revolutions of the sun, moon, and planets, and the like; just as in the ancient zodiacs of the Old World we find similar uncouth animals and impossible collocations of images presented. The great snakes which stretch across the pages of the codices mean time; the torches in the hands of figures, often one downward and one upward, indicate the rising and the setting of constellations ; the tortoise and the snail mark the solstices; the mummied bodies, the disappearance from the sky at certain seasons of certain stars, etc. A higher, a more pregnant, and, I believe, the only correct meaning is thus awarded to these strange memorials."

CHAPTER XIII
MYSTICAL BOOKS OF THE MAYA

The Maya manuscripts themselves afford us little light in the philosophy or practice of the arcane sciences, except as regards as- trology and the tonalamatl. It is rather from those books written by Christianized natives that we glean such knowledge as we possess of the spirit of Maya sorcery.

Unhappily these books, although published and translated into English in some cases, are now scarce and difficult to come by. The writer published in 1908 a small popular pamphlet dealing with the most important, "The Popol Vuh," and since that date several good English translations of this have appeared.

The Abbe Brasseur de Bourbourg had many years before translated it into French, and Daniel Garrison Brinton had in a similar manner dealt with the Book of the Cakchiquels and the Books of Chilan Balam. But Americanists as well as students of arcane knowledge still await the publication of a full-dress work dealing with these intensely interesting manifestations of the Indian mind.

None of the scanty native records of America which pre-date the discovery holds for us an importance so great, both from the mythological and historical viewpoints, as does the mysterious "Popol Vuh," the long-lost and curiously recovered sacred book of the civilized Maya-Quiche people of Guatemaa. The Book of the Cakchiquels and the Books of Chilan Balam are both of moment and great interest because of the historical data with which they provide the student of the Central American past. But neither contains a tithe of the rich mythological information treasured up in the "Popol Vuh."

The pity is that its mythology has not a very direct bearing upon that of the Maya proper as we know it from the manuscript paintings and sculpture of the Maya people of Yucatan, probably because it was written at a different period from the Maya heyday. In all likelihood it is more venerable, but precise criteria are lacking. But it is certainly supplementary to Maya belief, it casts a flood of light on the nature and actions of several gods of the Maya and Mexicans, sometimes under different or slightly altered names, and, above all, it gives us by far the clearest picture of Central American cosmogony and theology which we possess.

Whether it has been tampered with, sophisticated by late copyists, is a problem almost as difficult of solution as that of the alteration of the New Testament, but such indications of this as seem to exist can scarcely be dealt with faithfully in view of our slight knowledge of the whole question. The text we possess, the recovery of which forms one of the most romantic episodes in the history of American bibliography, was written by a Christianized native of Guatemala some time in the seventeenth century, and was copied in the Quiche language, in which it was originally written, by a monk of the Order of Predicadores, one Francisco Ximenes, who also added a Spanish translation.

The Abbe Brasseur de Bourbourg, a profound student of American archaeology and languages (whose interpretations of the Mexican myths are as worthless as the priceless materials he unearthed are valuable), deplored in a letter to the Due de Valmy, the supposed loss of the "Popol Vuh," which he was aware had been made use of early in the nineteenth century by a certain Don Felix Cabrera. Dr. C. Scherzer, an Austrian scholar, thus made aware of its value, paid a visit to the Republic of Guatemala in 1854 or 1855, and was successful in tracing the missing manuscript in the library of the University of San Carlos in the city of Guatemala.

It was afterwards ascertained that its translator, Ximenes, had deposited it in the library of his convent at Chichicastenango, whence it passed o the San Carlos library in 1830. Scherzer at once made a copy of the Spanish translation of the manuscript, which he published at Vienna in 1856 under the title of "Las Historias del origen de los Indios de Guatemala, par el R. P. F. Francisco Ximenes."

The Abbe Brasseur also took a copy of the original, which he published at Paris in 1861, with the title, "Vuh Popol: Le Livre Sacre de Quiches, et les Mythes de PAntiquite Americaine." In this work the Quiche original and the Abbe's French translation are set forth side by side. Unfortunately the Spanish and the French translations leave much to be desired so far as their accuracy is concerned, and they are rendered of little use by reason of the misleading notes which accompany them.

The late Dr. Edward Seler of Berlin was, prior to his death, engaged on a translation from the Quiche, but it appears to have been left unpublished. The name "Popol Vuh" signifies "Record of the Community," and its literal translation is "Book of the Mat," from the Quiche words "pop" or "popol," a mat or rug of woven rushes or bark on which the entire family sat, and "vuh" or "uuh," paper or book, from "uoch," to write.

THE MYSTERY OF THE POPOL VUH

The "Popol Vuh" is an example of a world-wide type of annals of which the first portion is pure mythology, which gradually shades off into pure history, evolving from the hero-myths of saga to the recital of the deeds of authentic personages. It may, in fact, be classed with the Heimskringla of Snorre, the Danish History of Saxo-Grammaticus, the Chinese History in the "Five Books," and the Japanese "Nihongi."

The language in which the "Popol Vuh" was written was, as has been said, the Quiche, a dialect of the great Maya-Quiche tongue spoken at the time of the Conquest from the borders of Mexico on the north to those of the present State of Nicaragua on the south. But whereas the Maya was spoken in Yucatan proper, and the State of Chiapas, the Quiche was the tongue of the peoples of that part of Central America now occupied by the States of Guatemala, Honduras, and San Salvador, where it is still used by the natives. It is totally different from the Nahuatl, the language of the peoples of Mexico; both as regards its origin and structure, and its affinities with other American tongues are even less distinct than those between the Slavonic and Teutonic groups.

Of this tongue the "Popol Vuh" is practically the only monument; at all events the only work by a native of the district in which it was used. At the period of their discovery, subsequent to the conquest of Mexico, the Quiche people of Guatemala had lost much of that culture, which was characteristic of the Maya race, the builders of the great stone cities of Guatemala and Yucatan. They were broken up into petty states and confederacies not unlike those of Biblical Palestine; yet seem to have retained the art of writing in hieroglyphs.

Whether or not the "Popol Vuh" was first written in their own script it is impossible to say, but the probability is that the record of it was kept mnemonically, or memorized by the priestly class, one of whose number reduced it to writing in European characters at a later date. In- deed, it seems unlikely that it was written down at all until penned in the sixteenth century by the Christianized native whose manuscript was found by Scherzer, and who, knowing most of it by rote, was doubtless inspired to preserve it much as Ixtlilxochit in Mexico set down the history and traditions of his race from patriotic motives.

The "Popol Vuh" is divided into four books, the first three of which are almost entirely mythological in their significance. The first book opens with an account of the Creation. At the beginning was only the Creator and Former, and those whom he engendered were Hun-Ahpu-Vuch, the hunter with the blowpipe; Hun-Ahpu-Utiu, the blow-pipe hunter, the coyote; Zaki-nima-Tzyiz, the white hunter, and the Lord, the serpent covered with feathers, the heart of the lakes of the sea.

There were also the father and mother gods, Xpiyacac and Xmucane. Concerning the first three we can only infer that they were among the numerous hunting-gods of the Maya-Quiche, who resembled the Maya archer-god Ahulane, whose shrine was situated on the island of Cozumel off the coast of Yucatan. "The serpent covered with feathers" is obviously Kukulkan or Quetzalcoatl, the Feathered Serpent of Yucatec and Mexican mythology, while the parental deities seem to be the same with the Mexican Cipactonal and Oxomoco, who may be described as the Adam and Eve of the human race, its first semi-divine progenitors.

Over the earth brooded the Creator and Former, the Mother, the Father, and the life-giver of all who breathe and have existence both in heaven, earth, or in the waters. All was silent, tranquil and without motion beneath the immensity of the heavens. All was without form and void. Here the Creator seems to be identified with the Feathered Serpent, and a little further on he takes plural form, like the Elohim, of Genesis. He is now "these covered with green and blue, who have the name of Gucumatz."

Gucumatz is merely the Quiche name of Kukulkan or Quetzalcoatl, but whether he was actually one and the same with the Creator we are left in doubt, as we are now told that he held converse with "the Dominator." The passage is confusing, and we are left with the impression that there were at least two deities of the Gucumatz type. They took counsel, and the dawn appeared. Trees and herbs sprouted. Then arose the Heart of the Heavens, Hurakan, the wind-god, from whom the hurricane takes its name, who is known to be the same as the Mexican Tezcatlipoca, the god of wind and fate.

Animals now appeared and birds great and small. But as yet man was not. To supply the deficiency the divine beings resolved to create manikins carved out of wood. But these soon incurred the displeasure of the gods, who, irritated by their lack of reverence, resolved to destroy them. Then by the will of Hurakan, the Heart of Heaven, the waters were swollen, and a great flood came upon the manikins of wood. They were drowned and a thick resin fell from heaven. The bird Xecotcovach tore out their eyes; the bird Camulatz cut off their heads; the bird Cotzbalam devoured their flesh; the bird Tecumbalam broke their bones and sinews and ground them into powder.

Because they had not thought on Hurakan, therefore the face of the earth grew dark, and a pouring rain commenced, raining by day and by night. Then all sorts of beings, great and small, gathered together to abuse the men to their faces.

The very household utensils and animals jeered at them, their mill-stones, their plates, their cups, their dogs, their hens. Said the dogs and hens, "Very badly have you treated us, and you have bitten us. Now we bite you in turn." Said the mill-stones, "Very much were we tormented by you, and daily, daily, night and day, it was squeak, screech, screech, for your sake. Now you shall feel our strength, and we will grind your flesh and make meal of your bodies."

And the dogs upbraided the manikins because they had not been fed, and tore the unhappy images with their teeth. And the cups and dishes said, "Pain and misery you gave us, smoking our tops and sides, cooking us over the fire, burning and hurting us as if we had no feeling. Now it is your turn, and you shall burn."

Then ran the manikins hither and thither in despair. They climbed to the roofs of the houses, but the houses crumbled under their feet; they tried to mount to the tops of the trees, but the trees hurled them from them; they sought refuge in the caverns, but the caverns closed before them.

Thus was accomplished the ruin of this race, destined to be overthrown. And it is said that their posterity are the little monkeys who live in the woods. There was now left on the earth only the race of giants, whose king and progenitor was Vukub-Cakix, a being full of pride.

The name signifies "Seven-times-the-color-of-fire," and seems to have had allusion to the emerald teeth and silver eyes, or golden and silver body of the monster. Vukub-Cakix boasted that his brilliance rendered the presence of the sun and the moon superfluous, and this egotism so disgusted the gods that they resolved upon his destruction.

He seems indeed to have been, like the Babylonian, Tiawath, the personification of earth or chaos, or the material as opposed to the spiritual, and, as the gods of the Babylonians sent Bel to destroy her, the creators of the Quiches decided to send emissaries to earth to slay the unruly titan. So the twin hero-gods, Hun-Ahpu and Xbalanque, were dispatched to the terrestrial sphere to chasten his arrogance. They shot at him with their blow-pipes and wounded him in the mouth, although he succeeded in wrenching off Hun-Ahpu's arm.

He then proceeded to his dwelling, where he was met and anxiously interrogated by his spouse Chimalmat. Tortured by the pain in his teeth and jaw, he, in an access of spite, hung Hun-Ahpu's arm over a blazing fire, and then threw himself down to bemoan his injuries, consoling himself, however, with the idea that he had adequately avenged himself upon the interlopers who had dared to disturb his peace.

But Hun-Ahpu and Xbalanque were in no mind that he should escape so easily, and the recovery of Hun-Ahpu's arm must be made at all hazards. With this end in view they consulted two venerable beings in whom we readily recognize the father-mother divinities, Xpiyacoc and Xmucane, disguised for the nonce as sorcerers.

These personages accompanied Hun-Ahpu and Xbalanque to the abode of Vukub-Cakix, whom they found in a state of intense agony. They persuaded him to be operated upon in order to relieve his sufferings, and for his glittering teeth they substituted grains of maize. Next they removed his eyes of emerald, upon which his death speedily followed, as did that of his wife Chimalmat.

Hun-Ahpu's arm was recovered, re-affixed to his shoulder, and all ended satisfactorily for the hero-gods. The sons of the giant had yet to be accounted for, however. These were Zipacna, the earth-heaper, and Cabrakan, the earthquake. Four hundred youths (the stars) beguiled Zipacna into carrying immense tree-trunks wherewith to build a house, and when he entered the foundation-ditch of the structure they overwhelmed him with timber.

They built the house over his body, but rising in his giant might he shattered it, and slew them all. But, his strength weakened by a poisoned crab, the divine brothers succeeded in dispatching him by casting a mountain upon him. In a similar manner they accounted for Cabrakan.

The Second Book takes for its first theme the birth and parentage of Hun-Ahpu and Xbalanque, and the scribe intimates that a mysterious veil enshrouds their origin. Their respective fathers were Hunhun-Ahpu, the hunter with the blow-pipe, and Vukub-Hunahpu, sons of Xpiyacoc and Xmucane.

Hunhun-Ahpu had by a wife Xbakiyalo, two sons, Hunbatz and Hunchouen, men full of wisdom and artistic genius. All of them were addicted to the recreation of dicing and playing at ball, and a spectator of their pastimes was Voc, the messenger of Hurakan. Xbaki-yalo having died, Hunhun-Ahpu and Vukub-Hunah-pu, leaving the former's sons behind, played a game of ball, which in its progress took them into the vicinity of the realm of Xibalba (the Underworld). This reached the ears of the monarchs of that place, Hun- Came and Vukub-Came, who, after consulting their counselors, challenged the strangers to a game of ball, with the object of defeating and disgracing them.

For this purpose they dispatched four messengers in the shape of owls. The brothers accepted the challenge, after a touching farewell with their mother Xmucane, and their sons and nephews, and followed the feathered heralds down the steep incline to Xibalba from the playground at Ninxor Carchah.

After an ominous crossing over a river of blood they came to the residence of the kings of Xibalba, where they underwent the mortification of mistaking two wooden figures for the monarchs. Invited to sit on the seat of honor, they discovered it to be a red- hot stone, and the contortions which resulted from their successful trick caused unbounded merriment among the Xibalbans. Then they were thrust into the House of Gloom, where they were sacrificed and buried.

The head of Hunhun-Ahpu was, however, suspended from a tree, which speedily became covered with gourds, from which it was almost impossible to distinguish the bloody trophy. All in Xibalba were forbidden the fruit of that tree. But one person in Xibalba had resolved to disobey the mandate. This was the virgin princess Xquiq (Blood), the daughter of Cuchumaquiq, who went unattended to the spot.

Standing under the branches gazing at the fruit, the maiden stretched out her hand, and the head of Hunhun-Ahpu spat into the palm. The spittle caused her to conceive, and she returned home, being assured by the head of the hero- god that no harm should result to her. This thing was done by order of Hurakan, the Heart of Heaven.

In six months' time her father became aware of her condition, and despite her protestations the royal messengers of Xibalba, the owls, received orders to kill her and return with her heart in a vase. She, however, escaped by bribing the owls with splendid promises for the future to spare her and substitute for her heart the coagulated sap of the blood-wart.

In her extremity Xquiq went for protection to the home of Xmucane, who now looked after the young Hunbatz and Hunchouen.

Xmucane would not at first believe her tale. But Xquiq appealed to the gods, and performed a miracle by gathering a basket of maize where no maize grew, and thus gained her confidence.

Shortly afterwards Xquiq became the mother of twin boys, the heroes of the First Book, Hun-Ahpu, and Xbalanque. These did not find favour in the eyes of Xmucane, their grandmother, who chased them out of doors. They became hunters, but were ill-treated by their uncles Hunbatz and Hunchouen, whom they transformed into apes. They cleared a maize plantation by the aid of magical tools and otherwise distinguished themselves thaumaturgically. But the rulers of the Underworld heard them at play and resolved to treat them as they had done their father and uncle.

Full of confidence, however, the young men accepted the challenge of the Xibalbans to a game of ball. But they sent an animal called Xan as avant-courier with orders to prick all the Xibalbans with a hair from Hun-Ahpu's leg, thus discovering those of the dwellers in the Underworld who were made of wood those whom their fathers had unwittingly bowed to as men and also learning the names of the others by their inquiries and explanations when pricked.

Thus they did not salute the manikins on their arrival at the Xibalban court, nor did they sit upon the red-hot stone. They even passed scatheless through the first ordeal of the "House of Gloom."

The Xibalbans were furious, and their wrath was by no means allayed when they found themselves beaten at the game of ball to which they had challenged the brothers. Then Hun-Came and Vukub-Came ordered the twins to bring them four bouquets of flowers, asking the guards of the royal gardens to watch most carefully, and committed Hun-Ahpu and Xbalanque to the "House of Lances" the second ordeal where the lancers were directed to kill them.

The brothers, however, had at their beck and call a swarm of ants, which entered the royal gardens on the first errand, and they succeeded in bribing the lancers. The Xibalbans, white with fury, ordered that the owls, the guardians of the gardens, should have their beaks split, and otherwise showed their anger at their third defeat.

Then came the third ordeal in the "House of Tigers" and the "House of Fire" without injury. But at the sixth ordeal misfortune overtook them in the "House of Bats," Hun-Ahpu's head being cut off by Camazotz, "Ruler of Bats."

The head was, however, replaced by a tortoise which chanced to crawl past at that moment and Hun-Ahpu was restored to life. Later the brothers performed other marvels, and, having conquered the Princes of Xibalba, proceeded to punish them, forbidding them the game of ball and reducing their lordship to government over the beasts of the forest only.

The passage probably refers to a myth of the harrying of Hades, and the defeat of a group of older deities by a new and younger pantheon, similar to the replacement of Saturn by Jupiter, the elder gods becoming "demons." With the object of proving their immortal nature to their adversaries, Hun-Ahpu and Xbalanque, first arranging for their resurrection with two sorcerers, Xulu and Pacaw, stretched themselves upon a bier and died. Their bones were ground to powder and thrown into the river.

They then went through a kind of evolutionary process, appearing on the fifth day after their deaths as men-fishes and on the sixth as old men, ragged and tatterdemalion in appearance, killing and restoring each other to life. At the request of the princes of Xibalba they burned the royal palace and restored it to its pristine splendour, killed and resuscitated the king's dog, and cut a man in pieces, bringing him to life again.

The Lords of Hell were curious about the sensation of death, and asked to be killed and resuscitated. The first portion of their request the hero-brothers speedily granted, but did not deem it necessary to pay any regard to the second. Throwing off all disguise, the brothers assembled the now thoroughly cowed princes of Xibalba and announced their intention of punishing them for their animosity against themselves, their father, and uncle.

They were forbidden to partake in the noble and classic game of ball a great indignity in the eyes of Maya of the higher caste they were condemned to menial tasks, and they were to have sway over the beasts of the forest alone. After this their power rapidly waned. These princes of the Underworld are described as being owl-like, with faces painted black and white, as symbolical of their duplicity and faithless disposition. As some reward for the dreadful indignities they had undergone, the souls of Hunhun-Ahpu and Vukub-Hunahpu, the first adventurers into the dark-some region of Xibalba, were translated to the skies, and became the sun and moon, and with this apotheosis the Second Book ends.

The Third Book opens with another council of the gods. Once more they decide to create men. The Creator and Former made four perfect men. These beings were wholly created from yellow and white maize.

Their names were Balam-Quitze (Tiger with the Sweet Smile), Balam-Agab (Tiger of the Night), Mahucutah (The Distinguished Name), and Iqi- Balam (Tiger of the Moon). They had neither father nor mother, neither were they made by the ordinary agents in the work of creation.

Their creation was a miracle of the Former. But Hurakan was not altogether satisfied with his handiwork. These men were too perfect. They knew overmuch. Therefore the gods took counsel as to how to proceed with men. They must not become as gods. "Let us so contract their sight so that they may only be able to see a portion of the earth and be content," said the gods.

Then Hurakan breathed a cloud over their eyes which became partially veiled. The four men slept, and four women were made, Cahu-Paluma (Falling Water), Choimha (Beautiful Water), Tzununiha (House of the Water), and Cakixa (Water of Aras or Parrots), who became the wives of the men in their respective order as mentioned above. These were the ancestors of the Quiches only.

Then were created the ancestors of other peoples. They were ignorant of the methods of worship, and lifting their eyes to heaven prayed to the Creator, the Former, for peaceable lives and the return of the sun. But no sun came, and they grew uneasy. So they set out for Tulan-Zuiva, or the Seven Caves, and there gods were given unto them, each man, as head of a group of the race, a god.

Balam-Quitze received the god Tohil. Balam-Agab received the god Avilix, and Mahucutah the god Hacavitz. Iqi-Balam received the god Nicahtagah. The Quiches now began to feel the want of fire, and the god Tohil, the creator of fire, supplied them with this element. But soon afterwards a mighty rain extinguished all the fires in the land.

Tohil, however, always renewed the supply. And fire in those days was the chief necessity, for as yet there was no sun. Tulan was a place of misfortune to man, for not only did he suffer from cold and famine, but here his speech was so confounded that the first men were no longer able to comprehend each other. They determined to leave Tulan, and under the leadership of the god Tohil set out to search for a new abode.

On they wandered through innumerable hardships. Many mountains had they to climb, and a long passage to make through the sea, which was miraculously divided for their journey from shore to shore. At length they came to a mountain which they called Hacavitz, after one of their gods, and here they rested, for they had been instructed that at that spot they should see the sun. And the sun appeared.

Animals and men were transported with delight. All the celestial bodies were now established. Following this many towns were established and sacrifices offered, and the narrative shades into tribal history mingled with legend.

The four founders of the Quiche nation died singing the song "Kamucu," "we see," which they had first chanted when the light appeared. They were wrapped together in one great mummy-bundle, the allusion being obviously an aetiological myth explanatory of the origin of mummification and wrapping in ceremonial bindings later prevalent among the Central American peoples.

The remainder of the account is genealogical and semi-historical. As regards the genuine American origin of the "Popol Vuh," that is now generally conceded. To anyone who has given it a careful examination it must be abundantly evident that it is a composition which has passed through several stages of development; that it is unquestionably of aboriginal origin and that it has only been influenced by European thought in a secondary and unessential manner.

The very fact that it was composed in the Quiche tongue is almost sufficient proof of its genuine American character. The scholarship of the nineteenth century was unequal to the adequate translation of the "Popol Vuh."

The twentieth century has as yet shown no signs of being able to accomplish the task. It is, therefore, not difficult to credit that if modern scholarship is unable to properly translate the work, that of the eighteenth century was unable to create it. No European of that epoch was sufficiently versed in Quiche theology and history to compose in faultless Quiche such a work as the " Popol Vuh," breathing as it does in every line an intimate and natural acquaintance with the antiquities of Guatemala.

The "Popol Vuh" is not the only mythi-historical work composed by an aboriginal American. In Mexico Ixtlilxochitl, and in Peru Garcilasso de la Vega wrote exhaustive treatises upon the history and customs of their native countrymen shortly after the conquests of Mexico and Peru, and hieroglyphic records, such as the "Wallam Olum," are not unknown among the North American Indians. In fact, the intelligence which fails to regard the "Popol Vuh" as a genuine aboriginal production must be more skeptical than critical.

At the same time it is evident that its author had been influenced to some slight extent by Christian ideas, though not to the degree believed in by some critics. Many of the seemingly Pentateuchal notions enshrined in the "Popol Vuh," such as the description of the earth as being "without form and void" (though these are not the actual terms employed), are common to more than one mythic system, and when we depart from the cosmogonic account there is little to strengthen the theory of Biblical influence.

COSMOLOGICAL BELIEFS OF THE MAYA

In the cosmogony of the "Popol Vuh" we can discern the sum of several creation-stories. A number of divine beings seem to exercise the creative functions, and it would appear that the account summarized above was due to the fusion and reconciliation of more than one cosmogonic myth, a reconciliation, perhaps, of early rival faiths, such as took place in Peru and Palestine.

We find certain traces of the cosmogonic belief common to both Maya and Mexicans that time had been divided into several elemental epochs governed by fire, water, wind, etc., each culminating in a disaster brought about by the governing element. For the first creative essays of the Quiche gods are destroyed in a manner reminiscent of the Mexican destruction of suns.

A disaster to mankind by fire is mentioned, and the legend of the giants serves to point to a similar overthrow by earthquake. But the belief is evidently in an elementary stage. This might afford grounds for thinking that in the "Popol Vuh" we have the remains of cosmogonic ideas considerably earlier than these formed either in Maya or Mexican myth, and the supposition that the material it contains is more ancient than either, pre-dating the fixed and carefully edited cosmogonies of Mexico and Yucatan.

The Maya, as can be gleaned from the Book of Chilan Balam of Mani, believed the world to consist of a cubical block, tern, "the altar" of the gods, on which rested the celestial vase, cum, containing the heavenly waters, the rains and showers, on which depended all life in their arid country. Within it grew the Yax che, the Tree of Life, bearing the life-fruit known as Yol.

In the "Codex Cortesianus" we find such a design. In the center rises the Tree of Life from the celestial vase. On the right sits Xpiyacoc, on the left Xmucane, the Adam and Eve of the Maya race.

The earth is alluded to in the "Popol Vuh" as "the quadrated castle, four-pointed, four-sided, four-bordered," so that it is plain that the same idea concerning its structure and shape was entertained by the author of that book as by the later Maya. As regards the mythology of the

"Popol Vuh," we must bear in mind that we are dealing with Quiche and not with Maya myth, but it is now possible to draw certain parallels.

For Hun-Ahpu and Xbalanque, the "hunters with the blow-pipe" or serbatana, I cannot conscientiously trace precise parallels in either Mexican or Maya myth. That they are hunting-gods seems probable, but they appear to me to have characteristics which might permit of comparison with the Dioscuri or the (very obscure) Cabiri.

They are divine brethren, the sons of Xpiyacoc and Xmucane, the Quiche "Adam and Eve." Hun-Ahpu means "magician" and Xbalanque "Little Tiger," and we know that the jaguar balam was regarded as a god among the Maya. The only parallel which occurs to me is that of the " twins "Uitzilopochtli and Tezcatlipoca, who also undertook a journey to the Underworld, and who are respectively associated with magic and the "tiger," or jaguar, and I consider it very probable that they had a common and remote origin.

A word may be ventured regarding Xibalba, the Quiche Underworld, described in the "Popol Vuh" as a shadowy subterranean sphere not unlike the Greek Hades. A hell, an abode of bad spirits as distinguished from beneficent gods, Xibalba was not.

The Maya Indian was innocent of the idea of maleficent deities pitted in everlasting warfare against good and life-giving gods until contact with the whites colored his mythology with their idea of the dual nature of supernatural beings. The transcriber of the "Popol Vuh" makes this clear so far as Quiche belief went. He says of the Lords of Xibalba, Hun-Came, and Vukub-Came: "In the old times they did not have much power. They are but annoyers and opposers of men, and, in truth, they were not regarded as gods."

If not regarded as gods, then, what were they? "The devil," says Cogolludo of the Mayas," is called by them Xibalba, which means he who disappears or vanishes." The derivation of Xibalba is from a root meaning "to fear," from which comes the name for a ghost or phantom. Xibalba was, then, the Place of Phantoms. But it was not the Place of Torment, the abode of a devil who presided over punishment.

The idea of sin is weak in the savage mind, and the idea of punishment for sin in a future state is unknown in pre-Christian American mythology. "Under the influence of Christian catechizing," says Brinton, "the Quiche legends portray this realm as a place of torment, and its rulers as malignant and powerful; but as I have before pointed out they do so protesting that such was not the ancient belief, and they let fall no word that shows that it was regarded as the destination of the morally bad. The original meaning of the name given by Cogolludo points unmistakably to the simple fact of disappearance from among men, and corresponds in harmless- ness to the true sense of those words of fear, Scheol, Hades, Hell, all signifying hidden from sight, and only endowed with more grim associations by the imaginations of later generations."

The idea of consigning elder peoples who have been displaced in the land to an Underworld, is not uncommon in mythology. The Xibalbans, or aborigines, were perhaps cave- or earth-dwellers like the "wee folk" of Scottish folk-lore, gnomish, and full of elvish tricks, as such folk usually are. Vanished people are, too, often classed with the dead, or as lords of the dead.

It is well known also that legend speedily crystallizes around the name of a dispossessed race, to whom is attributed every description of magic art. This is sometimes accounted for by the fact that the displaced people possessed a higher culture than their invaders, and sometimes, probably, by the dread which all barbarian peoples have of a religion in any way differing from their own.

Thus the Norwegians credited the Finns their predecessors in Norway with tremendous magical powers, and similar instances of respectful timidity shown by invading races towards the original inhabitants of the country they had conquered could readily be multiplied. To be tricked, the barbarian regards as a mortal indignity, as witness the wrath of Thor in Jotunheim, comparable with the sensitiveness of Hun-Ahpu and Xbalanque, lest they should be out-witted by the Xibalbans.

Still, the story of the visit of the younger hero-gods to Xibalba bears a close resemblance to other legends, pagan and Christian, of the "Harrying of Hell," the conquest of Death and Sin by Goodness, the triumph of light over darkness, of Ra-Osiris over Amenti. So, too, with the game of ball, which figures very largely throughout the Third Book.

The father and uncle of the young hero-gods were worsted in their favorite sport by the Xibalbans, but Hun-Ahpu and Xbalanque in their turn vanquished the Lords of the Underworld. This may have resembled the Mexican game of tlachtli, which was played in an enclosed court with a rubber ball between two opposite sides, each of two or three players. It was, in fact, not unlike hockey.

This game of ball between the Powers of Light and the Powers of Darkness is somewhat reminiscent of that between Ormuzd and Ahriman in Persian myth. The game of tlachtli had a symbolic reference to stellar motions. The books of Chilan Balam are native compilations of events among the Maya previous to the Spanish Conquest, and written by Maya Indian scribes in the characters invented and taught by the Spanish monks as suitable to the Maya tongue.

They embody the old traditions lingering in the memory of individuals concerning the doings of the Maya people before the coming of the Spaniards, though some belong to the end of the sixteenth and the first half of the seventeenth centuries. They exist in various transcripts in Yucatan, and were first copied by Dr. Hermann Behrendt, whose transcriptions were purchased by Dr. Brinton. They may be regarded as offshoots of the Maya MSS. and treat in general of matters given in portions of these; they contain also a substratum of historic information which has been preserved by tradition.

They are primarily brief chronicles, recounting the divisions of time, the periods known to the Mayas as katuns, which had elapsed since their coming to Mayapan. Spanish notices of what are known to the old his- torians as the prophecies of Chilan Balam are rare. The fullest is that of Villagutierre in his "Historia de el Itza, ye de el Lacandon." The prophecies purport to be those of the priest who bore the title not name of Chilan Balam, whose offices were those of divination and astrology.

Villagutierre's statement is to the effect that Chilan Balam, high priest of Tixcacayon Cabick in Mani, prophesied the coming of the Spaniards as follows: " At the end of the thirteenth age, when Itza is at the height of its power, as also the city called Tancoh, which is between Yacman and Tichaquillo, the signal of God will appear on the heights; and the Cross, with which the world was enlightened, will be manifested. There will be variance of men's will in future times, when the signal shall be brought. Ye priests, before coming even a quarter of a league, ye shall see the Cross, which will appear and lighten up the sky from pole to pole. The worship of vain gods shall cease. Your father comes, O Itzalanos! Your brother comes, O Tantunites! Receive your barbarous bearded guests from the East, who bring the signal of God who comes to us in mercy and pity. The time of our life is coming. You have nothing to fear from the world. Thou art the living God, who created us in mercy. The words of God are good: let us lift up His signal to see it and adore it: we must raise the Cross in opposition to the falsehood we now see. Before the first tree of the world now is a manifestation made to the world: this is the signal of a God on high: adore this, ye people of Itza! Let us adore it with uprightness of heart. Let us adore Him who is our God, the true God: receive the word of the true God, for He who speaks to you comes from heaven. Ponder this well, and be the men of Itza. They who believe shall have light in the age which is to come. I, your teacher and master, Balam, warn and charge you to look at the importance of my words. Thus have I finished what the true God commanded me to say, that the world might hear it."

It is not difficult to see in this account of the prophecy certain signs which at once mark it as spurious. The chief of these are the scriptural character of the language employed and the much too definite terms in which the prophecy is couched. These considerations lead us first to an examination of the books with a view to discovering whether or not they are genuinely aboriginal in character.

There can be no doubt that, as in the case of the Quiche "Popol Vuh," a genuine substratum of native tradition has been overlaid and colored by the Christian influence of the early Spanish missionaries. The genuine aboriginal character of this substratum is clear from internal evidence, matters being dealt with in a manner which betrays an aboriginal cast of thought, and knowledge of Maya manners being revealed in a way that no Spaniard of the period was capable of achieving.

At the same time, the evidence of priestly editing is by no means far to seek, and must be patent to the most superficial reader. The evidence of language also points to the authenticity of these productions. Such an idiomatic use of the ancient Maya tongue as they betray could have been employed by none but persons who had used it habitually from infancy.

The trend of thought, as displayed in American languages, differs so radically from that shown in European tongues as to afford almost no analogy whatever; and this is well exemplified in these curious books. Their authenticity has been called in question by several superficial students of the American languages, whose studies have been made at secondhand. But no authority of the first class has doubted their genuine aboriginal character.

As regards the authenticity of the prophecies, it is known that, at the close of the divisions of time known as katuns, a chilan, or prophet, was wont to utter publicly a prediction forecasting the nature of the similar period to come; and there is no reason to doubt that some distant rumors of the coming of the white man had reached the ears of several of the seers. So far as the reference to the Cross is concerned, it may be observed that the Maya word rendered "cross" by the missionaries simply signifies "a piece of wood set upright"; but cruciform shapes were well known to the Maya.

The natives were greatly disturbed at the destruction of their sacred records by the Spanish monks and, as many of them had acquired the European alphabet, and the missionaries had added to it several signs to express Maya sounds foreign to Spanish ears, a number of native scribes set to work to write out in the new alphabet the contents of their ancient records. In this they were, doubtless, aided by the wonderful mnemonic powers which were so assiduously cultivated by the American races, and they probably further relied upon such secretly preserved archives as they could obtain.

They added much new European lore, and omitted a considerable body of native tradition. The result of their labors was a number of books, varying in merit and contents, but known collectively as "the Books of Chilan Balam," these being severally distinguished by the name of the village where each was composed or discovered. It is probable that in the seventeenth century every village contained a copy of the native records; but various causes have combined to destroy the majority of them.

There still remain portions or descriptions of at least sixteen of these records, designated by the names of the several places where they were written, as, for example: the Book of Chilan Balam, of Chumayel, of Nabula, of Kaua, of Mani, of Oxkutzcab, of Ixil, of Tihosuco, of Tixcocob.

"Chilan," says Landa, second Bishop of Yucatan, "was the name of their priests whose duty it was to teach the sciences, to appoint holy days, to treat the sick, to offer sacrifices, and especially to utter the oracles of the gods. They were so highly honored by the people that they were carried on litters on the shoulders of the devotees."

The derivation of the name is from chij, "the mouth," and signifies "interpreter." The word balam means "tiger," and was used in connection with a priestly caste, being still employed by the Maya Indians as a name for those spirits who are supposed to protect fields and towns.

It is seldom that the names of the writers of these books are given, as in all probability the compilations, as we have them, are but copies of still older manuscripts, with additions of more recent events by the copyist. The contents of the various books of Chilan Balam may be classified under: astrology and prophecy, chronology and history, medico-religious practice, and later history and Christian teachings.

The astrology is an admixture of Maya stellar divination and that borrowed from European almanacs of the century between 1550 and 1650, which are no less superstitious in their leanings than the native products. Prophecies such as that quoted at length above abound.

The books of Chilan Balam are, however, chiefly valuable for the light they throw upon the chronological system and ancient history of the Maya. The periods of events in which they deal are designated katuns, and are of considerable length, but, their actual extent has not been agreed upon.

The older Spanish authors make their duration twenty years (the length of time alluded to in the text of the books), but marginal notes imply that they consisted of twenty-four years. As, however, these notes have been added by a later hand the original computation is possibly the correct one. But it is still more likely that the length of the katun was neither 20 nor 24 years, but 20X360 days. The cure of various diseases is exhaustively treated by the authors of the books. Landa relates that "the chilanes were sorcerers and doctors," and we shall probably not be far wrong if we compare them with the medicine-men of other American tribes.

The MSS. abound in descriptions of symptoms and hints for diagnosis, and suggest many remedies. The preparation of native plants and bleeding are the chief among these, but several appear to have been borrowed from a physic book of European origin.

Brinton states that Dr. Behrendt, who first copied these books, and who was himself a physician, left a large manuscript on the subject, entitled "Recetarios de Indios," in which he states that the scientific value of these remedies is next to nothing, and that the language in which they are recorded is distinctly inferior to the remainder of the books. He held that this portion of these records was supplanted some time in the last century by medical knowledge introduced from Europe.

This, indeed, is admitted by the copyists of the books, who probably took them from a mediaeval work on Spanish medicine known as "El Libro del Judio," "The Book of the Jew."

CHAPTER XIV
ARCANE PHILOSOPHY OF THE MEXICANS AND MAYA

The name Kab-ul, "the Great or Magic Hand," is one which should signify for us perhaps one of the most interesting and arresting figures in Maya mysticism. He is, of course, a type or phase of Itzamna, the personification of the East or the rising sun, which brought the beneficent mists and dews of the morning to the torrid land of Yucatan.

He was said to have come in his enchanted boat across the waters from the East, and therefore he presided over that quarter of the world and the days and years assigned to it. Says Brinton: "For similar reasons he received the name Lakin chan, 'the Serpent of the East,' under which he seems to have been popularly known. As light is synonymous with both life and knowledge, he was said to have been the creator of men, animals, and plants, and was the founder of the culture of the Mayas. He was the first priest of their religion, and invented writing and books; he gave the names to the various localities in Yucatan, and divided the land among the people; as a physician he was famous, knowing not only the magic herbs, but possessing the power of healing by touch, whence his name Kabil, 'the skilful hand,' under which he was worshiped in Chichen-Itza. For his wisdom he was spoken of as Yax coc ah-mut, 'the royal or noble master of knowledge.'"

His consort was the goddess Ix-chel, the Rainbow, also known as Ix Kan Leom, "the spider's web," which catches the dew of the morning. She was goddess of medicine, and her children were the Bacabs, the gods of the four cardinal points, who ruled over the calendar, and represented the worship of the four sections or houses of the heavens, each having different colors, cycles, and elements mythically and magically associated with them.

He is, so far as it is possible to judge, the "God K" of Schellhas, and the "doublet" of Kukulkan, or Quetzalcoatl, in the character of rising sun to Kukulkan's setting sun, much as Ra occupied the former place and Osiris the latter in the religion of Egypt. And, like Kukulkan, he is a great master of magic and a repository of magical thought. That a whole corpus of magical knowledge, well digested and quite philosophical in its character, centered in the idea of these twin deities who can doubt?

That this arose out of a nature symbolism, as it did elsewhere, seems certain. Indeed, the allegory of nature symbolism lies at the root of all early magical and philosophical lore.

The knowledge of the Maya, their entire system of thought, was founded on the operations of the celestial bodies and fixed on the temporal appearance and reappearance of these bodies, and the processes of growth. The immovable brilliance of the fixed stars must have imprinted itself upon the eye and the imagination of man almost from the first, must have intrigued and puzzled him, or have been accepted by him without emotion as a phenomenon duly to be explained away in terms of myth.

He seems to have invested the planets not only with godhead but with sex as well. The Sun was male and the Moon female. But as he advanced in knowledge and observation, he included the lesser lights in the celestial family. He found that Venus and Mercury never traveled beyond a certain limit, and these he associated with the Sun as wife and son respectively.

Still later, taking the Earth as the center of the universe, he arranged the Moon, Mercury, and Venus to the dexter side of the Sun, regarding their alternation as morning and evening stars as fortunate or the reverse. Mars, Jupiter, and Saturn, which seemed to him less under the control of the central luminary, he relegated to the sinister sphere, permitting to Jupiter, however, a less bad eminence because of his chiefship among the three an exception which finally resulted in something of a beneficent reputation being achieved for that planet.

Mars and Saturn, however, were definitely evil, the first a quick-moving, restless orb of destructive tendencies, the other an ancient wizard of dire proclivities. The life of early man was closely interrelated with the incidence of solar and lunar phenomena.

Changes of temperature and weather affected his hunting expeditions. The behavior of the Moon and its connection with the tides must have strongly influenced his imagination, and in the event begot a whole folk-lore of its own. It is now clear, too, that she was regarded as the repository of magic, the great tank or reservoir whence the mystic influence of mana, orenda, or faery emanated, and she had influence upon childbirth as the place whence new souls were supposed to be sent to inhabit earthly bodies.

The idea that the stars are gods or great men translated to the heavens, is widespread among savages and, in a measure, lies at the very roots of astrological belief. The constellations are frequently supposed to represent personages, and some, especially in Australia, are chiefly connected with the totemic system of several of the tribes.

The stars, among primitive people, have a useful significance and perform a more important function than the Sun, for by their movements the times of feasts and ceremonies are determined, and they serve as a kind of calendar by means of which the savage agriculturist can regulate the cultivation of the soil. Thus they came to have a very real meaning for early man.

Strange omens and signs connected with them had, also, a significance which, naturally, could not be ignored. The germ of astrological belief is certainly to be found among many savage peoples.

Thus Shortland discovered that the Maories, when about to attack a position, professed to be able to foretell the result by the relative appearance of Venus and the Moon. If the planet were above the Moon, the attackers would be victorious; if beneath, the defenders would triumph.

Once the idea of personality, of godhead, had been connected with the planets, they were regarded as powerful enchanters or deities who were constantly striving to direct the actions of man in such a manner as to bring them into harmony with some vaster plan of their own. The idea of a cosmic symphony had been established. Man must work in harmony with the higher powers. But in due course it was observed that the lesser planets differed from the great luminaries of day and night in one important respect.

The paths of the latter were circular, while those of the planets proper executed a curved line or epicycle. They waxed and waned in magnitude. In the course of a single night the early man of Europe or Asia could behold almost all the stars visible in our latitude. He fixed two lines for observational purposes, one running east and west, the other north and south from where he stood, and discovered a stationary point in the North Pole and the star lying nearest to it.

When he had ascertained the eastern and western points of his horizon and his meridian, he began to relate the paths of the planets to these. This naturally resulted in the division of the heavens into "houses," in which the constantly changing courses of the planets might be observed. The Mexicans and Maya divided the heavens into four quarters, and these are reflected in their tonalamatls, or "Books of Fate." Thus they have really only four "houses" of astrological significance.

But, like the peoples of Asia and Europe, they believed in the repercussion of the planets on the various parts of the human body. The several day-signs, which were obviously stellar in their origin, were supposed to govern the several human limbs and organs, as we have seen in the chapter on Mexican Astrology.

We thus see how this species of arcane thought began to take shape and to develop into a definite system with amazing ramifications. But can we go farther and discover in it a still deeper significance than that which seems to have sprung merely from a slowly evolved belief in the physical effects of the heavenly bodies?

THE CULT OF QUETZALCOATL

For this we certainly must look, for its beginnings, at least, to the figure of Quetzalcoatl, or Kukulkan. He is, as Seler says, "the embodiment of the cult which in its essentials was solely established for the purpose of obtaining for the people the rain needed for their crops in sufficient quantity and at the right time. As the beginnings of this cult and the development of the priestly order certainly dated from hoary prehistoric times, or at all events were supposed to do so, Quetzalcoatl himself further became the king, priest, and tribal god of the nation of the Toltecs, who were regarded as the first settlers, the inventors of all culture, of all arts and knowledge. Indeed, it is quite conceivable that to this association of ideas corresponds a measure of historic truth that in this first notion the rain-dispensing deity and the rain-making priest were merged in one, and by it this special conception of the deity was transmitted to the fol owing generations. In any case it accords with this view that the same god was later regarded as the inventor of all other priestly arts of vatication, witchcraft, calendric lore, and astronomy, and was, in fact, identified with the Morning Star, the orb, which, as we have seen, became the initial point of the system of day-counts based on the combination of the numerals 13 and 20. On the other hand, a second feature which is amongst the most prominent in the myth of this god his wandering forth to the land on the Atlantic seaboard, the Tlillan Tlapallan, the Tlatlayan, 'the land of the black and of the red color,' 'the place of conflagration,' his death there, combined with the expectation of a future return may have its explanation partly in actual historical events, partly in other mythological notions."

Out of these ideas, then, arose the figure of Quetzalcoatl, the great magician, and a specific lore came to be associated with him. He was said to be the creator-god, and in other places the son of the creative deities. He was also the Morning Star, Venus, to the course of which the duration of the tonalamatl or "Book of Fate" stands in relationship. His direct opposite is Tezcatlipoca, the dark god.

We have thus a system of duality, in which Quetzalcoatl is the white magician and Tezcatlipoca the black magician. All the lore of light sprang from the former, all the magic of the lower cultus from the latter. They fight, as do Ormuz and Ahriman in Persian myth, and when Quetzalcoatl retires, drought and evil naturally follow. But Quetzalcoatl will return and with him the good days. So what had once a merely seasonal significance came also to have an arcane meaning.

At the time of the Spanish conquest of Mexico Quetzalcoatl's star was certainly not in the ascendant, his priesthood seems to have been rather under a cloud, and the evil notion that Tezcatlipoca had conquered for a while led to those abominable holocausts of humanity in sacrifice which have blackened the name of the ancient Mexicans. The people really believed themselves to be under the sway of the black magician Tezcatlipoca, and when Cortes arrived they were joyful at first because they were under the impression that the beneficent Quetzalcoatl had actually returned.

They were, of course, speedily disillusioned, but that is beside the question. Assuredly Quetzalcoatl returned every rainy season to water the crops. But there was another and a spiritual sense in which he did not return, and that this was realized by the Mexicans is revealed by the fact that at the period of the Conquest they relied much more on human sacrifice and the shedding of blood to the maize gods to ensure good crops than on the ancient rain-making ritual associated with Quet- zalcoatl's cult.

All Mexico sighed for his reappearance, and saw his advent in the coming of Cortes. When Montezuma learned of the Conquistador's arrival he actually sent him the four costumes appropriate to Quetzalcoatl, and it was only when he heard of the barbarities committed by the Spaniards that he forbade their approach to the city of Mexico.

This makes it clear that the thinking classes of Mexico and Yucatan were desirous of Quetzalcoatl's return, that they practiced his cult, and probably made every endeavor to hasten his advent by magical means. The priesthood of Tezcatlipoca, on the other hand, strenuously opposed the idea, and there is some evidence that they had been engaged in doing so for a considerable time.

Quetzalcoatl is said to have closed his ears with both hands when human sacrifices were mentioned, and the wise Nezahualcoyotl, the poet-king of Tezcuco, not only prophesied the return of Quetzalcoatl, but cast doubt on the ability of the sanguinary gods to aid him, saying: "Verily, these gods that I am adoring, what are they but idols of stone without speech or feeling? They could not have made the beauty of the heaven, the sun, the moon, and the stars which adorn it, and which light the earth, with its countless streams, its fountains and waters, its trees and plants, and its various inhabitants. There must be some god, invisible and unknown, who is the universal creator. He alone can console me in my affliction and take away my sorrow."

Strengthened in this conviction by a timely fulfillment of his heart's desire, he erected a temple nine stories high to represent the nine heavens, which he dedicated "to the Unknown God, the Cause of Causes." This temple, he ordained, should never be polluted by blood, nor should any graven image ever be set up within its precincts.

What then resided at the heart of this dualism, what was the particular nature of the philosophy which inspired a belief in the wisdom-religion or magic of beneficence, and what, alternatively, lay at the roots of the magic of evil so prominent in Mexico? The "white magic" of Quetzalcoatl was evidently the outcome of an imported system, possibly allied to Buddhism, possibly to some European mystical system.

The Polynesian peoples cultivated a species of debased Buddhism, but that which seems to have penetrated to Central America appears to have been of a more exalted type. The one alternative to the theory of importation from Asia is that of the introduction of some form of European mysticism, Celtic or Mediterranean.

Yet the peculiarly Asiatic character of the statues of Kukulkan, Quetzalcoatl's Yucatecan type, and the similarity of Maya architecture and art to Asiatic forms rather discount the latter theory. If we do not accept the idea of importation we are left with the hypothesis of the native development of the Quetzalcoatl cult, a highly improbable contingency, having regard to all the circumstances.

Whatever its origin, the Quetzalcoatl philosophy must inevitably be regarded as of the nature of a wisdom-religion inculcating the dogmas of the higher mysticism, and founded on Mexican soil by an actual person. It taught the belief in the return of the soul to earth after a sojourn in a place of refreshment.

The whole circumstances of Quetzalcoatl's myth bear such a strong resemblance to the rites and doctrines of initiatory ceremonies as found elsewhere that we cannot surely be mistaken in equating them with these as regards their general character. Quetzalcoatl, before passing to Tollan-tlapallan falls sick, that is, the initiate is undergoing the usual mental stress which precedes the ceremony, the longing for Otherwhere. He is given a draught from the sacred cup, and becomes "intoxicated," that is, rapt in spiritual contemplation. He abandons his palaces, his gold and silver, the treasures of this world, as did the Greek mystics, and becomes "old" in arcane experience.

Preceded by flute-players, the typical instrumentalists of the Mysteries, he proceeds on his "journey," reaches the river of the initiates, which is similar to the Styx of the Greek Mysteries, or to that crossed by the heroes in the "Popol Vuh," and crosses it by a bridge. He is next met by sorcerers who ask him to abandon his knowledge of the mechanical arts. Here it is plain that the hierophants or presiding priests of the Mysteries have been changed into "wizards."

He obeys them. Another "magician" then insists upon his drinking a draught which he could give "to none of the living," that is, the cup of forgetfulness employed in all initiations at a certain phase.

He loses his senses after the draught, precisely as did the Greek initiates, and when he awakes "tears his hair," perhaps in a divine frenzy. Next he passes between a mountain of snow and a volcano. This is an analogy with the passage of the neophyte through the infernal regions.

Here his attendants "die," that is, the epopts and musicians leave the neophyte at this particular point. The memorials of his progress were a court, in which the mystical ball-game of tlachtli was played, and a cross, which he made by transfixing one tree with another symbols of psychic stages traversed in the Mexican Mysteries.

Likewise he constructed subterranean houses, which resemble those cells dug in the ground employed in Britain by the Druidical mystics for contemplation, and elsewhere he balanced a great rolling stone, which was also part of the initiatory apparatus of the Druids. Then in his raft of serpents he seated himself as in a canoe to reach the land of Tlapallan, a passage which renders it most clear that the whole myth of his departure describes the initiatory process, the voyage resembling that of the neophytes of the British Mysteries in the "rite of the coracle," which seems to have taken place in Cardigan Bay, or the Eleusinian rite of "Mystics to the Sea."

If we tabulate the circumstances of Quetzalcoatl's myth, we shall find that they bear a striking resemblance to the known facts of initiation in Egypt, Greece, and Britain. They are: The state of longing for perfection. The draught from the sacred cup. Spiritual "intoxication," i.e. rapt contemplation. Abandonment of the things of this world. Recognition of arcane experiences. Journey of the soul, accompanied by musicians. Crossing of the "Styx" into the land of the Dead. Abandonment of worldly knowledge at the behest of the Subterranean powers. The draught of oblivion. Divine frenzy. Passage through the infernal regions. Departure of accompanying epopts. Passage through various psychic stages. Contemplation in subterranean cell. The rite of the rocking-stone. Passage across water to the place of new life. Regeneration in the place of new life. Return to the mundane sphere as an initiate.

These stages are not arranged in the myth of Quetzalcoatl in the same incidence as in the case of the Greek and British mysteries, but the majority of the circumstances known to have been connected with initiation in Greece and Britain are here present. It is clear, then, that we must look for a mystical system connected with the Quetzalcoatl cult which had an almost precisely similar dogma and outlook to those current in Britain and Greece.

Do we actually discover this to be so? Comparing first the mystical cosmogony of Britain with that of Mexico,, we find the Universe divided into three planes.

In Mexico we find nine heavens arranged as different planes of psychic progression. We find Arthur in British myth descending into Annwn, or Hades, to seek the Cauldron of Inspiration, just as Quetzalcoatl in Mexico proceeds to Tlapallan to seek the Fountain of Refreshment. But another myth makes the Mexican god penetrate to Hades or Mictlan to seek for maize, just as Arthur sought the generating mistletoe in Annwn.

It is precisely in British and Mexican myth that we find the two best-known examples of the "Harrying of Hell" and the triumph of the gods of light over those of darkness. The "Popol Vuh," which provides the transatlantic evidence of this belief, is indeed a great book of American initiatory experience.

Having thus satisfied ourselves that the outlines of British and Mexican mysticism display similar beliefs; do we find this to be the case as regards the Greek and American systems? Generally speaking, we can at once state this to be so. Both were fundamentally based on the primitive idea of vegetable growth, out of which sprang the allegory of the rebirth of the soul of men.

Demeter the Corn-mother is reborn as Core, precisely as the Mexican Maize-mother is reborn as Cinteotl, the son, and as

Quetzalcoatl, the rain-spirit, the "finder" of maize, is "reborn" in Tlapallan, the place of bright colors. More particularly, we must ask ourselves if we can trace any system similar to that of the philosophy of the Greek or Egyptian Mysteries in Mexico, where the fragments only of such a system are apparent.

The outward form of the Greek and Egyptian mystical philosophy was expressed chiefly in dramatic rite, and in the festivals of Mexico we observe circumstances so obviously resembling these that we cannot but believe in an ancient common origin. But as regards dogma, we find a similar belief in the phenomenon of rebirth, as expressed in the return of Quetzalcoatl, the notion of a regenerating fountain of the soul, as found also in Egypt, and the belief that man had fallen and must be "reborn."

Mexican myth, like Greek and Egyptian arcane myth, was fulfilled of this idea of the fall of man and the necessity for his regeneration. Xochiquetzal, the Mexican Venus, is said in the "Codex Telleriano-Remensis" to have been "the first sinner," and is represented in a picture in that MS. as "weeping for her lost happiness," having been driven from Paradise because she had broken a flower.

On the occasion of her festival the people fasted on bread and water because of her mortal sin, and we have seen that the same myth held good of Itzpapalotl. We may then feel that we are on fairly certain ground if we state positively that the idea underlying the cult of Quetzalcoatl was the regeneration, the rebirth of man, just as it underlay the British, Greek, and Egyptian mysteries.

That the possibility of regeneration in Egypt applied in more ancient times to the Pharaoh alone I have made plain enough in "*The Mysteries of Egypt*," and that some such belief also obtained in Mexico is also evident. The soul of the Pharaoh, after death, was thought of as winging its flight to the sun-land, and we find a Mexican legend which recounts how Montezuma, the ill-fated Emperor of Mexico, flew to Tamoanchan, the place of the setting sun.

Another link between the Hellenic and Mexican Mysteries is that provided by the cult of the god Tlaloc, which seems to resemble that of the Cretan monster, the Minotaur, who appears in the Greek Mysteries, with his tribute of youth. Children were annually "devoured" by the water-god, that is they were drowned in the Lake of Tezcuco, and a specific tribute of specially selected victims was paid to him, while to his Maya equivalent virgins were sacrificed by drowning in the cenotes or great reservoirs of that arid land.

That Tlaloc was developed from the form of such a monster we can scarcely doubt, having regard to his enormous tusks and large rolling eye. He was probably the great serpent or dragon which lay in the cavernous depths of the lake in wait for drowning people, just as the Minotaur was the fiendish bull-man who made the labyrinth of Gnossos his den, that is, he was an earth-monster (for the bull is symbolic of the earth and the earthquake), just as Tlaloc was a water-monster, and both must be placated with human sacrifice.

Whatever their origin, the Mysteries of Mexico display a decided resemblance to these of the Old World, and it is therefore permissible to argue that the system of arcane knowledge which they inculcated was much the same in essence as that in vogue in the Eastern Hemisphere, yet interpenetrated by novel and localized ideas. We must then think of the cult of Quetzalcoatl as a mystery cult, having a distinct initiation ceremony, and that this survived in the practices of the Nagualist Society is also obvious enough.

It appears to have had as its central object the rebirth of man and the regeneration of his spirit in a sphere of Otherwhere, whence he might return to earth for another existence. Of this cult Quetzalcoatl seems to have been the Dionysus or Osiris. The rite of the Zapotec high priest who took the human form of Quetzalcoatl is eloquent of the fact that a certain measure of orgiastic frenzy was associated with his cult, and this reveals the Bacchic resemblance.

The Osirian association is also clear enough. Quetzalcoatl, like Osiris, fares across the water to seek regeneration in another sphere, to drink of the fountain of youth. His opponent is Tezcatlipoca, in Central America Hurakan, the representative of Black Magic and all evil, the protagonist of the worship and ritual of the lower cultus.

GOOD AND EVIL

In Mexico we find, indeed, as perhaps nowhere else save in Persia, a distinct dualism of good and evil. The amazing thing is that the ball-game between the good and evil deities which figures so largely in Iranian myth as having been played by Ahura Mazda, or Ormuzd, and Ahriman, is reflected in the Mexican myth given by Mendieta, which tells how Tezcatlipoca let himself down from the sky by means of a spider's web, and coming to Tollan, engaged in a game of tlachtli, or ball, with Quetzalcoatl, in the midst of which he transformed himself into a jaguar, and chased Quetzalcoatl to Tlapallan.

The olli, or ball, with which they played is the symbol of light and darkness, as its bright and shaded sides show. It was the symbol of the god Xolotl.

One of the hymns or songs given in the Sahagun MS. says of Xolotl: "Old Xolotl plays ball, plays ball On the magic playing-ground." The Mexican game of tlachtli symbolized the movements of the moon (but more probably of both sun and moon). This, perhaps the favorite Mexican amusement, was a ball-game, played with a rubber ball by two persons one at each end of a T-shaped court, which in the manuscripts is sometimes represented as painted in dark and light colors, or in four variegated hues.

In several of the manuscripts Xolotl is depicted striving at this game against other gods. For example, in the "Codex Mendoza" we see him playing with the moon-god, and can recognize him by the sign ollin which accompanies him, and by the gouged-out eye in which that symbol ends.

Seler thinks "that the root of the name olin suggested to the Mexicans the motion of the rubber ball olli and, as a consequence, ball-playing." It seems to me to have represented both light and darkness, as is witnessed by its colors. Xolotl is, indeed, the darkness that accompanies light. Hence he is "the twin," or shadow, hence he travels with the sun and the moon, with one or other of which he "plays ball," overcoming them or losing to them.

He is the god of eclipse, and naturally a dog, the animal of eclipse. Peruvians, Tupis, Creeks, Iroquois, Algonquins, and Eskimos believed the dog to be so, thrashing dogs during the phenomenon, a practice explained by saying that the big dog was swallowing the sun, and that by whipping the little ones they would make him desist. The dog is the animal of the dead, and therefore of the Place of Shadows.

Thus also Xolotl is a monster, the sun-swallowing monster, like the Hindu Rahu, who chases the sun and moon. As a shadow he is "the double" of everything.

The axoloil, a marine animal found in Mexico, was confounded with his name because of its monstrous appearance, and he was classed along with Quetzalcoatl merely because that god's name bore the element coatl, which may be translated either "twin" or "snake." Lastly, as he was "variable as the shade," so were the fortunes of the game over which he presided.

At the same time he seems to me to have affinities with the Zapotec and Maya lightning-dog peche-xolo and may represent the lightning which descends from the thunder-cloud, the flash, the

THE MAGIC AND MYSTERIES OF MEXICO

reflection of which arouses in many primitive people the belief that the lightning is "double," and leads them to suppose a connection between the lightning and twins, or other phenomena of a twofold kind.

As the dog, too, he has a connection with Hades, and, said myth, was dispatched thence for the bones from which man was created. He is also a traveling god, for the shadows cast by the clouds seem to travel quickly over plain and mountain. As the monstrous dwarf, too, he symbolized the palace-slave, the deformed jester who catered for the amusement of the great, and this probably accounts for the symbol of the white hand outspread on his face, which he has in common with Xochipilli and the other gods of pleasure.

He bears a suspicious resemblance to the mandrake spirits of Europe and Asia, both as regards his duality, his loud lamentation when as a double-rooted plant he was discovered and pulled up by the roots, and his symbol, which may be a reminiscence of the mandrake. Now all this seems to me to throw light on the dualistic character of Mexican arcane thought. Xolotl is the "twin" of Quetzalcoatl, that is, he is Quetzalcoatl in another guise, as the ball-player, but he wears nearly all Quetzalcoatl's symbols and his dress, to say nothing of his long beard.

He is also the divine dog of the Mexican Mysteries, their Anubis, so to speak, and in most of the Codices he is seen taking on a canine appearance. He is also one of the "dwarfish servants" of the god.

Quetzalcoatl, the alien and "civilized" god or magician, the protagonist of white magic and the civilizing mysteries, found Mexico unready for him. He was "driven out," and his cultus remained on sufferance and as an aristocratic and priestly one only. Tezcatlipoca, the native god of obsidian, and the Ahriman of Mexico, presided over a ritual not unlike that of Siva in India. Mexico groaned beneath his bloodstained rites. Small wonder that he came to be known by names so awful as "The Hungry Chief" and "The Enemy".

Montezuma seems to have felt the justice of Cortes's rebuke that his gods were devils, and his acceptance of the Christian faith appears to have been sincere enough and to have come to him as a great relief in the end. But, like that of Quetzalcoatl, the cult of Tezcatlipoca had its own mysteries, degraded as they were.

These were the Mexican equivalents of the Black Mass. A graceful young man was selected from among the war captives and was during a whole year permitted to lead a life of unrestricted pleasure. He was clad in the finest robes, he ate and drank of the best, he was hailed by the populace as a great lord, he was given a harem of beautiful women, but at the end of the year he must perish.

It is the story of Faust in a Mexican setting, the legend of the man who has sold himself to the Devil. At the end of the year he was immolated by having his heart (soul) torn out and cast before the idol of Tezcatlipoca.

For just as the legend of Faust reflects the traditional remembrance of a rite in which a man was sacrificed to a demon, the story of the Mexican victim of Tezcatlipoca affords us the description of that rite itself. In the Faust legend the person "sells" himself to the Devil; in the Mexican rite he is "selected." And that Tezcatlipoca was sufficiently demonic, we know from the old Spanish chroniclers.

"The Mexicans," says Sahagun, "believed that he was invisible and was able to penetrate into all places, heaven, earth, and hell . . . and that he wandered over the earth stirring up strife and war and setting men against one another."

He also remarks that, "he was a true giver of prosperity, and extremely capricious." Is this not Mephistopheles in propria persona?

And, to complete the picture, Tezcatlipoca is a friend of witches and, like the German demon, and the fiends in the Welsh-legends of the Grail, is lame. Faust, under the guidance of Mephistopheles, visited "the Mothers," the Chonthian deities of growth, who dwelt beneath the Earth, and who were represented in the Mysteries of ancient Eleusis.

At the Teotleco, a movable feast sacred to Tezcatlipoca, the footprint of the god was assiduously looked for by the priests in a heap of maize. When it appeared, the chief attendant cried, "The master has arrived."

On the following day a huge fire was prepared and captives were burnt alive. Young men disguised as demons danced round it, hurling the unhappy victims into the flames. Is this not the myth of Satan and hell-fire dramatized?

Tezcatlipoca in his cock shape (we will recall that Mephistopheles wore a cock's feather) was the fiend who deceived the first woman. But not only did he deceive Hueytonantzin, "our great mother," but, with the help of other demons he slew her, "founding with her the institution of human sacrifice," offering up her heart to the sun.

In many ancient Mexican myths we find both Tezcatlipoca and Quetzalcoatl posing as creators, aiding each other in framing the world. Both are said to be the sons of Tonacatecutli and Tonacaciuatl, "who had existed from the beginning, both in turn became (or ruled) the sun for an "age." But Tezcatlipoca fell from heaven, or Tamoanchan, like other gods, he transgressed by plucking the roses and branches of that delectable place.

This has, of course, an arcane significance, and implies that these deities broke the sex-taboo placed upon the gods, for it is distinctly stated that the Mexican deities, although many of them had female counterparts, were not united in marriage, nor had they any marital relations whatever. Tezcatlipoca and his erring brothers and sisters, the Tzitzimime, were therefore like Milton's angels, cast out of heaven, some into "hell," others upon the earth, to become the adversaries of mankind, and as I have already said, Tezcatlipoca's minor names, Yaotl, "Enemy," and Yaomauitl, "Dreaded Enemy," make his character and position clear in this respect.

We can trace, then, the process by which the barbarous obsidian cult of the Nahua tribes came to be regarded by the more enlightened Mexicans as definitely evil, whilst the civilized cultus of Quetzalcoatl was identified with all that was good and delectable. Not that the faith of Tezcatlipoca was altogether bad, for it certainly possessed elements of goodness and progress, but its association with human sacrifice gradually occluded most of these, and in the end the worship of the god substituted terror for conscience.

To sin against Tezcatlipoca was only to offend, and caused him no sorrow but vindictive anger, which was speedily assuaged by horrible punishment. To be a priest of Tezcatlipoca was to be a black magician in every sense of the word, an associate of witches, a shape-shifter, an invoker of demons.

The priesthood of Quetzalcoatl, on the other hand, was philosophical and spiritual in its outlook. We see here, clearly, then, not so much a religious state and condition in Mexico, but one in which an opinion much more purely magical had developed. Mexican "religion," in a word, was not so much the worship of a pantheon of deities mainly beneficent, with a corresponding fear and hatred of a comparatively small number of evil deities, as in Greece or Egypt, or Babylon, nor was it even an acknowledgment of "powers" of rather indefinite character, as among the Teutons or the early Celts.

It was a well-defined national or tribal recognition of a good pantheon in opposition to an evil one, in which the ignorant accepted perforce the rule of the darker deities and the enlightened the path of the higher gods, although even these were compelled by popular opinion and for political reasons to "bow the knee to Mammon," and to participate in the horrid orgies of supernatural beings of a type almost wholly debased lest they arouse popular clamor through their neglect of forces which, it was believed, might withhold sustenance and vindictively bring the whole human race.

The myths of the Nootka Sound Indians, however, seem to point to an early version of this dualism. In them the gods Quautz and Matlox are represented as the good and bad principles and seem to me the prototypes of Quetzalcoatl and Mictlan. To irretrievable ruin were they not periodically placated with sacrifices of the most revolting character.

Such a possible condition early European Christianity dreaded and foresaw did it not deal faithfully and manfully with the paganism it outrooted. Yet it was even compelled to make certain terms with that paganism, accepting by the famous bull of Pope Gregory some of the less offensive rites and customs of the lower faiths it had displaced.

The colonial priesthood of Spain has frequently been blamed for the ferocity of the measures it adopted in Mexico and Central America. But if we cannot excuse its destruction of manuscripts and of some of the more innocent monuments, we can but applaud the forthright valor with which it extirpated the abominable demonism of old Mexico and cast down its sanguinary high places. In time it came to recognize that the wretched peoples to whom it had been sent to minister were, for the most part, only too willing to believe in and accept its comparatively mild tenets, as the noble and Christ-like Las Casas discovered and demonstrated to the confusion of his more fanatical countrymen.

Yet even he, a second Quetzalcoatl, might not altogether destroy the awful dread which generations of besotted slavery to the doomful spirits of evil which had obsessed them had bred in the terrified folk, caught in a maze of inextricable ritual and beset by a thousand menacing taboos. Quetzalcoatl fell with Tezcatlipoca, the good that might not prevail, along with the evil that had prevailed too long. But even his overthrowers recognized the essential divinity of his serene and blameless cult, and came to identify him with St. Thomas, who, they thought, must have arrived in America, carrying with him the Cross and the rite of Baptism.

Yet who will fail to admire the noble effort of the priesthood of Quetzalcoatl, surrounded as it was by the forces of death and hell? When the good finds itself in opposition to evil overwhelming and inveterate, what may it accomplish save by fighting wrong with its own weapons, by opposing magic with magic, as did St. Columba, St. Patrick, and even the Founder of Christianity Himself, by wielding the divine science, the true Magic, as a weapon to destroy the false?

This did Topiltzin Quetzalcoatl, the St. Columba of Mexico. In Guatemala and Yucatan he seems to have succeeded. In Mexico he might well have sung to his Father the Sun as did the Hindu priest to Agni, the deity of the sacrificial fire, as we find in "The Rigveda" "Bright-gleaming warrior lord, Protect us in the fray From this dense devilish heathen horde And all that scheme to slay. A welcome light to loyal hearts, But terrible to face for those that deal in magic arts, And all the Atri race.

"For what Quetzalcoatl essayed was the conquest of demons as we find it outlined in the Brahmanas where the confusion of the Asuras is alluded to. The Asuras performed at the sacrifice all that the Devas performed. The Asuras became thus of equal power with the Devas, and did not yield to them.

"Thereupon the Devas had a vision of the 'silent praise.' The Asuras, not knowing it, did not perform the 'silent praise.' This 'silent praise' is the latent essence of the hymns. Till then whatever weapons the Devas used against the Asuras, the Asuras used in revenge against them; but when the Devas had a vision of the 'silent praise,' and raised it as a weapon, the Asuras did not comprehend it.

"With it the Devas aimed a blow at the Asuras, and defeated them, for they had no comprehension of this weapon. There-upon the Devas became masters of the Asuras. He who has such a knowledge becomes master of his enemy, adversary, and hater."

In that, in piety and right-thinking, reside the true, the real magic, which is even proof against the horrors of the infernal world. Virtue, humble piety, simple goodness constitute within themselves a magic of such invincible potency that all the powers of Hell, rushing to their overthrow, avail no more than the boiling surf against the adamant of the sea-cliff.

A great and salutary lesson is to be learned from Old Mexico, for our world is still demon-haunted, the powers and principalities of Black Magic beset it, as never before. We imagine, perchance, that which we know as civilization may save us from evil that mere material knowledge may serve as amour of proof against embattled evil.

Futile hope, for earthly knowledge is not of the nature of true enlightenment, nor has it any guarding sanction. We cannot fall to such depths as did Old Mexico, we believe. Yet, relatively, according to the light vouchsafed us, have we already done so. Evil is tireless.

All evil works through a magic of its own, a black magic which expresses itself in forms so numerous and so protean that it is frequently undistinguishable from goodness and beauty. The priests of Tezcatlipoca assured the Aztecs that unless they rendered holocausts and human blood-sacrifices to the gods these would withhold sustenance from them and they would perish.

In a like manner does the priesthood of the modern Mammon terrify the people by the doctrine that they must indulge not in legitimate competition, which is the soul of prosperity, but in base commercial strife in which the most sordid expedients are resorted to, otherwise they will starve.

In the bloodstained shrines of Tezcatlipoca fantastic rites were enacted which men believed essential to human continuance and sustenance. "These were the masks which Tezcatlipoca assumed," says the old chronicler, "to play with the people, to have his sport with the people."

In such wise do the false gods of our age tantalize and torment humanity. Tezcatlipoca, Asmodeus, Belial, Satan, by whatever name you choose to call him, is the same in all times and in all lands. That Satan had empery in Old Mexico who can doubt? His personality is so obvious in the guise of Tezcatlipoea that it is not to be gain-said.

The missionary priests of Spain only too shrewdly realized this. The worship and philosophy of Tezcatlipoca are scarcely to be distinguished from diabolism or devil-worship. He is the great black man of the witch-cult, who presides at their ceremonies, the demon to whom the profane render praise and sacrifice in blood-stained sanctuaries, the Master of Sin, the Terrifier and Lord of Phantoms, the patron of thieves, and with his twin brother Uitzilopochtli, the fosterer of war and strife.

The military side of Aztec life was associated with immorality, the young women as yet unmarried being companions of the youthful warriors. The entire manifestation and content of the cult of Tezcatlipoca and his brother were evil unalloyed evil, which, notwithstanding its might, seems to have found as worthy antagonists in darkest Mexico as in more fortunate Europe.

SPECIAL REPORT
Does The Mayan Calendar Predict
The End of the World in 2012?
By Commander X

What will happen on December 21, 2012? This date is significant because according to the Maya "Long Count" calendar, this marks the end of a 5,126-year era. The Long Count is a great cycle of 13 baktuns (roughly 5,126 years), where the use of 13 may again represent the growth of the moon from new to full. The current cycle began on 13.0.0.0.0 4 Ahau 8 Cumku which correlates to Aug. 13, 3114 BC.

In Mayan mythology each Long Count cycle is a world age in which the gods attempt to create pious and subservient creatures. The First Age began with the creation of the Earth, and it had upon it vegetation and living beings. Unfortunately, because they lacked speech, the birds and animals were unable to pay homage to the gods and were destroyed. In the Second and Third Ages the gods created humans of mud and then wood, but these also failed to please and were wiped out. We are currently in the Fourth and Final Age of mankind.

The Mayans prophesied that starting from 1999 we have 13 years to realize the changes in our conscious attitude and to stop our self-destructive ways. We then need to move onto a path that opens our consciousness to integrate with the universe. The Mayans knew that our Sun, or Kinich-Ahau, every so often synchronized with the central of our galaxy, the Milky Way. From this center will come a "spark" of light/energy which causes the Sun to shine more intensely producing solar flares and changes in the Sun's magnetic field. The Mayans say that this happens every 5,125 years, but also that this causes a displacement in the Earth's rotation, which also creates great catastrophes from Earth changes such as shifts in the Poles.

The Mayans believed the universal processes, like the "breathing" of the galaxy, are cycles that never change. What changes is the consciousness of man that passes through it, always in a process toward more perfection. Based on their observations, the Mayans predicted that from the initial date of the start of their civilization, 4 Ahau, 8 Cumku which is 3113 B.C., after one cycle being completed 5,125 years in their future, December 21, 2012.

THE MAGIC AND MYSTERIES OF MEXICO

The Sun, having received a powerful ray of synchronizing light from the center of the galaxy, would change its polarity which would produce a great cosmic event that would propel human kind to be ready to cross into a new era, The Golden Age. It is after this, that the Mayans say we will be ready to go through the door that was left by them, transforming our current civilization, which is based on fear, to a higher harmonic vibration.

Only from our individual efforts can we avoid the path to great cataclysms that our planet will suffer at the start of the new era. In the last cataclysm of the Mayas, their civilization was destroyed by a great flood that left few survivors. Our Biblical story of Noah's great flood is our ancestral memory from this time. The Maya believed that having known the end of their cycle, mankind can prepare for what is to come. The Maya believed that the coming changes will permit us to make a quantum leap forward in the evolution of our consciousness to create a new civilization that will manifest great harmony and compassion to all humankind.

Their first prophecy talks about "The Time of No-Time," a period of 20 years, which they call a Katún. The last 20 years of the Sun's cycle of 5,125 years, this cycle is from 1992 - 2012. They predicted that during these times, solar winds would become more intense, and that this would be a time of great realization and great change for mankind. It would also be a time when mankind realizes the damage it has done to the planet through pollution, greed and a lack of respect for the beauty of our world. According to the Mayans, these changes will happen so that mankind comprehends how the universe works and allow us to advance to superior levels, leaving behind superficial materialism and liberating ourselves from suffering.

The Mayans say, that seven years after the start of Katún, 1999, we would enter a time of darkness which would force us to confront our own conduct. They say that this is the time when mankind will enter "The Sacred Hall of Mirrors," where we will look at ourselves and analyze our behaviors with ourselves, with others, with nature and with the planet in which we live.

This is a time in which all of humanity, by individual conscious decision, decides to change and eliminate fear and lack of respect from all of our relationships. The Mayans prophesied that the start of this period would be marked by a solar eclipse on August 11, 1999, known to them as 13 Ahau, 8 Cauac, and would coincide with an unprecedented planetary alignment, the "Grand Cross" alignment.

This would be the last 13 years of the Katón period; the last opportunity for our civilization to realize the changes that are coming at the moment of our spiritual regeneration. For the Mayans, everything is numbers and the time of the 13 sacred numbers started in August 1999. They predicted that along with the eclipse, the forces of nature would act like a catalyst of changes so accelerated and with such magnitude that mankind would be powerless against them. Also, that our technologies in which we rely on so much would begin to fail us.

We will no longer be able to learn from our civilization in the way that we are organized as a society. They said that our internal, spiritual development would require a better place along with a better way to interact with more respect and compassion.

The first prophecies were attained by the Maya's study of the Sun. They discovered that the entire solar system moved that even our universe has its own cycles, repetitive periods which begin and end like our day and night.

These discoveries lead to the understanding that our solar system rotates on an ellipse that brings our solar system closer and further from the center of the galaxy. In other words, according to the Mayans, our Sun and all of its planets rotate in cycles in relation to the center of the galaxy or Hunab-Kú, the central light of the galaxy.

It takes 25,625 years for our solar system to make one cycle on this ellipse. One complete cycle is called a galactic day. The cycle is divided into two halves similar to our day and night. The half closest to the central light, is our solar system's 'day' and the half furthest away is its "night." Each day and each night lasts 12,800 years, meaning that the central galaxy is the Sun for our entire solar system.

The Mayans discovered that every grand cycle has its minor cycles that carry the same characteristics. One galactic day of 25,625 years is divided into five cycles of 5,125 years. The first cycle is the galactic morning, when our solar system is just coming out of the darkness to enter the light.

The second cycle is the midday, when our solar system is closest to the central light. The third cycle is the afternoon, when our solar system begins to come out of the light. The fourth cycle is the late-night, when our solar system has entered its furthest cycle from the central light. And the fifth and last cycle is night before dawn, when our solar system is in its last cycle of darkness before starting again. This is the cycle we are currently coming out of.

The Mayan prophecy tells us that in 1999, our solar system began to leave the end of the fifth cycle which started in 3113 B.C. and that we find ourselves in the morning of our galactic day, exiting darkness and on the verge of being in plain day of our central galaxy in 2012. They say that at the beginning and end of these cycles, which is to say, every 5,125 years, the central sun or light of the galaxy emits a ray of light so intense and so brilliant that it illuminates the entire universe. It is from this burst of light that all of the Suns and planets sync.

The Mayans compare this burst to the life pulse of the universe, beating once every 5,125 years, each life pulse lasting 20 years, a Katún. These pulses mark the end of one cycle and the beginning of the next.

So we come back to what they call "The Time of No Time," an evolutionary period, short but intense, inside the grand cycles where great changes take place to thrust us into a new age of evolution as individuals and as mankind. The Mayans believed that as individuals, we will have to make decisions that will affect us all.

John Major Jenkins, author of *Maya Cosmogenesis 2012: The True Meaning of the Maya Calendar End Date*, finds the end of the Long Count conveys hope rather than destruction.

"Personally, I think it's about transformation and renewal. It's certainly nothing as simplistic as the end of the world," he told *New York Times Magazine*.

"A lot of people are talking about apocalypse right now, but there's a deeper meditation that can and should happen around the end date. At any end-beginning nexus - at the dawn of a new religion or a spiritual tradition - you have this amazing opening. Revelations come down. There's a fresh awareness of what it means to be alive in the full light of history."

THE HINDU KALI YUGA

According to author J. Krishnamurti, one of the most interesting calendar coincidences in relation to the Mayan 2012 information, is the similarity between the start dates of the last long count cycle of the Mayan system and the Hindu's Kali Yuga. Yuga's are vast periods of time, epoch's that relate to the Earths journey around a cosmological central sun. The four Yuga (Satya Yuga, Treta Yuga, Dvapara Yuga and Kali Yuga) together make up an entire world age between creation and destruction events, held to be around 4,320,000 years in total duration.

The current Long Count calendar cycle started at 3114 B.C., the Kali Yuga, a predicted era of moral decent and spiritual bleakness, began in the year 3102 B.C., a mere 12 years' difference for systems on different sides of the planet. The Brahma Vaivarta Purana Sutra from ancient India depicts a period which has many of the failings visible in our modern society; such is the backdrop of the spiritual decline in the Kali Yuga.

Krishnamurti says that despite the similarities, it is a mistake for people to seek a link between the Mayan 2012 end date and the closing of the Kali Yuga. The Kali Yuga is set to continue on for a vast period of time, at least 432,000 years, well eclipsing the 5126 years of the Mayan Long Count. Scholars from philosophies such as Buddhism, and from religions such as Brahmanist Hinduism, often discuss ages as many millions of years long, entire vast Kalpa of time is addressed.

The Buddhist philosophy does not tend to hold with the idea that a time of any great universal significance will happen in our near future. Every moment carries the same inherent problems and their solutions. The only significant events predicted or prophesied are the ending the vast epochs, or the extremely intermittent arising of new Buddha's.

There have been suggestions in relation to 2012, that the next Buddha will arise at this time in a rather Judeo-Christian end of days scenario. Anyone educated in Buddhist teachings will know that it is made clear that Buddha's only arise millions of years apart.

Buddhism is prophesized to completely disappear during the Kali Yuga, and that during that time it will be virtually impossible for seekers to find any opportunity for spiritual realization at all by any system we might be able to consider now. Only when such utter darkness has shrouded the world will another being become fully realized wholly by their own efforts, without any guidance, and become the next Buddha, named Maitreya.

There are numerous interpretations on what will actually happen in December of 2012, however, if history is to be any guide on what will occur it is probably safe to say that mankind will still be here on Planet Earth on December 22, 2012.

Keith Prufer, assistant professor of anthropology at the University of New Mexico says that the Mayan calendar isn't in widespread use outside of Guatemala, and that the end of the calendar's long cycle does not imply an apocalypse, but rather an anniversary similar to the millennium, though for a period of more than 5,000 years.

"It's not the end of the world," he said.

Only time will tell for sure.

Quetzalcoatl

If you enjoyed this book, write us for our free catalog:

Global Communications
P.O. Box 753
New Brunswick, NJ 08903

E-mail: mrufo8@hotmail.com

Visit our website:
www.conspiracyjournal.com

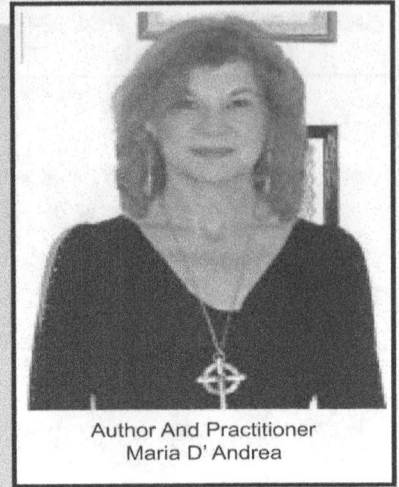

www.ingramcontent.com/pod-product-compliance
Lightning Source LLC
Chambersburg PA
CBHW062100090426
42741CB00015B/3285